TRAGIC
PASSAGES

Jean Racine's Art of the Threshold

Roland Racevskis

Lewisburg
Bucknell University Press

Associated University Presses
2010 Eastpark Boulevard
Cranbury, NJ 08512

The paper used in this publication meets the requirements of the American National Standard for Permanence of Paper for Printed Library Materials Z39.48-1984.

Library of Congress Cataloging-in-Publication Data

Racevskis, Roland, 1971–
    Tragic passages : Jean Racine's art of the threshold / Roland Racevskis.
        p.   cm.
    Includes bibliographical references and index.
    ISBN 978-0-8387-5684-3 (alk. paper)
    1. Racine, Jean, 1639–1699—Criticism and interpretation.   2. Tragedy.   I. Title
PQ1905.R25   2007
842'.4—dc22   2007017925

PRINTED IN THE UNITED STATES OF AMERICA

For my parents

When the inquirer, having pushed to the circumference, realizes how logic in that place curls about itself and bites its own tail, he is struck with a new kind of perception: a tragic perception, which requires, to make it tolerable, the remedy of art.

—Nietzsche, *The Birth of Tragedy*

Contents

Acknowledgments   9

Note on Translations   11

Introduction   15

1. *La Thébaïde:* From the Thresholds of Power to the Limits of
   Identity   38

2. *Alexandre le Grand* or the Ends of the Earth   61

3. Generational Transition in *Andromaque*   73

4. Life in an Antechamber: Time, Space, and Power in
   Britannicus   91

5. The Tragic Time of Self in *Bérénice*   104

6. *Bajazet* or the Dagger of Damocles   115

7. Not Going Out to Meet Destiny in *Mithridate*   128

8. Subjective Dispersion in *Iphigénie* or the Unbearable
   Fullness of Being   143

9. *Phèdre:* Leaving the Shores of Self   159

Conclusion   182

Notes   187

Bibliography   210

Index   216

Acknowledgments

THIS STUDY WAS ENRICHED BY A NUMBER OF CRITICAL READINGS OF the manuscript and discussions of different aspects of the project. My thanks go to Juliette Cherbuliez, Louise Horowitz, Michael Koppisch, Jeffrey Peters, Lorraine Piroux, Karlis Racevskis, Derek Schilling, Steven Ungar, and to my reader at Bucknell University Press. I thank Jennifer Howell for excellent research assistance.

I had the opportunity to devote a semester in fall 2001 to research for this book thanks to the generous support of the University of Iowa College of Liberal Arts and Sciences and the University of Iowa Obermann Center for Advanced Studies. I am thankful also for the generous support of the University of Iowa Office of the Vice President for Research.

Finally, I gratefully acknowledge permission to reprint material, in modified form, from the following articles:

"*La Thébaïde* de Racine, des seuils du pouvoir aux limites de l'existence." *Australian Journal of French Studies* 42.2 (Summer 2005): 87–105.

"Subjective Dispersion in *Iphigénie* or the Unbearable Fullness of Being." *French Forum* 27.2 (Spring 2002): 13–27.

"The Time of Tragedy: *Andromaque, Britannicus, Bérénice.*" In *Racine et/ou le classicisme,* Edited by Ronald W. Tobin, 113–23. Tübingen: Narr (*Biblio 17* —129), 2001.

"Time, Space and Power: A Foucaultian Reading of *Britannicus.*" *Romance Notes* 40.3 (Spring 2000): 279–85.

"Generational Transition in *Andromaque.*" *Dalhousie French Studies* 49 (Winter 1999): 63–72.

Note on Translations

Unless otherwise indicated, the translations of *ANDROMAQUE*, *Britannicus*, *Bérénice*, *Phèdre*, and *Athalie* (and the prefaces and dedications) are taken from *Jean Racine, Five Plays*, trans. Kenneth Muir; translations for all remaining plays are cited in *Complete Plays*, trans. Samuel Solomon. For other primary and secondary sources, unless a specific translation is referenced, all translations are my own.

TRAGIC PASSAGES

Introduction

"N'ALLONS POINT PLUS AVANT" [LET'S GO NO FURTHER].[1] PHÈDRE'S
first words present a contradiction. Though she ostensibly refuses to go
on—to continue living, speaking, standing, and acting—Racine's infamous heroine is here only ironically sounding the first notes of a command performance. What we witness between Phèdre's initial refusal
to live and her eventual demise is a self in suspension between life and
death and between inaction and action. Phèdre, who can only give expression to her identity by calling for the disintegration of that very
identity, adopts a paradoxical attitude that reappears, in different ways,
in a number of Racine's tragedies. Time and again, Racine places his
characters in positions of limbo, between the self and the other, between
what is onstage and what is offstage, between existence and oblivion,
the transcendent and the terrestrial. Racine's tragedies play out on
thresholds.

In what follows I argue that Racine articulates a unique vision of
identity in suspension and subjects trapped in the indefinite moment of
their own becoming. An idea central to this study is that Racine's secular tragedies most effectively represent the human predicament of being
caught in between states of being. While a number of scholars have ex-
amined transitional time and space, conflicts between duty and desire,
and ambiguities of identity in essays on Racine's individual plays, there
has not yet been a systematic study of how these topics contribute to a
liminary esthetics.[2] The goal of this book is to begin describing this art
of in-betweens, with the hope that this inquiry may shed more light on
a dramatic corpus that elaborates a sustained textual meditation on
transitional times and places, sites not only of action but also of inaction, mixing utterance and silence.

Why do Racine's characters so often fail to do what they intend to
do? Why do they so often do nothing? An insightful reader in many
respects, Thierry Maulnier misses something fundamental to Racine's
art when he claims that "[s]omeone like Racine has no use for the weak,
the misfits, or the down-and-out, or—worse still—mediocrities whom
grand sentiments are inevitably forced to relegate to everyday human-

15

ity. He means to endow inner life with its exact and perfect expression, not the inexact and imperfect expression that is their human expression."[3] On the contrary, I will argue, it is precisely the weak and ill adapted that Racine shows us in great detail on the stage and page. Maulnier's admiration for Racine's art leads this critic into a rhetoric of perfection, purity, and totality that disregards the complexity of the unsaids and in-betweens that are the common currency of Racine's problematic fictional beings. Along with their overwhelming passions and crystalline poetic statements, we are repeatedly confronted with these characters' inadequacies, their guilt feelings, the painfully human moments of longing that afflict them as they attain, it is true, a kind of perfection, but only paradoxically, through their all too human imperfection.

While at times they move about in shame-driven agitation on the stage, at other times, as M. J. Muratore has remarked, Racine's characters sink into complete inactivity: "On the descriptive surface, Racine does in fact appear to imbue his characters with movement as they bolt about, persistently prey to the contortions of indecisiveness and instability. Yet, the erratic behavior, the verbal spasms, the inconsistencies, in all their meaningfulness, remain in and of themselves, fundamentally meaningless: they are surfacial phenomena, un-progressive gyrations, spurts of uncontrollable emotion. In fact, Racine's is essentially a theater of non-evolution: the characters travel over and over the same ground, ending precisely where they begin."[4] Against the grain of this analysis, I propose that it is this very "non-evolution" of dramatic situations that we must examine more closely in order to grasp the full complexity of Racine's art. Muratore's equation of nonaccomplishment with meaninglessness ignores the possibility that lacks, failures, and lacunae may paradoxically, by way of their very negativity, generate new kinds of meanings. This type of fictional signifying undermines the positivist, production-oriented thinking that posits verifiable external activity as the sole criterion for meaning. It is in fact one of the singular merits of Racinian drama to question implicitly the ethics of productivity that calls for concrete action as the ground for meaning.[5]

Though Muratore's analysis misses the mark in its summary dismissal of dramatic nonaccomplishment as meaninglessness, it has the merit not only of underlining the prominence of that nonaccomplishment but also of connecting these failures of action, "erratic behavior," to failures in communication, "verbal spasms." Characters' language, like their movements, also serves as a medium of frustration and incompletion, of suspension and obstacles to self-actualization. And yet far from being nebulous or frustratingly impoverished, as it is to readers who may find fault with Racine's limited vocabulary, Racine's language brings us to a reflection on the very conditions and limits of utterance. An inescapable difficulty of enunciation, rather than hollowing out characters' speech, contributes to its esthetically suggestive power. Between silence and utterance, stasis and departure, the terrestrial and the transcendent, Racine's characters are also often, quite meaningfully, at the threshold to self-actualization.

Richard Goodkin puts the problem in terms of individuation, a process which can always only remain incomplete in Racine's secular tragedies: "What the Racinian hero is at pains to do is to break out of himself, to create himself as a being without ambivalence, a creature of a single value, the supreme heroic gesture."[6] For Goodkin, what makes Racine's characters tragic is the fact that they are caught in a middle ground of becoming, in a process that can have no end in the tragedies leading up to and including *Phèdre:* "The lesson of Phèdre's self-revelation is that in Racine heroic individuation, the constitution of a coherent unit of character, is only a potential, a process by which one moves toward unity of personality."[7] Racine's characters are truly beings in progress, in some sense never fully formed. If Pierre Corneille's tragedies stage what Eugène Vinaver calls the "Cornelian exaltation of being," Racine's tragedies explore the painful nuances of becoming.[8] Characters are perpetually (only) on the way to being themselves. If in Corneille heroic individuation is a distinct possibility, in Racine it is merely a potential.

By constructing characters as mixed, conflicted, and incomplete beings, Racine found a unique way to fulfill the Aristotelian requirement that tragic man remain a hybrid of positive and negative qualities, somewhere between the good or sound man and the wicked man as described in the *Poetics:*

> Since, then, the putting together of the most beautiful tragedy should be not simple but of a complex weave, and what is more it should be imitative of fearful and pitiable things, first, just as it is clear that the sound men ought not to be shown changing from good to bad fortune, so the wicked ought not to be shown changing from misfortune to good fortune any more than the very evil man ought to appear to fall from good fortune to ill fortune. The one between these, then, is left. He who is neither distinguished by virtue and justice nor changing to bad fortune on account of vice and wickedness is of this sort, but one who changes on account of some mistake and is one of those in great repute and of good fortune such as Oedipus, Thyestes, and notable men of families of this sort.[9]

Racine extends Aristotle's guidelines into a dramaturgy that captures moments of the tragic hero's development, on the way to achieving greatness or to descending into darkness, but never fully getting there. If Néron in *Britannicus* is destined to become the supreme villain, in the play itself we witness only a brief sequence in his process of becoming. If Andromaque is to be sovereign of Epirus, we can see her only on the verge of ascending to this station. Whether they are going upward or downward, Racine's most memorable characters fade from view like an arrow in midair. They are the theatrical and fictional embodiment of that ancient philosophical image, which Goodkin examines in detail: "Zeno's paradoxes essentially pose the question of the relation of the middle—the halfway point, the point of being on the way, or in the process, or in the instant of change—to the ends. The search for the middle term is the search for the moment of change in itself, and reflects the desire to seize becoming and process in their essence."[10] The present study draws on Goodkin's analysis of the philosophical question of mediation in its relevance to dramaturgy in order to highlight the moments of becoming, of change, and of in-betweenness that Racine brings to the fore.

While there are certainly instances in which Racine uses theatrical situations and devices that can be found elsewhere in early modern theater, I argue that Racine's focus on liminary moments of becoming and on the difficulty of crossing these borders is unique to his dramatic art. My interstitial reading distinguishes Racine's dialogues from the complex political inquiries and heroic identity formations in Corneille as well as from the polyphonic virtuosity of Shakespeare. Although Hamlet finds himself caught in a state of indecision that bears a superficial resemblance to a Racine character, as Lisa Hopkins points out *"Hamlet* famously concentrates not on moving or becoming but on *being* or not *being."*[11] The focus on being in *Hamlet* does, however, entail a great many representations of liminary spaces and zones of passage between worlds. But unlike the existential boundaries that so often entrap Racine's characters, in *Hamlet* "[t]he boundaries between the worlds of the living and the dead . . . are . . . fluid, unstable, and easily permeated, but to troubling rather than titillating or energizing effect."[12] As in *Macbeth*, in *Hamlet* ghosts appear to the world of the living, and living characters see and directly interact with the world of the dead. Frequently in Shakespeare, characters abruptly die—take for example Macduff's son in 4.2 of *Macbeth*—while the action moves on; in Racine, the passage to death tends to be purposefully deferred, magnified as an object of dramatic inquiry, and at times, as in *La Thébaïde*, remains unaccomplished at the fall of the curtain.

Perhaps the closest Shakespeare comes in his liminary esthetics to Racine is with *King Lear*, which, as Hopkins points out, "is clearly a play about borders, set on a number of literal and metaphorical edges[;] in it the link between literal and spiritual borders is vividly actualized as a man contemplates suicide on the edge of a cliff explicitly described in the new landscape-language of perspective."[13] In *King Lear*, "[u]ncertainty about the end of life is particularly associated with edges and liminal places."[14] The most fully developed of these transitional sites is "the dread summit of this chalky bourn" where Edgar drags Gloucester back from the brink of death: "Give me your hand. You are now within a foot / Of th'extreme verge. For all beneath the moon / Would I not leap upright."[15] Edgar and Gloucester will indeed make it back from the edge in this scene; Racine's characters tend to be caught there.

In the construction of tragic situations, Racine draws on meager linguistic resources compared to Shakespeare. As Goodkin explains, "Racine uses few words, and unlike Shakespeare, whose elaborate and inventive language spans many registers, he limits himself almost exclusively to quite common words, repeating them in endlessly varying combinations, like a kind of kaleidoscope made up of few colors which become all the more striking as they appear to take on different qualities in different contexts."[16] Next to Shakespeare's inexhaustible repertoire of verbal variations, Racine's characters seem, in Christopher Braider's words, to be trapped in a state of "quasi-autistic" repetition and introversion.[17] Goodkin's image of the kaleidoscope accurately accounts for the way in which Racine uses limited linguistic means to create a wide variety of meanings. In the chapters that follow I analyze both the potential meanings of Racine's characters' variations on key terms and the gaps between their moments of anguished self-expression. Part of the central hypothesis of this book is that, along with what remains undone, what remains unsaid holds the potential to be richly meaningful.

My reading is thus not one that looks for plenitudes of utterance. Nor does it seek to anchor all of Racine's works, concepts, and expressions unequivocally in a seventeenth-century sociohistorical context. It is thus an approach to Racine's language that focuses on polysemy and paradox, on an esthetics of unsaids and in-betweens that take stylized form in the tragedies. While in certain specific contexts I refer to early modern sociopolitical conditions in order to offer directions for further inquiry, I maintain a focus primarily on the esthetic dimensions of the plays, rather than on their historical contexts—the latter have been and continue to be explored much more thoroughly and suggestively than can be done here.[18] A study of liminary spaces in terms of the nationalistic political meanings of early modern cartography—the kind of project that Lisa Hopkins has recently carried out for Shakespeare—also lies beyond the scope of this book.[19]

One task that the present project has in common with Hopkins's study, however, is the hermeneutic inquiry into borders, margins, edges, and interstices on a number of levels, from the subjective to the eschatological. One of the most intriguing but also potentially ambiguous aspects of thresholds and other abstract and concrete liminary spaces is the flexibility of their conceptualization combined with the diversity of their locations. From the internal thresholds of self-actualization in *Britannicus* to more concrete but richly symbolic dramatic sites like the sacrificial altar of *Iphigénie*, places of passage abound in Racine, from the ineffably metaphorical to the concrete. The polymorphous prevalence of this concept in Racine gains effective explanation in the work of Antoine Soare, who discusses how Racine's verse contains myriad permutations of key ideas by means of the technique of sylleptic projection. Soare defines the procedure as "the reprise of a term or of an image within the same play and at different levels of meaning, these meanings being defined by oppositions including literal/figurative, exterior/interior, and concrete/abstract."[20] This flexible poetic art of exploring multiple levels of signification for the same terms "attests to a specifically Racinian desire . . . to double the dramatic imagination with a material imagination, and to make both minds and things speak the same language."[21] It thus contributes to what Goodkin might call the kaleidoscope effect of Racine's minimalism.

By looking at the various manifestations of the in-between in Racine's secular tragedies, then, I propose a modest reopening of the texts. I aim to offer a set of readings that remain as close as possible to these texts in order for the highly flexible central hypothesis to retain the specificity necessary to advance an interpretation. As Hopkins puts it in her study of Shakespeare, "this is a difficult balancing act, and yet also a productive one, for it has as a benefit that while borders and points of contact may be excessively overdetermined, they can, by the same token, also be seen to bear on a number of issues simultaneously."[22] These issues include humanity's situation between terrestrial existence and an intuition of divine will, the dynamic relationship between interior life and the exterior world, and the nature of dramatic space and time. To explore these questions, I will be looking at key moments of in-betweenness, snapshots of Racinian characters' entrapment in esthetically suggestive moments of their (often failed) becoming.[23] The underlying characteristic of all the major scenes I examine is their irreducibility and their infinite suggestiveness for readers and spectators of Racine's tragedies across the centuries.[24] Further, there is a sense in which my approach to this author must itself remain on the threshold to its conclusions, in a self-questioning stance, proposing readings on the basis of textual evidence but at some level always merely on the way to a new understanding of Racine.

The phrase "on the way" is a borrowing from the work of Martin Heidegger, whose writings on the idea of the threshold, specifically in its relevance to the nature of poetic language, subtend the pages that follow. For Heidegger, what remains unsaid is not only a legitimate object of inquiry; meaningful silences, particularly in poetry, bring us as close as we can get to "the possibility of undergoing a thinking experience with language."[25] To approach the meaning of the unsaid is indeed to deal with an aspect that inheres in language: "Everything spoken stems in a variety of ways from the unspoken, whether this be something not yet spoken, or whether it be what must remain unspoken in the sense that it is beyond the reach of speaking."[26] For Heidegger, every great poet (he pursues this argument in reference to Georg Trakl) makes a single statement, present in every line of his/her verse but in the end inaccessible to direct apprehension by the poet's readers: the site of this fundamental utterance lies beyond language. But the thinking on this inacessible poetic statement "aims to call forth the *nature* of language."[27] Thus a sustained inquiry into what remains most significantly unsaid in poetry contributes to a search for the experience of language as such.

This approach requires methods radically different from the thinking of cause and effect and the kinds of calculations that lead us to expect dramatic characters to act above all productively, or in line with their sociopolitical setting, under the lens of our direct observations and assessments: "When we reflect on language *qua* language, we have abandoned the traditional procedure of language study. We now can no longer look for general notions such as energy, activity, labor, power of the spirit, world view, or expression, under which to subsume language as a special case. Instead of explaining language in terms of one thing or another, and thus running away from it, the way to language intends to let language be experienced as language."[28] In Racine, the failure of characters to utter thoughts successfully or to accomplish anticipated departures or other actions initiates a sustained meditation on the nature of the very poetic language that develops characters, plots, and the idea of tragic destiny. Thresholds, both concrete and abstract, spatially frame the most significant failures of Racine's protagonists. Like Orpheus, they arrive at key crossings without being able to complete them. As Nancy Mardas explains:

> At the threshold of Hades, Orpheus fails to be true to his destiny as a poet. He does not allow for errancy. Instead of listening, heeding, and praising, Orpheus looks back. In looking back to Eurydice, Orpheus speaks the silent but undoing word of will, of willful desire. This is the moment of her physical death, and his psychic death, the failure to . . . let Being come into unconcealment in the ebb and flow of fate. Instead of allowing history to come into presence through destiny, Orpheus tries to fix the moment with his gaze. He tries to prolong the moment, to linger, to stay beyond the time allotted by fate. This activity is an instance of what Heidegger calls the "essential process" of disjunction on which human being always stumbles. The disjunction of lingering turns out to be a fundamental trait of what is present in human being, which is never Being, but rather always Becoming, and is so with will, willfully.[29]

Trapped in an Orphic mode of becoming, Racine's characters ceaselessly interrogate their destinies, both looking forward and back, but frequently without being able to make the critical crossings that would resolve their tragic situations.[30] It is this moment of unrealized passage that Racine's poetry so often highlights. Perhaps ultimately it is as Gaston Bachelard says: "In this 'horrible inside-outside' of unuttered words and unfulfilled intentions, within itself, being is slowly digesting its nothingness."[31] If Racinian characters' failures to act and speak reveal an internal vacuity, this very failure continues to generate multiple layers of meaning in a poetic language that explores the limits of the human condition. Truly, in Racine's case, "[t]he poet speaks on the threshold of being."[32]

As we see time and again in Racine's tragedies, the threshold is a painful place to occupy. For Heidegger, the pain of the threshold creates the possibility for an irreducible oscillation generative of difference, or what he calls dif-ference. This insight originates in an extensive reading of a specific line (in italics below) from Trakl's *A Winter Evening*, where a wanderer peers from the snowy cold into a brightly lit house that he makes to enter:

> The threshold is the ground-beam that bears the doorway as a whole. It sustains the middle in which the two, the outside and the inside, penetrate each other. The threshold bears the between. What goes out and goes in, in

the between, is joined in the between's dependability. The dependability of
the middle must never yield either way. The settling of the between needs
something that can endure, and is in this sense hard. The threshold, as the
settlement of the between, is hard because pain has petrified it. But the pain
that became appropriated to stone did not harden into the threshold in order
to congeal there. The pain presences unflagging in the threshold, as pain.

But what is pain? Pain rends. It is the rift. But it does not tear apart into
dispersive fragments. Pain indeed tears asunder, it separates, yet so that at
the same time it draws everything to itself, gathers it to itself. Its rending, as
a separating that gathers, is at the same time that drawing which, like the
pen-drawing of a plan or sketch, draws and joins together what is held apart
in separation. Pain is the joining agent in the rending that divides and gathers. Pain is the joining of the rift. The joining is the threshold. It settles the
between, the middle of the two that are separated in it. Pain joins the rift of
the difference. Pain is the dif-ference itself.

Pain has turned the threshold to stone.[33]

Combining in their tension the movements of dispersion and gathering,
the space of the threshold thus marks an irreducible in-between, a site
where interior and exterior become indistinguishable. This site of difference, the contemplation of which requires a thorough questioning of
the binary oppositions, like exterior/interior, that become blurred there,
is the site of poetic language. In signifying along this borderline, the
words of the poet undertake an inquiry into the nature of language
while also undermining the clear oppositional categories that ground
the logic of identity and difference.

Further developing Heidegger's explorations of the nature of language, in the "Double Session" Jacques Derrida reads *Mimique*, a short
prose text by Mallarmé, in conjunction with a passage from Plato's *Phi-
lebus*. Mallarmé's disturbing scene of the mime Pierrot who "murders"
his wife by tickling (in a sense pleasuring) her to death, functions in
this deconstructive reading to question the notion of mimesis inherited
from Plato. The major problems posed by Mallarmé have to do with the
nature of theatrical and textual representation and of action as presented by fiction. Drawing on Heidegger's conceptualization of the
threshold, Derrida theorizes the concept of the hymen, a similar idea of
irreducible in-betweenness:

A folding back, once more: the hymen, "a medium, a pure medium, of fiction," is located between present acts that don't take place. What takes place
is only the *entre*, the place, the spacing, which is nothing, the ideality (as
nothingness) of the idea. No act, then, is *perpetrated* ("hymen . . . between
perpetration and remembrance"); no act is committed as a crime. There is

only the memory of a crime that has never been committed, not only because on the stage we have never seen it in the present (the Mime is recalling it), but also because no violence has been exerted (someone has been made to die of laughter, and then the "criminal"—bursting with hilarity—is absolved by his own death), and because this crime is its opposite: an act of love. Which itself has not taken place. To perpetrate, as its calculated consonance with "penetrate" suggests, is to pierce, but fictively, the hymen, the threshold never crossed. Even when he takes that step, Pierrot remains, before the doors, the "solitary captive of the threshold."[34]

The scene questions both the nature of action—what has been done or not done?—and mimetic representation. The mime stands between action and nonaccomplishment, in a conceptual space that leads Derrida to a reflection on "the pure medium of fiction." To Heidegger's theorization of the threshold as a space of perpetually renewed difference, Derrida adds the notion of captivity in this kind of space. Although the situation of representation in Racine is obviously not nearly as abstract or free from historical reference as the mime scene in Mallarmé, I would nonetheless argue that a similar situation of entrapment in an interstitial space of irreducible difference obtains in numerous moments of Racinian characters' tragic experience.

My reading of Racine in the light of Heidegger and Derrida's thoughts on thresholds does not aim to exaggerate the importance of threshold space in comparison with other elements of Racinian dramaturgy. To overstate the case of the threshold would be paradoxically to fetishize and even to fossilize a component of Racine's poetics that is by its very nature irreducible, elusive, and always at least two-sided. As Derrida explains, the in-between space of the hymen, on the verge of the actualization of being but not quite there, evades potential reductive assessments of it:

The mirror is never passed through and the ice never broken. At the edge of being.

At the edge of being, the medium of the hymen never becomes a mere mediation or work of the negative; it outwits and undoes all ontologies, all philosophemes, all manner of dialectics. It outwits them and—as a cloth, a tissue, a medium again—it envelops them, turns them over, and inscribes them. This nonpenetration, this nonperpetration (which is not simply negative but stands between the two), this suspense in the antre of perpenetration, is, says Mallarmé, *"perpetual"*: *"This is how the Mime operates, whose act is confined to a perpetual allusion without breaking the ice or the mirror: he thus sets up a medium, a pure medium, of fiction."*[35]

The unaccomplished in-between reveals itself to be integral to fictional representation, questioning the latter's conditions of possibility and generating an endless dynamics of meaning. Derrida's heuristic concept of the hymen functions by means of unexpected inversions. Perhaps the most significant of these reversals is the transformation of negativity into signification. Unaccomplished action is thus "not simply negative" but rather marks a point of interest that lies at the heart of the fictional text, somewhere between the lines of what that text signifies.

At the basis of the kind of interstitial space that frustrates attempts to force the literary text into reductive categories lies a fundamental ambiguity.[36] This kind of uncertainty is what Heidegger sees as the crucial openness of poetry: "This language is essentially ambiguous, in its own fashion. We shall hear nothing of what the poem says so long as we bring to it only this or that dull sense of unambiguous meaning."[37] Heidegger goes on to say, however, that ambiguity is by no means tantamount to "lax imprecision."[38] On the contrary, it is from the very rigor with which the poet constructs that unsayable statement that grounds his/her poetry that ambiguity arises.

The more compelling and decisive the poetic voice, the more potential meanings the poetry generates. Racine is a case in point. Ample evidence for the multiplicity of interpretations of the tragedies can be found in the vast secondary bibliography on Racine, of which the references in this book can only provide a cross section. As John Campbell has recently pointed out, "[t]he fact that no general Racine bibliography is available to scholars cannot hide the sheer number of well-researched and well-argued points of view that are on offer. Each of the multiple hundreds of studies that have appeared in the past decades contributes its own distinctive piece to what is a fascinating mosaic. In other words, Racine's tragedies defy attempts to contain them within a single perspective."[39] Ever wary of the tendency to force Racine's individual works into restrictive critical paradigms, Campbell even goes so far, as the title of his study indicates, as to question whether we can even talk about "Racinian tragedy" as a coherent entity. Citing the many and varied ways in which the term "Racinian" has been used and misused to launch critical paradigms that do not always account for the complexity of a given play, Campbell goes directly against the tide of much Racine scholarship. Instead of attempting to give a global picture of something artificially construed to be "Racinian tragedy," the book highlights the specificity of each of the plays, for "it seems hazardous to speak in terms of a 'Racine' that can be analyzed like some inert substance."[40] This strong questioning of the presuppositions that drive so much Racine criticism brings a fresh perspective to a field of inquiry that is in constant need of renewal. Campbell's readings of the tragedies reopen these works and bring to them a sharply skeptical perspective.

There is no doubt that we must be wary of approaches to Racine that tend to lump the uniqueness of the tragedies into one synthetic but potentially reductive vision; I nonetheless part ways in this project with Campbell's radical questioning of whether an oeuvre called "Racine" even exists. In the pages that follow, I implicitly accept the idea that Racine's secular tragedies form an esthetically coherent whole. I think that Lucien Goldmann was right when he said that "the universe of his plays . . . is one of the most rigorously coherent to be found in world literature."[41] As I aim to show in the body chapters of this book, the resonances from play to play, the coherence of language, and the repetition with variation of dramatic and esthetic techniques from one secular tragedy to another establish an esthetic cohesiveness that many Racine scholars have emphasized. As Campbell points out, however, some exegetes have taken that coherence too far in the direction of an overarching, artificially synthesizing conception of "Racine."

Goldmann's claim of an unequivocal "vision du monde" in Racine's works, a worldview that resonates unambiguously with sociopolitical realities of the seventeenth century and with the religious movement of Jansenism, is a clear example of the kind of theorizing that has recently come under increasing criticism. Campbell seeks alternatives to the sweeping explanations and categorical statements of Racine's most influential twentieth-century readers. Over against the rigid psychoanalytical schemata of Charles Mauron, the bold summations of Barthes or the all-too-powerful vision of Goldmann, twenty-first-century readers may look for more nuance and flexibility in their approaches to Racine:

> Not only is there another way to proceed than to see Racine's plays as necessarily manifesting some grand design. The validity of such a coherent whole can be challenged, at least implicitly, by the scrutiny of particular issues in particular plays, each of which can be seen to pose different problems. This is not to divide up "Racine" into a series of autonomous republics: it would be self-evidently absurd to propose that no links exist between plays, written by the same author, that broadly adhere to an accepted set of dramatic conventions. There is, however, a fundamental distinction to be made between seeing such links and, on the other hand, maintaining that the separate plays derive their identity from an ideal centralized state.[42]

Campbell's argument is particularly valuable in that it so forcefully challenges many previous approaches. The critical demonstration runs

into difficulty, however, when there are overwhelming similarities between tragedies that Campbell wants somewhat artificially to treat as if
they were fundamentally unrelated. For example, Campbell so stresses
the uniqueness of the temporality of waiting in *Mithridate* that he ne-
glects to mention *Iphigénie*, the quintessential tragedy of anticipation. In
a discussion of *Athalie* and *Britannicus*, Campbell reluctantly mentions
that there is indeed a similarity in representations of sovereignty in the
two plays.[43] Why not see a similarity, and for that matter an oeuvre,
where there is one? Campbell has good heuristic reasons for not doing
so, and his purpose is to go as far as possible toward debunking the idea
of "Racinian tragedy" and the insufficiently nuanced interpretations
that have grown out of the notion. This questioning accomplishes the
significant goal of reopening these works in all their individual complexity. But it is only by means of a kind of critical atomism that
Campbell can arrive at this supremely skeptical vision. As a result, the
tragedies, which have so often been bent to the shapes of overarching
visions, in Campbell appear at times to be cut off from closely related
texts or at other times lumped together a few at a time to draw contrasts
with others—this happens with *Andromaque* and *Britannicus*, which are
treated in tandem to contrast with the uniqueness of *Bérénice*. *Andromaque* acts as a foil to show a sharp break between its focus on frenetic
activity on the one hand and the inactivity of *Bérénice* on the other. But,
as I will ask in my third chapter, what might be the significance of inactivity and unaccomplishment in *Andromaque?* The issue is elided, as
Campbell opts for the particularity of the single work over against the
tyranny of the all-too-commonly theorized oeuvre.

Both the strength and the weakness of the grand structuralist theo-
ries of the mid-twentieth century lay in the fact that certain core insights into the texts led their authors to make sweeping statements that
are increasingly being contested in the light of the evidence drawn from
irreducible primary sources. In Goldmann's argument for a purely Jansenist Racine, "God's voice no longer speaks directly to man. This is
one of the fundamental points of tragic thought. 'Vere tu es Deus ab-
sconditus,' quotes Pascal. The hidden God."[44] Goldmann's synthesis of
Pascal's Jansenist philosophies and the dramatic world of Racine's
tragedies has profoundly marked Racine criticism. How better could
one describe the world in which Phèdre interrogates the gods who
weigh so heavily on the tragic universe but never show themselves?
How better to account for the pain that Agamemnon and Iphigénie experience at the threshold between invisible yet inexorable divine will
and the trapped world of suffering humanity?

Richard Goodkin extrapolates on the comparison between Pascal and Racine to describe the predicament of Racinian man:

> The Jansenist middle, the unbearable feeling of being in a middle state as unacceptable as it is irremediable, forces humanity to feel the existence of the two extremes, but allows it to do nothing to reconcile them. Humanity becomes poised above a treacherous void, a situation which the Jansenists exacerbate by reducing the mediating capabilities of the clergy and placing man, unprotected, at the mercy of a severe and judging divinity. The middle position between fallen humanity and God, the position which might potentially define humanity's greatness, the position of heroism, straddling the mortal and the divine, is reduced to the pure perception of a problem, a break, a fundamental discontinuity. Jansenist man is made to inhabit a kind of vacuum, or rather a whirlwind: it is no more possible to regulate the middle than to escape from it.[45]

Goldmann evokes the fear and trembling of a consciousness caught between human imperfection and an inaccessible divine will: "This is why the tragic mind is constantly haunted by both hope and fear, why it is always full both of fear and trembling and of hope, and why it is forced to live in uninterrupted tension, without either knowing or accepting an instant of repose."[46] No critic has more effectively evoked the quaking, intermediary position of a character like Phèdre.

And yet the core insight of *Le Dieu caché*, which we retain in order better to appreciate the tragic predicaments of Racine's characters, leads Goldmann to categorical claims that seem to foreclose the possibility of interstitial complexity in Racine's dramatic art: "The languages of authenticity and inauthenticity, of clarity and ambiguity, are not only mutually incomprehensible but mutually inaudible. The only person to whom tragic man can address his words or ideas is God, but this God, as we know, is dumb and absent and never replies. This is why the only possible means of expression for tragic man is the monologue—or, more accurately, since this monologue is addressed not to himself but to God—what Lukàcs calls the 'solitary dialogue.'"[47] This strong statement, though it elucidates selected moments of Racinian tragedy, remains nonetheless far too rigid to describe the complexity of the plays themselves. While at times they lash out at a hidden, incomprehensible God, like Jocaste in *La Thébaïde*, at other times Racine's characters remain obsessed only with one another. While at times they engage in poignant monologues, clearly at other times pointed dialogues light up the stage and advance the tragic action. Far from dealing in a single form of expression, Racine's characters play on many scales and modes,

albeit with a limited number of initially sounded notes. Further, between moments of clear utterance, pockets of silence and troublesome
areas of unspoken ambiguity create intermediary registers of quizzical,
potential meanings. For Goldmann, to the contrary, "the tragic mind
sees neither transitions [the term in the French is *passages*] nor degrees."[48] If for Goldmann Racine is to be found in absolutes, I propose
here that we have much to learn in the tragic passages situated in spaces
between what is claimed, done, or understood. This is not to say that
core insights, like the hidden God, no longer apply. It is rather a matter
of recognizing that even Goldmann, though he tells us much that is crucial, cannot tell the whole story (nor can the present study).

It is inescapable, no matter how skeptical we are of psychobiography,
that Jansenism had an impact on the works of a playwright who grew
up in an atmosphere permeated by the theology of Port-Royal.[49] But
the extent to which Jansenism unequivocally explains the religious dimension of Racine's secular tragedies is at the very least debatable:

> Are Racine's tragedies thus "Jansenist"? The very concept deserves some
> pause for thought. After all, the theology of grace is notoriously controver-
> sial and slippery, and the relationship between grace and human freedom is
> a problem still awaiting resolution . . . Bernard Beugnot has reminded his
> readers gently of the almost irrecoverable complexity of religious life in
> seventeenth-century France. No less complex is the history of how many
> hundreds of subtle minds in that century addressed the issues raised by a
> burning question: how can divine love, foreknowledge, and omnipotence co-
> exist with human responsibility for evil, in a context where happiness is an
> aspiration and suffering a reality?[50]

The key term here is "slippery." The problematic nature of early modern theology contradicts easy answers on what Racine may or may not
have been saying in religious terms. There is no doubt that Jansenist
elements can be identified in Racine, but, as Maurice Delcroix has con-
vincingly shown, so can classical, pagan elements.[51] It thus becomes increasingly difficult to accept Goldmann's assertion that "after the
amoral and a-religious period of rationalism and empiricism, the tragic
vision represents a return to morality and religion, of religion in the
wider meaning of faith in a set of values which transcend the individual."[52] Such a view on the religious question in Racine's works cannot
explain away the profound ambivalence in them regarding the transcendent. A reading sensitive to this ambivalence finds above all a multiplicity of meanings in Racine, from the terrestrial to the metaphysical.

Discussing liminary representations of eschatology in Shakespeare's world, Hopkins points to the importance of ambiguity expressed in spatial terms:

> So even as eschatological meanings thus become written into the very fabric of the world, uncertainty about the true path to spiritual salvation remained as great as ever, and the many signs of faith-changing or of covert allegiances to the old religion testify to both the attractiveness and the difficulty of hedging one's bets.
>
> Eschatological concern is reflected in an intense focus on edges in a variety of art forms, from mannerism's breaking of the frame to musical destabilizations of closure in the new fashion whereby "phrases are incomplete in any one voice and the sense is made only in the polyphony."[53]

Similarly, the focus in Racine on humanity's positioning between earthbound blindness and intuition of divine will reveals an underlying uneasiness about the way to salvation. Along with Jansenist, more generally Christian, and pagan elements, Racine includes strong albeit implicit voicings of agnosticism. To follow on Hopkins's musical analysis, it is in the polyphony of potential religious meanings that we may more fully explore the theological dimension of Racine's secular tragedies. To this polyphony corresponds a multivalent, highly complex representation of space, from the abstract interior spaces of subjective experience to concrete stage space. As metaphysical uncertainty challenges the Racinian subject, so this uncertainty also takes shape on the stage. The eschatological exploration of the liminary corresponds to the dramatic-spatial exploration of in-betweens, margins, edges, borders, and thresholds. The study of the ambivalence of Racine's dramatic metaphysics must necessarily include, then, an analysis of the construction of space in the plays.

As is the case with their language, the places Racine's characters inhabit seem to be strictly limited, even apparently impoverished. But, like Racine's kaleidoscopic language, the stylized minimization of the stage serves to highlight the figurative multivalence of the few concrete sites and objects that are represented there. Some of the most significant of those relatively few places are loci of transition and in-betweenness that externalize the anguished experience of Racine's tragic personae.

To look at some of these existential and eschatological borderlines, it is essential that we take into account the ways in which the significance accorded to these places of transition influences the staging of the tragedies. While a full treatment of the staging of the in-between in Racine would require extensive theatrical analyses beyond the present investigation, my study of thresholds and other in-between spaces requires a brief consideration of how theorists of stage space have conceived of these crucial intermediary zones in performances of Racine's works.[54] Thresholds and other in-between sites can be conceptualized in terms of what Patrice Pavis terms *scenic space,* the space of the stage, as opposed to *dramatic space.* Pavis defines the latter as "the space represented in the text that it is up to the spectator to construct in his/her imagination."[55] He explains further that dramatic space "belongs to the dramatic text and can only be visualized in the metalanguage of the critic—and of any spectator—who undertakes the activity of the construction, by way of the imaginary (of symbolization) of dramatic space."[56] Ultimately, "dramatic space is the space of Fiction."[57]

Though this fictional space will be our main area of interest, the multiple layers of meaning evident in any part of Racine's work require critical consideration of the entire spectrum of meanings, from the concretely theatrical to the ineffably abstract. The space of the threshold is no exception. In eschatological terms, one of the most significant transitional zones in the Racinian tragic universe is the point of passage from the world of the living to the world of the dead. This mythic space appears in references to the somber shores of the River Styx, the gateway to the netherworld. It is a significant transitional site for staging the unrealized search for truth through the experience of death. As David Maskell points out, this abstract but highly evocative space presents significant problems for the performance of the tragedies:

Three characters—Atalide, Mithridate, and Phèdre—are seen to be at death's door rather than actually dead (*Baj.* Act V, Scene xii; *Mit.* Act V, Scene v; *Phè.* Act V, Scene vii). Corpses on stage were neither plausible nor decent. The verb *expirer* was used to indicate the character's physical condition. It meant to breathe one's last. It was a convenient way of fudging the issue of whether the person was actually dead. Like fainting or losing consciousness, "breathing one's last" had all the theatrical impact of death, whilst preserving decorum and plausibility. Atalide is seen to stab herself, Mithridate is covered with blood and dust, Phèdre's poison is seen working on her. The words "il expire" or "elle expire," applied to these characters, are almost the last words uttered in the tragedy. These "deaths" raise the problem of when the final curtain was closed.[58]

That the word "deaths" has to be put in quotation marks when discussing these scenes indicates that Racine experimented with the borderline between the living experience of his characters and their (most often unaccomplished) crossing to the world of the dead. The other side to this experiential passage remains inaccessible to Racine's readers and spectators, just beyond the horizon of the stage, the curtain, and of the words that express a character's last moments. Death is both onstage and fundamentally elsewhere. Why do a number of Racine's characters exit our perceptions of them in a moment of unaccomplished dying? While adherence to the *bienséances* that prohibit the kind of onstage bloodletting characteristic of the "tragédie sanglante" [sanguinary tragedy] provide one explanation, an examination of the conceptual space of the threshold may yield yet other insights into the tragic situation of the individual caught in the moment of passage from the world of the living to the world of the dead. In a sense, Racine's characters often walk the stage as the living dead, assessing their immediate situation with one eye off in the inaccessible distance.

In Jean-Louis Barrault's staging of *Phèdre*, the eponymous protagonist suggests an evacuation of stage space by focusing on an unattainable world offstage. As Œnone speaks to her in her opening scene, "Phèdre's gaze gets lost in a far-off place, as she faces the audience. Her nervous state predisposes her to hallucination."[59] In all of Racine's tragedies, "[t]he characters are 'imprisoned,' psychologically enveloped, *captivated* by their passions; thus we must have before our eyes a far-off but luminous point of possible departure, a piece of the sky that figures a permanent desire."[60] For Jean Emelina, the consistent focus on alternative imaginary spaces corresponds to the abstraction of the Racinian stage: "It remains true that this space is fascinating, if not for the general public, at least for those who are interested in classical dramaturgy, for its very narrowness and quasi-abstract fixity; it remains true that an *elsewhere* is spoken, albeit not seen; it remains true that we must take into account a set of spaces that are imagined more than once by means, first and foremost, of the portrayal of passions."[61] Space, then, constitutes an abstract entity born of individual desires, and the stage itself is often only minimally developed in comparison to the spatial richness of characters' imaginations. The present study aims to explore and to elucidate some of these imagined zones, by focusing on the in-betweenness that traps the characters who fictionally and figuratively inhabit Racine's stage.

Though it can become a complex conceptual area for the reflection on the nature of humanity's existence in the world, the in-between space of passage also serves a crucial practical function in the art of staging.[62] As Maskell explains in an analysis of Pierre Peyron's illustration of *Mithridate*, entrances and exits and the tensions generated by movements onstage point to the doubly theatrical and textual nature of Racine's tragedies:

Poised athletically on one foot, Mithridate points off stage with his left hand, while his right hand urges Monime to accompany him. Less assertive but equally determined, Monime gestures forcefully in the opposite direction. Thus Peyron focuses on the movements of the two characters each urging the other to leave the stage. This linking of verbal and visual action is a constant feature of Racine's drama. Characters deploy the art of persuasion to detain on stage a character who is impatient to leave, or to urge a character away who is reluctant to depart. This exploits the characteristic feature of seventeenth-century French drama, the frequency with which characters enter or leave the stage.[63]

The image of characters caught between opposing movements places them in an interstitial zone of frustration, neither entirely there nor yet departed from the scene. The visual nature of staging points to a significant aspect of the subjective experience of the Racinian character, caught between conflicting desires at the indeterminate site of the threshold.

The tension expressed in what might be termed the caught-ness of Racine's characters arises from their desire to act, though more often than not this desire remains unfulfilled. Anne Ubersfeld explains the significance of dramatic actors' perpetual striving in this way: "[T]he conative function is decisive in theatre. Each protagonist tries to make something happen to someone else (to satisfy his or her own desires), with the help of orders, promises, prayers, supplications, threats, blackmail, all of which amount to a conative function."[64] The atmosphere of tense anticipation and unrealized activity manifests itself physically, as Maskell points out: "The gap between potential and actual bodily contact can generate theatrical tension. Suspense is created when an arrest in anticipated, because the spectator has a visual image of actual arrest, conditioned by his previous experience. The same kind of tension can be generated in the case of embraces, which may be seen on stage or may be the focus of expectant anticipation."[65] The corporeal tensions that can be elucidated in the theatrical subdiscipline of proxemics find their verbal analogue in the interplay between utterance and silence in interrogative dialogue, another significant source of dramatic tension: "Interrogation in all its forms generates suspense. It stands between mystery and revelation, ignorance and knowledge. On stage it engages the spectator in the quest for truth."[66] This journey proves to be unending in Racine, and it is the very unaccomplishment of this quest that generates the greatest diversity of meanings in the secular tragedies.

The reaching and striving of characters takes concrete shape in their attempts to move about in the stage space. Both obstacles and potential

sites for transition, doors play a significant role in the staging of the
Racinian imaginary. They have most notably been explicated by Roland
Barthes: "Here one waits, here one trembles; to enter it is a temptation
and a transgression."[67] As Emelina points out, in a more general sense,
Racine's dramaturgy consistently focuses on the periphery of the scene
of action. Doors, spaces between columns, hiding places, and spaces
separating private chambers tend to elicit strong emotions in characters
and spectators. Key entries and exits occur at these points of passage
which mark the uncertain separation between interior and exterior
space.[68] Doors especially "figure, in a simultaneously concrete and symbolic way, the tensions and the stakes" that are represented in the
drama.[69]

Antechambers, also key intermediary spaces, become veritable "are-
nas where entire lives are played out in movements that are majestic,
minute, contained, but decisive."[70] Emelina situates the discussion of
movements and staging within a Racinian esthetics of minimalism. Racine makes something out of practically nothing by generating maximum tension and tragic emotion out of a minimum of detailed
movement. Barthes sees in the antechamber a space of static frustration
and an arena for agitated motion, a site both connected to and separate
from the chamber, or the seat of power:

> The Chamber is contiguous to the second tragic site, which is the Antecham-
> ber, the eternal space of all subjections, since it is here that one *waits*. The
> Antechamber (the stage proper) is a medium of transmission; it partakes of
> both interior and exterior, of Power and Event, of the concealed and the
> exposed. Fixed between the world, a place of action, and the Chamber, a
> place of silence, the Antechamber is the site of language: it is here that tragic
> man, lost between the letter and the meaning of things, utters his reasons.
> The tragic stage is therefore not strictly secret; it is rather a blind alley, the
> anxious passage from secrecy to effusion, from immediate fear to fear ex-
> pressed. It is a trap suspected, which is why the posture the tragic character
> must adopt within it is always of an extreme mobility.[71]

The movements of Racine's characters are not always accomplished
with facility, however, if they are accomplished at all. Barthes's categorical adverb "always" does not take account of the extreme immobility
that so often afflicts Racine's characters. But the merit of Barthes's discussion of doors and antechambers has been to highlight the significance of these transitional spaces for the development of dramatic
action.

From doors between palace chambers to points of passage separating the world of the living from the world of the dead, Racine's tragedies repeatedly, in many different but related ways, stage a drama of the threshold, which it is my aim to highlight. In this book's chapters, I examine Racine's secular tragedies sequentially, in the chronological order of their performances. It may be objected that this chronological order does not necessarily follow any thematic argument on thresholds and other in-betweens in Racine. What I have tried to do, in viewing the secular tragedies as a coherent oeuvre, is to make this study accessible to readers interested in individual plays or in the corpus of profane tragedies as a whole. Each play is introduced by a plot summary, to refresh our memory as we begin discussion of these works and to appeal to readers who may be experiencing some of Racine's tragedies for the first time.

The opening chapter centers on *La Thébaïde* (1664), Racine's first play. I argue that the conflict of the *frères-ennemis*, an adaptation of the tale of enmity between brothers found in Sophocles' *Œdipus Rex* and *Antigone*, places us at the point of transition between one identity and another and highlights the conflicts that inhere in human relationships. Perhaps the most memorable image in *La Thébaïde* evokes Etéocle and Polynice already waging a vicious war against one another inside their mother's womb. The tragedy exposes a classic case of interpersonal animosity at the heart of familial relationships, a tension on the borderline between interrelation and alienation.

After depicting the violence of ancient Thebes, Racine turned to a more heroic subject, situated in a more expansive fictional universe. In *Alexandre le Grand* (1665), Racine recasts the myth of Alexander by elaborating a kind of global poetics, a representational practice that paints a picture of a world and a conqueror of that world. As a military leader Alexandre tests the geographical limits of the spaces known to humankind and inspires reflections on what may lie beyond the shadowy borderlines of human exploration. While this play has been criticized for its languid love plot, I maintain that the portrayal of world, world limits, and other worlds constitutes an underestimated component of a flawed but intriguing example of dramatic art.

Racine attained a new level of dramaturgical success in 1667, veritably launching his career with an exploration of tragic mediocrity. Chapter 3 explores the theme of generational transition, of the genealogical in-between space in which the characters of *Andromaque* act and speak, in the shadow of their ancestry and serving an unknown future. My reading of the temporal construction of *Andromaque*, in which no one is at home with their identity in the present, emphasizes representations of the future in this play and thus breaks sharply with a body of scholarship that has, following on the work of Georges Poulet, almost categorically described this drama as an account of the overwhelming weight of the past.[72]

Both time and the dynamics of space structure the argument of the fourth chapter, on *Britannicus* (1669). This section draws on Michel Foucault's historical study of penal practices in the early modern and modern world to analyze Racine's representation of Rome under Nero. The dynamics of power, which play out at the threshold between self and other, and between one room of Nero's palace and another, take on a mechanistic shape in *Britannicus*, a play which, while referring to the ancient history of Rome recounted in Tacitus's *Annals*, implicitly comments on the workings of power in anticipation of the modern state.

The following chapter, on *Bérénice* (1671), probes more deeply into the nature of the Racinian individual. The limbo in which Bérénice finds herself, as she waits for Titus to make a definitive decision on whether to marry this foreign queen or relinquish her in order to adhere to his duties as emperor, portrays a detailed kind of subjective experience, focused on minute increments of time. The construction of character and of plot are central to this analysis of Racine's most minimalist play, a drama of the individual that painstakingly recounts a single situation—that of a woman trapped in her own becoming and oscillating between hope and despair, waiting for her fate to be determined.

A year after this masterful meditation on inaction, Racine's theater took a sharply different turn with an Orientalist depiction of violent and claustrophobic spaces. *Bajazet* (1672), a modern tale of Turkish intrigue, takes us through a labyrinthine poetics of the seraglio. A drama of captivity and suffocation, *Bajazet* places a powerful female character, Roxane, on center stage, in a sadistic meditation on the liminal experience of the passage between life and death. This deadly reflection can only end (and does) in a bloodbath.

The play of life and death in *Mithridate* proves more subtle. This intricately wrought tragedy of 1673, performed the year after Racine was elected to join the ranks of the Académie Française, explores the myth of Mithridates, the rebel king who repeatedly foiled attempts by the Romans to subdue him and cheated death (and those around him) until he finally made the crossing to the world of the dead. The difficulty of this final transition is rendered in a dramatic representation that elaborates an ornate threshold esthetics.

Chapter 8 advances a detailed reading of the art of the liminary in *Iphigénie* (1674). Waiting for the wind to blow and for fate to force their hand, the Greeks and their sacrificial lamb, the eponymous character, take stock of their situation in a space between observable phenomena and the intangible forces of destiny. *Iphigénie* is the tale of action suspended, resolution deferred, and identity challenged. Full to overflowing with a vague but ominous sense of their destinies, the dramatis personae feel compelled to give voice to their pain and frustration, and when language fails them they willingly undergo a kind of desperate disintegration of identity that throws into the question the limits of selfhood and life.

The last of Racine's mythological plays, *Phèdre* (1677), further explores the contours of the tragic self. In my final chapter, I pay particular attention to representations of in-between times and spaces, summed up in the image of the "rives de Trézène" (3.5.929), those fatal seashores that brought Hippolyte to the center of the tragic situation in which his stepmother Phèdre would both fall madly in love with him and demand that his father Thésée condemn him to death. When a sea monster summoned by Neptune at Thésée's behest rears up from the deep, Hippolyte is dragged on the rocks and dismembered by his panicked horses. The young hero, unrecognizable from his wounds, utters his last words, from a state between life and death, between punishment and innocence, in a space between earth and sea.

A concluding section includes syntheses of the preceding studies and an assessment of the Judeo-Christian treatment of thresholds in *Esther* (1688–89) and *Athalie* (1691). With the sacred tragedies, Racine makes the transition to an ordered cosmology, a world structure in which all references to transcendence are univocal. The shadowy borderline between humans and divine will disappears, such that by time of *Esther* and *Athalie*, the crossing to the heavens has been made, and the poetic inquiries of his theater pursue new, more pious objectives.

In the secular tragedies, however, Racinian humanity remains haunted by points of passage that it cannot cross. While the path to knowledge of divine will remains permanently blocked, the gods hover no less menacingly over the lives of mortals. Racine creates a stage space with no exit for these tormented beings. By means of a kaleidoscopic esthetics of minimalism, this tragic dynamics of entrapment generates infinite shades of meaning over time and through different readings. Even *La Thébaïde*, Racine's rough-hewn theatrical début, still has much to tell us, about the ancient world, about Racine's times, and about our own. It is to the grim setting of ancient Thebes and to the family conflicts on the threshold to a throne that we now turn.

1

La Thébaïde: From the Thresholds of Power to the Limits of Identity

WHEN *LA THÉBAÏDE* PREMIERED AT THE PALAIS-ROYAL THEATER ON June 20, 1664, Racine was on the verge of launching an illustrious career, but he was still far from being a recognized dramatist. As Antoine Adam has pointed out, "the play's initial reception was not just mediocre; it was pitiful"[1]—witness the performances' meager earnings, which dropped from 370 livres at the premiere to 130 livres at the fourth staging. To this day, when citing the play, we tend to be more familiar with its shortcomings than with its merits.

And yet Jules Brody reminds us of how Racine's readers have perhaps unfairly castigated the author of *Phèdre* for having written a play that, had it come from the pen of a lesser-known dramatist, may have been viewed with more clemency: "People seem not so much dissatisfied with the play itself as with Racine for having written it."[2] In a close reading of *La Thébaïde,* Brody opts for a critical approach according to which the text reveals nascent elements of Racine's mature tragic vision. From this perspective, *La Thébaïde,* though it has significant structural flaws, holds keys to understanding Racinian esthetics. Following Brody's lead, I focus in this chapter on the beginnings of Racine's art of the threshold, a significant component in the construction of dramatic action and of characters that emphasizes intermediary, indeterminate spaces and temporalities of becoming.

Often situated at the multiple thresholds that separate the world of the living from that of the dead, earthbound life from the transcendent will of the gods, the present from a future unknown yet suspected, the characters of Racine's profane tragedies, starting with *La Thébaïde,* undergo the tragic tensions of the experience of the threshold. In *La Thébaïde,* the enemy brothers Etéocle and Polynice strive to occupy the same site, the throne of Thebes. Their father Œdipus had decreed that the brothers should alternately occupy the seat of sovereignty, but when Etéocle's term is up, he finds himself unwilling to relinquish the throne. Polynice arrives on the scene to claim the power and position that are rightfully his, and he has an army to back him up. Meanwhile, their uncle Créon aims to capitalize on their conflict, which will take the lives of both of his sons, Ménécée and Hémon, in order to pursue his quest for sovereign power. Jocaste, Polynice and Etéocle's mother, and Antigone, their sister, express powerless anguish as they watch the warring brothers progressively approach the inevitable outcome of their mutual annihilation. In the midst of these harrowing events, Antigone cultivates her love for her cousin Hémon before becoming the object, near the end of the tragedy, of the scheming Créon's unwanted advances. But like Hémon and Ménécée, who die while trying to break up the fight between the enemy brothers, Antigone and her mother Jocaste will burn themselves out in the struggle, finally taking their own lives out of utter despair. Although he has finally reached the throne in the midst of the bloodbath he has helped to create, Créon states in the final scene that, after losing Antigone, he feels ready to pass into the world of the dead as well.

In the end, no one actually manages to occupy the cursed seat of power in Thebes. Créon, who values this position more than his sons' life, appears ready to relinquish it at the end. Etéocle and Polynice both toy with the threshold of power, but they are never able to cross it because their feud makes the throne's attribution an uncertain subject of dispute. The theatrical representation of the tragic destinies of these characters starts with the points of access to sovereignty. In this chapter, starting with a study of the limits of this throne, I examine how with *La Thébaïde* Racine launched a kind of dramaturgy based in no small part on multiple in-between spaces in which the dramatis personae must live out their destinies, trapped in an anguished and violent process of failed becoming.

The widespread figurative presence of the threshold in Racine's first tragedy indicates that, as Brody suggests, components of Racine's more accomplished art are already present with *La Thébaïde*, albeit in embryonic form. Taking as a point of departure the first published version of the play (1664), which Georges Forestier's 1999 Pléïade edition presents along with the numerous variants from the collective editions of 1675–97, we may identify some of the prominent images and conceptual constructs of Racine's theater at a moment when the dramatist himself was still on the verge of entering the literary arena.

Striving for the Throne

At the center of *La Thébaïde*, the throne of Thebes draws those who pretend to power with a quasi-magnetic force. From the beginning to the end of this tragedy, the seat of sovereignty structures spatial relationships and interpersonal dynamics. Much of the action takes place precisely on the threshold to this throne. The enemy brothers and Créon constantly circle around this privileged site and ask themselves repeatedly who will occupy it, how he will get there, and what the consequences will be for the Theban people.[3] Jocaste and Antigone intervene in order to explain what is at stake in this struggle, and Créon's sons try to mediate the conflict that drives the dramatic action. Créon, who is at once the most savvy and the most bloodthirsty of all the characters, will eventually accomplish his primary objective, eliminating competition for the throne, and he will attempt, in a kind of half-hearted afterthought, to mix love with power in the tragedy's dénouement. In spite of the events that befall all of the play's characters (including Créon), Créon navigates the system of spatial and intersubjective relations that structure access to the throne with a certain degree of success.

Barthes sees Créon, in anticipation of Pyrrhus (*Andromaque*), as one of the emancipated characters of the Racinian world, a liberated individual who breaks with the past and with tradition.[4] He enjoys an immunity to the forces of heredity like the hatred that consumes the enemy brothers. Free from genealogical or transcendent determinisms, the autonomous Créon represents, for Barthes, the first Racinian *individual*. He defines himself in contrast to the brothers, who remain tragically interdependent and who never manage to escape from their family history; indeed, they return to it obsessively. Créon, for his part, concerns himself above all with the empirical, observable world, with his amorous and political objectives (even if he fails to attain all of them) in this world.

In the 1664 edition, Jocaste reveals her knowledge of Créon's motives and strategies in terms of the latter's spatial relation to the throne:

> Mais avouez Créon, que toute votre peine,
> C'est de voir que la Paix rend votre attente vaine,
> Et qu'en vous éloignant du Trône où vous tendez,
> Elle rend pour jamais vos desseins avortés.
>
> (1.5.259–62)[5]

> [Confess, however, Creon, your sole care
> Is lest peace nullify your craven hope,]

[Distancing you from the throne you seek, (*my translation*)]
[And smash the trap by which you lie in wait.]

Absent from the editions of 1675–97, which give the third verse of this passage as "Qu'elle assure à mes Fils le Trône où vous tendez" [Securing to my sons the throne you seek], is the idea of the distance that separates Créon from the throne to which he aspires. In the 1664 version, the symmetry between "éloignant" at the hemistich and "tendez" in rhyming position creates the image of repulsion in space, an antipathy that emanates from the center of power, a force that operates directly against the concerted, esthetically mannerist effort of the aspiring sovereign.[6] The focus on the spatial relation between the throne and the would-be ruler creates a hybrid between a geometrical, classical esthetics on the one hand and a corporeal, stylized, mannerist tension on the other.

As a catalyst of violent political transformation, Créon defines his own identity by referring to the activity of striving for the power that he will eventually attain by means of his machinations: "Je ne fais point de pas qui ne tende à l'Empire" [I take no step that leads not to the throne] (3.6.948). He also proves capable, in his rationalism, of strategies and calculations worthy of the ultimate classical tyrant, the Néron of *Britannicus.* Créon describes the way he plays one of the enemy brothers against the other in order to calculate and manipulate spatial relations close to the center of power:

> D'Etéocle d'abord j'appuyai l'injustice,
> Je lui fis refuser l'Empire à Polynice,
> Tu sais que je pensais dès lors à m'y placer,
> Et je le mis au Trône afin de l'en chasser.
>
> (3.6.951–54)

[At first I joined the unjust Eteocles,
Making him bar the throne to Polynices.
You know since then I aimed myself to mount it;
And put him on it but to drive him thence.]

The generalizing concept of empire quickly boils down, in Créon's rhetoric, to the spatial and figurative specificity of a synecdoche, the throne. The 1697 edition substitutes "le Trône" for "l'Empire" in line 952 cited above in order to emphasize the locative specificity of the "y" and "en" in the verse that appears as "Et je l'y mis, Attale, afin de l'en chasser" in the final edition. Thus, while the 1664 version highlights the spatial figuration of empire and the esthetic tendency toward the specificity of the throne as a site of contestation, the definitive edition sheds light on the means Créon uses in order to occupy this space, so that he may then place Etéocle there, only to remove him. In both cases, the central idea is that of the battle for and around the throne and of the strategies by means of which Créon controls access to this privileged place while trying at the same time to get there himself.

Toward the beginning of the play, Etéocle tells Jocaste of the struggle between the two brothers for the central position of authority:

> Polynice à ce titre aurait tort de prétendre,
> Thèbes sous son pouvoir n'a point voulu se rendre,
> Et lorsque sur le Trône il s'est voulu placer,
> C'est elle et non pas moi qui l'en a su chasser.
>
> (1.3.127–30)

> [No, Madam, he must no more claim to rule.
> Thebes has not wished to yield to this decree;
> And when he wished to sit upon the throne,
> She it was and not I who drove him hence.]

In this scene, Racine highlights the key moment when Polynice was on the verge of occupying the throne. The dramatic effect of this image takes on a particular intensity because it evokes an uncertain time when power had not yet been decisively attributed.

We may recall in this context a similar scene in *Britannicus* where Agrippine describes how Néron excluded her from the center of power and, by means of a treacherous act of affection, revoked her past privileges: "L'Ingrat d'un faux respect colorant son injure, / Se leva par avance, et courant m'embrasser / Il m'écarta du Trône où je m'allais placer" [Gilding his insult with a false respect, / The wretch stood up and, with a swift embrace, / Barred me from the throne I was about to mount] (1.1.108–10). The Racinian figuration of the struggle for power will culminate in 1669 with the maneuverings of Narcisse and Néron and the lamentations of Agrippine and Britannicus. In *La Thébaïde,* and this is especially striking in the 1664 version, Racine poeticizes the battle on the threshold to power. The throne, the metonymic center of the narratives by means of which the characters describe their aspirations, gives imagistic form and geometric structure to the movements of the dramatis personae. Racine uses these themes and images in a far more effective way in his masterpiece of 1669. And yet spatial struggles around the throne, which becomes a vortex of its pretenders' aspirations, are even more widespread (with an experimental insistence) in the dramatic action and dialogue of *La Thébaïde*.

Fully in anticipation of the acerbic debate between Néron and Britannicus on the inheritance of sovereign power (3.8), the stichomythia that Etéocle and Polynice exchange in the immense third scene of the fourth act of *La Thébaïde* develop the theme of the spatial battle for power. A dynamics of occupation and expulsion takes shape (as it does in 1.3.129–30) in the rhyming pair of the verbs "placer" and "chasser":

> POLYNICE
> Tu sais qu'injustement tu remplis cette place.
> ETEOCLE
> L'injustice me plaît pourvu que je t'en chasse.
> POLYNICE
> Si tu n'en veux sortir, tu pourras en tomber.
> ETEOCLE
> Si je tombe, avec moi tu pourras succomber.
>
> (4.3.1111–14)

> [POLYNICES
> Unjustly, as you know, you sit upon it.
> ETEOCLES
> Unjust or no, so long as you're not on it.
> POLYNICES
> If you will not step down, you'll fall from high.
> ETEOCLES
> If I fall, with me you shall surely die.]

Racine complements the three-dimensional geometry of occupied and limited space by adding the vertical axis descriptive of the climb to the throne and the possible fall from this position. Polynice presents Etéocle with the scenario according to which the latter may become the victim of the inexorable force of gravity that trumps Icarian presumptuousness; Etéocle responds by threatening to take his brother down with him. This counterthreat derives entirely from the fact that the two brothers are inseparable, in terms of blood and destiny, that what happens to the one can easily happen to the other—they are caught in the same spiral of intransitive becoming.[7]

Their mother understands their mutual interdependence and sees in their combativeness the possibility, not only of their mutual destruction, but also of the eventual destabilization of the social order that they both aim to control. In a desperate attempt to convince Polynice to let go of his rights to the throne, Jocaste recognizes that "Le Trône vous est dû, je n'en saurais douter, / Mais vous le renversez en voulant y monter" [The throne to you is due, I cannot doubt it; / But you are toppling it, wishing to mount it] (4.3.1141–42). Though she is conscious of the promise that has been made to Polynice, Jocaste chooses to focus on the functional nature of power relations and on the potential concrete consequences (which are expressed figuratively) of the struggle that threatens to destroy her family. Using the vertical metaphor of ascension toward and descent from the throne, Jocaste envisages the chaotic possibility of the destabilization and inversion of the privileged site that structures power at Thebes.

Later in the same scene, she goes even farther and opens a disabused, critical reflection on the nature of sovereignty:

> Ce Trône fut toujours un dangereux abîme,
> La foudre l'environne aussi bien que le crime,
> Votre Père et les Rois qui vous ont devancés,
> Sitôt qu'ils y montaient s'en sont vus renversés.

(4.3.1283–86)

> [This throne has ever proved a perilous chasm;
> Girt both with thunderbolts as well as crime:
> Your father and the kings preceding you,
> Scarce seated on it, have been overthrown.]

In other words, the throne does not deliver all that it seems to offer. Jocaste's gaze penetrates the exterior, the pretext of power that ornaments the threshold to the throne, and reaches the subterranean, unstable foundations of this site. Thus she brings to light the conditions of possibility and the somber realities at the bases of power. She reveals these treacherous underpinnings by painting the vertical, dark and cavernous picture of the "abîme" into which her sons may fall. In the following verse, Jocaste sketches a horizontal axis, marked by the dangers that surround the throne. This spatial construct prefigures the return to the vertical concept of the dangerous climbs and disastrous drops undergone by those who have vied for the throne in the past. The antithetical pair "montaient" and "renversés" places two strongly opposed movements in direct tension. Thus Jocaste's description evokes the unlimited and chaotic space of the chasm that opens underneath the throne, while also identifying the horizontal and vertical axes descriptive of the dangers, attempts, and misfortunes that play themselves out on the threshold to the throne.

For Corneille, the throne can also be situated above an abyss. In *Rodogune* (1644–45), Cléopâtre casts a skeptical gaze on the seat of power and on the marriage, of one of her sons with Rodogune, that will permit access to the Syrian throne: "L'hymen semble à mes yeux cacher quelque supplice, / Le trône sous mes pas creuser un précipice" [This marriage seems to me to hide disaster, / This throne to reveal a precipice beneath my steps].[8] Like Jocaste in *La Thébaïde*, Cléopâtre sees through the pretext of sovereignty and locates the dangers hidden behind the throne. But the major difference between the role of the mother in Corneille and in Racine lies in the fact that Cléopâtre is still queen. She has a very real power over her sons and over Rodogune. Even though rights to the throne remain undecided in the initial acts of *Rodogune,* the seat of power is by no means empty; it remains occupied by a queen who intends to impose her will and who possesses a formidable "art de me venger" [art of vengeance] (4.5.1397), a set of strategies and rhetorical techniques that she deploys in order to determine the political course her country will take: "Aucun des deux ne règne, et je règne pour eux" [Neither of the two reigns, and I reign for them] (2.2.446).[9] The verb in the indicative, "je règne," sums up the situation. Cléopâtre's sons, Antiochus and Seleucus, who love one another in spite of their political and amorous competition, present a united front against their powerful mother. In contrast to the empty and inaccessible space of the Theban throne of *La Thébaïde*, the throne in *Rodogune* is occupied and will be reassigned following on the events of the tragic day at hand— Seleucus will fall victim to his mother's machinations and Antiochus, who will be saved from death by the gods, will finally reign in a dénouement that establishes coherence in both political and cosmological terms. The competition of the allied brothers of *Rodogune* ends as a result of the violent and all too effective actions of an overpowering mother.

By contrast, the mother of the enemy brothers of Thebes does not have the power to influence tragic action. The brothers themselves will have to resolve their struggle for sovereignty in a fight to the death. In his description of the high stakes of this battle, Etéocle draws our attention to the spatially exclusive nature of the central seat of power in Thebes:

> Jamais dessus le Trône on ne vit plus d'un Maître,
> Il n'en peut tenir deux quelque grand qu'il puisse être;
> L'un des deux tôt ou tard se verrait renversé,
> Et d'un autre soi-même on y serait pressé.

Jugez donc par l'horreur que ce méchant me donne,
Si je puis avec lui partager la Couronne.

(4.3.1299–1304)

[No throne did ever more than one lord see;
Two do not fit, however broad it be!
One, late or soon, must needs come tumbling down,
His other self would press from him the crown.
Judge by the spleen with which I view this fool
If I with him can ever share my rule.]

The metonymic double of "Trône," "Couronne," appears much less frequently in this play than the central seat the rivals aim to occupy.[10] This
may well be because the throne as a figurative construct presents more
possibilities for representing sovereign power and the battles that take
place around this symbolic center. This space is more extensive than
that occupied by a single object such as a crown, but, as Etéocle points
out, it is a strictly limited space, "quelque grand qu'il puisse être." For
Barthes, "their father's decree has condemned them to fulfill the same
function, and this function (the royalty of Thebes) is a *place:* to occupy
the same throne is, literally, to occupy the same space; to fight over this
throne is to dispute the site in which they wish to lodge their own bodies; it is to break, finally, that law which has made them twins."[11] To
follow on this analysis, the corporeal nature of this dispute constitutes
the essential aspect of the war between the enemy brothers. Just as they
painfully shared the uterine space of the maternal body, they now find
themselves in a similar situation in regard to the throne.[12] Etéocle occupies it, and Polynice has arrived at its threshold to dispute its attribution. The brothers fight in the ambiguous space of this threshold, which
is a kind of antechamber in relation to the throne itself. Because, as
Etéocle states, the throne can only be occupied by a single individual,
the space they are condemned to cohabit is not, as Barthes suggests, the
throne itself, but rather this in-between space of battles, ambiguities,
and dangers. In this atopical margin, the brothers coexist without being
able to tolerate each other's presence. According to Richard Goodkin,
"[t]he twins' mutual repugnance is, ironically, the only thing they agree
on and are willing to imitate in each other: it is a paradoxical attraction
that brings them together and repels them."[13] The originality of Racine's representation of power struggles in this tragedy lies in the creation of this paradoxical, transitional space of suspense and tension.
The margins to the throne, a poetic and dramatic creation that fuels the
action of *La Thébaïde,* become a privileged object of tragic representa-

tion, an implicit geometry of frustrated aspirations to power that structures the uncomfortable world these characters inhabit.

Polynice takes to their logical conclusion the spatial dimensions of the hatred between the two brothers by designating the whole world as a space too restricted to accomodate them: "Et moi je ne veux plus tant tu m'es odieux, / Partager avec toi la lumière des Cieux" [So loathsome are you now, I cannot bear / Heaven's light with you a moment more to share] (4.3.1305–6). Antigone explains the situation in her own way, by establishing a kind of cosmic borderline, between the world of the living and that of the dead, a boundary that may finally separate the twin combatants:

> Le Trône pour vous deux avait trop peu de place,
> Il fallait entre vous mettre un plus grand espace,
> Et que le Ciel vous mît pour finir vos discords,
> L'un parmi les vivants, l'autre parmi les morts.
>
> (5.2.1381–84)

> [The throne for both of you was much too cramped;
> There had to be a greater space between you;
> So heaven had to end your clash by placing
> One with the living, the other with the dead.]

The throne and all that is exterior to this privileged space is set in direct analogy to the world of mortals and to Hades respectively. The threshold of the throne, where the brothers are fighting, thus evokes the shadowy borderline between life and death, the most uncertain spatiality in the Racinian universe.

Between life and death, between power and exclusion, between the rise of the curtain and the end of the tragic day, the characters of *La Thébaïde* circulate around the throne of Thebes, disputing and interrogating their destinies while inexorably caught in the vortex of their becoming. Even Etéocle, who supposedly holds this seat, does not occupy it fully because this position is currently being strongly contested. Nor has he left the seat of power entirely. In a virtual manner, he has partially descended from the throne in order to defend what he considers to be his legitimate prerogative to rule over Thebes. In contrast to *Rodogune* or *Britannicus*, where power is held by the formidable Cléopâtre and Néron respectively, the action of *La Thébaïde* circulates around the vacuous throne of Thebes. Far from being a concrete reality, this site, one of the privileged figurative constructs of the play, points to a void, a mystery, as inscrutable as the future, destiny, and the will of the gods.

Cléopâtre and Néron (and Agrippine) have a profound knowledge of
the functioning of power. As Terence Cave has explained, this kind of
coherent knowledge does not exist in *La Thébaïde*. Even Créon, who has
specific political ambitions and looks at the throne strategically, does
not manage to formulate or to deploy political knowledge. For Cave,
"knowledge is fractured and scattered throughout the action."[14] *La Thébaïde* is thus also a tragedy about the failure of political knowledge in a
milieu dominated by intersubjective tensions that destroy any attempt
at political understanding or action. To take this interpretation one step
further, Racine's début can be seen as a theatrical representation of numerous interconnected forms of tragic blindness. Just as they fail to
occupy the seat of power, Racine's characters are frustrated by the
opaqueness of their future, of their destinies, and of the will of the gods.
Blindness, contradiction, and vacuity reign in this play at all levels, from
the political to the cosmological. The radical uncertainty that results for
the individual is incarnated by a new kind of fictional character—
Racine's thoroughly modern Jocaste.

COSMIC AND TEMPORAL THRESHOLDS

In the opening scene of *La Thébaïde*, Jocaste's first words reveal a
profound metaphysical uncertainty:

> Ô toi, qui que tu sois qui rends le jour au monde,
> Que ne l'as-tu laissé dans une nuit profonde?
> A de si noirs forfaits, prêtes-tu tes rayons,
> Et peux-tu sans horreur voir ce que nous voyons?
>
> (1.1.23–26)

> [O thou . . . who giv'st the world its light,
> Why hast thou not left it in deepest night!
> On such dark crimes wilt thou shine dazzlingly
> And not shrink back when seeing what we see?]

Paradoxically, the figure of apostrophe, and the second-person personal
pronoun that accomplishes this direct address to the heavens, takes its
place next to the skeptical relative clause "qui que tu sois" in the first
hemistich of line 23 in the play's first (1664) version. The repetition of
"qui" in the second hemistich, the part of the verse that describes the
illuminating effects of the divine forces that have wrought the tragic
day, underlines once again what Constant Venesoen considers to be the

fragility of the "religion du désarroi" [religion of discomfiture] practiced by Jocaste.[15] The mother of the enemy brothers directly calls out
to transcendent entities whose exact nature and identity remain mysterious.

As Jean Dubu's analysis of differences between the 1664 and 1697
versions shows, Racine would by 1697 remove the metaphysical uncertainty of Jocaste's words and change line 23 cited above to "O toi, Soleil, ô toi qui rends le jour au monde" [O thou, Sun, thou, who giv'st
the world its light].[16] For Dubu, this was in order to "eliminate any hint
of skepticism, indeed of agnosticism, in Leibnitzian times."[17] In the 1664
text, Jocaste's certainty of the gods' role in creating the tragic day
emerges in direct tension with her radical uncertainty. This ambiguity
takes figural shape in the chiaroscuro of daybreak, the moment when
this *mater dolorosa* laments the opening of the tragic day and nostalgi-
cally evokes the "nuit profonde" in which she would rather have this
tragedy disappear.

The focus on the threshold to the day at hand and on the last moments of the preceding night already suggests the beginning of *Iphigénie*,
where Agamemnon, accompanied by Arcas, begins to question his own
destiny and the will of the gods, whose nature remains just as mysterious as it is for Jocaste in *La Thébaïde*.[18] The development of the dramatic
idea of the borderline between the terrestrial and the transcendent thus
extends to Racine's masterpiece of 1674, before culminating in the apotheosis that Poulet has so eloquently discussed in his study of *Phèdre*.[19]
Jocaste will return in the third act of *La Thébaïde* to the idea of her
tragic ignorance of the gods' will. A tirade that expresses the frustration
of being situated on the threshold between her terrestrial life and her
guesses about a great beyond opens with the line "Connaissez mieux du
Ciel la vengeance fatale" [Learn to know better Heaven's dire revenge]
(3.3.767). But this vengeance and this fate remain unknown to her,
even though she vaguely senses their immediacy. The sky is just as inaccessible to the characters of this dramatic universe as the future, the
time frame these personae interrogate with a similar kind of relentless-
ness.

There is thus a considerable difference between the Racinian Jocaste
and the same character in Corneille. In *Œdipe* (1659), Jocaste accepts
the will of the gods as an unequivocal explanation of her world. At the
end of the third act, she explains to Thésée that, should he turn out to
be her son, he will undoubtedly have committed the crimes the gods
have foreseen:

Si ce fils vit encore, il a tué son père:
C'en est l'indubitable et le seul caractère;
Et le ciel, qui prit soin de nous en avertir,
L'a dit trop hautement pour se voir démentir.

(3.5.1137–40)

[If this son still lives, he has killed his father:
True to his character, and without any doubt;
And the heavens that carefully informed us of this,
Have spoken too clearly to be contradicted.]

The voice of the heavens is loud and clear in the dramatic world of *Œdipe*. It is not to be questioned and not to be doubted; one knows what it says. In *La Thébaïde*, however, such knowledge of the gods' will can nowhere be expressed without a potential questioning or rebuttal. The knowledge of the heavens that Racine's Jocaste seeks remains as inaccessible as sovereign power over Thebes, as mysterious as the future of this city, which all its inhabitants examine in frustration. Without the help of the gods, the Racinian character can only speculate, alone and anguished, on his/her own destiny.

When Polynice describes the people's attitude toward him, he is examining his future, thus acting in parallel to the people, who forebode the hardships of living under a tyrant:

La raison n'agit point sur une populace,
De ce Peuple déjà, j'ai ressenti l'audace,
Et loin de me reprendre après m'avoir chassé,
Il croit voir un tyran dans un Prince offensé.

(2.3.539–42)

[Reason may never move a multitude.
I've brooked, before, the black looks of this mob,
Who drove me off and, far from greeting me
As King, look on their injured prince as tyrant.]

The adverb "déjà" and the verbal construction "croit voir" designate this activity of anticipating, of interrogating the immediate future, the time frame that so often occupies Polynice's mind. Characters' temporally liminal status, located as they are at a point between present and immediate future, constitutes one of the central elements of the subjective and temporal esthetics of *La Thébaïde*.[20] In the words that Créon addresses to Etéocle, the ramparts of Thebes give concrete form to this positioning of the subject in time:

Seigneur, votre sortie a mis tout en alarmes,
Thèbes qui croit vous perdre est déjà toute en larmes,
L'épouvante et l'horreur règnent de toutes parts,
Et le Peuple effrayé tremble sur ses remparts.

(1.4.203–06)

[My lord, your sortie has spread gloom around:
Dreading your death, Thebes is in tears already;
On every side panic and horror reign,
The frightened people tremble on her ramparts.]

The vantage point of the populace atop the ramparts, complemented by their physical destabilization (their trembling), creates the image of the Theban collectivity on the threshold of their future, on the verge of seeing what the tragic day will have brought them. But they have not yet arrived there, even though they are already (*déjà*) on the brink of understanding their collective destiny. They find themselves in a terrifying liminal space that puts everything into question. This trembling people is situated at the limits of the city, at the border between ordered city life and the threat of what can come from elsewhere (from Argos), between order and disorder, interior and exterior, the familiar and the foreign, the present reign and a future one. The pervasive fear has a global effect on this population: "L'épouvante et l'horreur règnent de toutes parts."

Etéocle, for his part, has a different experience, though it is esthetically complementary to the threshold constituted by the ramparts of Thebes (for him, the people's fear is but a "vaine frayeur" [needless terror] [1.4.207]). He perceives these borders in a manner that contributes to the definition of his own valor:

Je n'ai que trop langui derrière une muraille,
Je brûlais de me voir en un champ de bataille,
Lorsque l'on peut paraître au milieu des hasards,
Un grand cœur est honteux de garder des remparts.

(1.3.63–66)

[I have for too long languished behind a wall.
I longed to be in a battlefield.
When one can go forth into the dangers of battle,
A brave heart is ashamed to stay at the ramparts (*my translation*).]

This intermediary status of the people and main characters lies at the center of the tragic construction of the plot of the enemy brothers in the first version of the play (this last passage does not appear in the 1697 edition). Racine's project consists in meticulously dragging out the moment of anticipation, the temporal experience of the threshold that will be at the basis of all the action in *Iphigénie*, the tragedy par excellence of waiting. As I discuss in chapter 8, the 1674 tragedy will be played out in the intimate and anguished space of the subjectivity of that play's main characters, Agamemnon and Iphigénie herself. Although Racine's first play does not evoke individual experience with the force or detail evident in his later works, *La Thébaïde* contains the initial elements of a subjective esthetics of anticipated transition, of the crossing in progress between domains of individual experience.

One of the privileged experiences of *La Thébaïde* is, of course, criminality. Jocaste calls out again to the gods, accusing them, not of committing crimes, but rather of bringing mortals to the verge of delinquency:

> C'est vous dont la rigueur m'ouvrit ce précipice.
> Voilà de ces grands Dieux la suprême justice,
> Jusques au bord du crime ils conduisent nos pas,
> Ils nous le font commettre, et ne l'excusent pas.

(3.2.691–94)

> [Your spite, it was, that brought me to the abyss:
> The vaunted justice of the gods is this!
> They lead our footsteps to the edge of crimes
> They make us perpetrate, unpardoned paradigms!]

As Jocaste indicates, the gods have placed her on the edge, but without pushing her beyond it. If the gods seem to make one commit crime (*faire commettre*), it is still humans on earth who commit (*commettent*) the act. The gods have opened up the precipice and brought the individual to the edge, but in the end it is up to that individual to fall. In lamenting her fate, Jocaste designates the liminal space of individual choice, one for which she refuses to take responsibility. She therefore describes the situation in which a human being acts, having been brought to the brink of transgression, in order afterward to blame the gods for the final, decisive, human action. Her confusion is thoroughly modern. As Forestier explains, "Jocaste's complaint has progressively solidified in the form of a denunciation of the culpability of the gods: thus the rhetoric of this monologue of lamentation has taken precedence over the Greekness of the character, who does not retain here the ambiguous status characteristic of the oppressed heroes of Greek tragedy, who are conscious of the injustices of unpredictable divinities but still accept that injustice."[21] Through her lamentations, which serve to develop a theme inherited from ancient Greece, Racine's Jocaste brings us to a new form of subjectivity, the Racinian individual, who interrogates the gods from an ambiguous position between certainty and uncertainty and condemns them from an anguished and self-centered point of view.

Créon, for his part, cultivates a cynicism that allows him to understand his misdeeds in a larger, diachronic context. He looks not only at the isolated act but also at the timeline of a whole career in crime: "Tous les premiers forfaits coûtent quelques efforts, / Mais, Attale, on commet les seconds sans remords" [All first offences take a little force; / But one commits the next without remorse] (3.6.1001–2).[22] The *efforts*, the pains of the choice of crime, tax the subject on the verge of the initial criminal act. Once this threshold has been crossed, this subjective drama ceases, and the deleterious becomes habitual, worthy of relatively little interest or concern. But in this tragedy, just as we find ourselves on the threshold to the throne of Thebes, we also circulate around the edge of a crime, the one that must be committed in order to resolve the dramatic action, so that Thebes may pass from the uncertain order of Etéocle's reign to a new order. This place of passage is associated with twilight, with the opening of the temporal frame of tragic action, also with the uncertain perspective provided by the ramparts of the city, and finally with death. All of these dramas are to a certain extent subjective in nature.

The ultimate personal trial in tragedy is the passage from life to death. This ontological threshold, a commonplace of the genre, plays a prominent role in *La Thébaïde*. The play ends with the virtual death of Créon, who already suffers the consequences of his treachery:

> Polynice, Etéocle, Iocaste, Antigone,
> Mes Fils, que j'ai perdus pour m'élever au Trône,
> Tant d'autres malheureux dont j'ai causé les maux,
> Font déjà dans mon cœur l'office des bourreaux.
> Arrêtez, mon trépas va venger votre perte,
> La foudre va tomber, la Terre est entrouverte,
> Je ressens à la fois mille tourments divers,
> Et je m'en vais chercher du repos aux Enfers.
>
> (5.6.1649–56)

> [Polynices, Eteocles, Jocasta, Antigone,
> My dear sons, I have lost to mount the throne,
> So many others I have wronged in life,

Jab in my heart the executioner's knife.
Stop . . . My death will redeem your own death spasm;
The bolt is falling, earth's a yawning chasm;
I feel my thousand torments still increase
And now sink down to hell in search of peace.]

Line 1655 explains what is taking place in Créon's heart. Although Créon casts the play's most cynical figure, he nonetheless goes through a complex subjective experience. The play's ending brings us to the moment of/before his death, and Créon's comments describe this intermediary instant at which he has not yet crossed the borderline separating the world of the living from the world of the dead. Does he die at the end of this final scene? These last lines of verse seem to suggest it, but Racine's staging directions in the text of the play ambiguously point out only that in the end he falls "entre les mains des Gardes" [into the hands of the Guards].[23] In either case, we see him on the verge of crossing over into the realm of the dead, but not yet able to do so.[24] The final scene thus gives us the ultimate example in this tragedy of the dramatic emphasis on the last moment of a character's life.

What is the exact function of the esthetic valorization of the moment of death, a tragic commonplace, in the dramaturgy of Racine? A look at the ending of *Rodogune* provides an informative counterexample to the conclusion of *La Thébaïde*. In the last act of *Rodogune*, Cléopâtre, who has already killed Seleucus, tries to poison Antiochus and Rodogune. Antiochus is rescued at the last moment by the arrival of news of his brother's death. After an exchange of accusations and explanations between Rodogune and Cléopâtre, Antiochus refuses the poisoned cup from which Cléopâtre then drinks. Saved on the very threshold of death, Antiochus, who will become king of Syria, receives the following explanation of his survival from the supporting character Oronte:

Dans les justes rigueurs d'un sort si déplorable,
Seigneur, le juste ciel vous est bien favorable:
Il vous a préservé, sur le point de périr,
Du danger le plus grand que vous puissiez courir;
Et par un digne effet de ses faveurs puissantes,
La coupable est punie et vos mains innocentes.

(5.4.1831–36)

[In the just rigors of a deplorable fate,
Sire, the justice of the heavens has smiled upon you:
It has saved you, on the verge of death,

From the greatest danger you can ever face;
And as a rightful outcome of its powerful favors,
You are exonerated and the guilty punished.]

The tragic action is thus resolved in the space between life and death, a site controlled entirely by the will of the gods whose justice shines on the destiny of the characters. In the conclusion of *La Thébaïde*, Créon's ambiguous ontological status leaves the question of life and death unanswered, just as the question of the attribution of sovereign power remains unresolved. As Cave has pointed out, Créon's ambition amounts to nothing, and the borderline that separates life from death, a conventional space highlighted in tragedy, takes on a particular negative significance in Racine. This ontological threshold, far from constituting a place of resolution and divine intervention as it does in Corneille, becomes with Racine a site of contradiction and irresolution. Here knowledge and order recede definitively from view, fragmented, crushed under the weight of blind tragic destiny.

Christian Biet analyzes the quizzical conclusion of *La Thébaïde* in terms of political theory. What establishes the specificity of Racine's treatment of the myth of the house of Œdipus is the fact that "this play does not seem to propose any acceptable solution for saving the city. Dominated by fatality, the story leads to an emptying of the stage, to the point where the last words of the text are stage directions indicating Créon's demise."[25] In *Rodogune*, the dramatic valorization of the borderline between life and death leads to a new state of order in a dramaturgical tour de force; in *La Thébaïde*, this borderline turns into an abyss, taking us to a void at the last moment of the tragedy. Thus we are abandoned, bereft of resolution and of solutions, in political and in subjective terms. For Corneille, the ontological threshold leads to the accomplishment of a political transition; for Racine, it leads to a progressive evacuation of the stage.[26]

In the mortal combat of the enemy brothers, the space between life and death only serves to give tautological expression to the hatred that continues to devour this family from within. Polynice uses the threshold between the life and death of his brother to proclaim his victory and his superiority: "*Traître songe en mourant que tu meurs mon Sujet*" [Remember, traitor, that you now die as my subject (*my translation*)] (5.3.1504). The lack of punctuation in this line of verse suggests a rapid rhythm of enunciation, an effort to sound these words before the other is incapable of hearing them and recognizing their meaning. But Etéocle remains alive, waiting for the chance to bring his brother to the same point of passage:

L'ardeur de se venger flatte encor ses désirs,
Et retarde le cours de ses derniers soupirs.
Prêt à rendre la vie il en cache le reste,
Et sa mort au Vainqueur est un piège funeste,
Et dans l'instant fatal que ce Frère inhumain,
Lui veut ôter le fer qu'il tenait à la main,
Il lui perce le cœur, et son âme ravie,
En achevant ce coup abandonne la vie.

(5.3.1511–18)

[He harbours still the passion for revenge,
With all his strength delaying his last sighs.
About to yield his ghost, he clings to life,
And his death becomes the victor's trap of doom:
In the fateful moment, when his monstrous brother
Is poised to pluck the sword to which he clings,
He stabs him in the heart; his gloating soul,
Having achieved this stroke, gives up his life.]

Instead of utilizing the last moment of life to vent his animosity, Etéocle manipulates the minimal temporality of his remaining breaths in a strategic manner. His hatred gives him the energy to extend these final moments, permitting Racine to drag them out in poignant and painstaking verse. Though he has little time, he knows how to use it and "en cache le reste." Etéocle deploys the vestiges of his existence to accomplish the most important act of his life, the one by which he kills his brother.

Conclusion: The Thresholds of Identity

The final battle between the enemy brothers consummates a hatred that began even before they were born. The inception of this fundamental animus dates from the same moment when the identities of Etéocle and Polynice were formed. In the 1664 version, Etéocle recounts the origins of this fraternal conflict as follows:

Nous avons l'un et l'autre une haine obstinée,
Elle n'est pas, Créon, l'ouvrage d'une année,
Elle est née avec nous, et sa noire fureur,
Aussitôt que la vie entra dans notre cœur.
Nous étions ennemis dès la plus tendre enfance,
Et déjà nous l'étions avecque violence,

Nous le sommes au Trône aussi bien qu'au berceau,
Et le serons peut-être encor dans le Tombeau.

(4.1.1015–22)

[Our hatred for each other is fanatic;
And has not just been fashioned in a year;
Such hate was born with us; and its dark fury
With life itself flowed deep into our hearts.
From tenderest infancy we stood forth foes,]
[And already we harbored a violent hatred.
We hate each other on the throne just as we did in the cradle.
Perhaps this will even extend to the grave (*my translation*).]

In the context of this account, the brothers' ultimate battle, the fight that brings them both to the last moments of their existences, takes its place in the more extended diachrony of the tragic story of their entire lives. As Etéocle points out, their hatred was born at the moment of their entry into the world of the living. The brothers made the crossing between nonexistence and life at the same moment when they conceived their fraternal hatred. Lines 1021 and 1022 in the 1664 edition give spatial form to this tragic trajectory, by means of the designation of the privileged places where this animosity played out. Three sites are specified: the throne, the cradle, and the tomb. These three places all have thresholds, modes of access or angles of approach that also constitute privileged sites for the advancement of tragic action. The threshold to the cradle, the moment of entry into the world of the living, marks a space that the two brothers immediately vie to occupy exclusively. As I have shown above, the thresholds to power, all of the possible modes of access to the throne, have a structural importance for the play. Finally, the threshold to the grave is the ultimate site for the total actualization of the brothers' hatred and for the linguistic and dramatic evocation of the subjective experience of these characters.

The 1697 edition, which does not include the triple spatial designation *berceau/trône/tombeau,* instead provides the biblical image of an intrauterine war between the twins:[27]

Nous étions ennemis dès la plus tendre enfance,
Que dis-je? nous l'étions avant notre naissance.
Triste et fatal effet d'un sang incestueux.
Pendant qu'un même sein nous renfermait tous deux,
Dans les flancs de ma Mère une guerre intestine
De nos divisions lui marqua l'origine.

Elles ont, tu le sais, paru dans le berceau,
Et nous suivront peut-être encor dans le tombeau.

(4.1.919–26)

[From tenderest infancy we stood forth foes,
Indeed, we were so even before our birth:
Fatal and tragic brood of incestuous blood!
While one same womb was still enclosing both,
In our mother's flesh, intestinal war
Engraved on her the source of our contentions.
You know how they burst forth within the cradle,
And in the grave perhaps will follow us.]

In his last revisions of *La Thébaïde*, Racine removed the throne as a privileged site in the context of the life's story of the enemy brothers' hatred.
This revision undoubtedly served to attenuate the repetition of this term
(see note 10 above). With the final version, the dramatist also managed
to associate the terms "berceau" and "tombeau," which metonymically
figure the beginning and end of life respectively, all the more closely by
eliminating the intermediary term ("trône") indicative of the struggles
of adult life. Origins and end are thus juxtaposed in rhyming position,
while we lose the triple form evocative of the fuller diachrony of origins,
life's struggles, and death that appeared in the first printed edition of
the play. The added image of intestinal war provides the reader and
spectator with a great deal of figurative specificity for the origins of the
brothers' animosity. This figurative turn enriches our understanding of
the ontological nature of the hatred that structures Etéocle and Polynice's relationship.

For Gérard Montbertrand, the image of the originary struggle of the
brothers in their mother's womb is central to what comes to pass in the
action of *La Thébaïde:* "Politics and the fight for power over Thebes,
which the brothers nonetheless discuss constantly, are no more than a
pretext, a ritualized form of this hatred and the battle it provokes. The
real war is located in the viscera: it is biological, not political."[28] What
renders this hatred inexorable is thus its visceral nature. The physical
effects of the animus that dominates Etéocle and Polynice structure the
struggle for power, and thus the effort to occupy the throne is no more
than a means of manifesting a fundamentally biological antipathy. Following on Barthes and Montbertrand, then, the concept of the "guerre
intestine" points to an excessive closeness. Just as they cannot occupy
the same place, when they are too close to one another, their positioning
in space produces violent effects. After having recounted the origins of

his struggles with Polynice, Etéocle describes the force generated by the spatial proximity of his brother:

> Et maintenant, Créon, que j'attends sa venue,
> Ne crois pas que pour lui ma haine diminue,
> Plus il approche, et plus il allume ses feux,
> Et sans doute il faudra qu'elle éclate à ses yeux.
> (4.1.1027–30)

> [And Creon, now that I await his coming,
> Do not believe my hate for him will wane,
> The nearer he, the more I find him odious;
> And this must doubtless strike him in the face.]

The 1664 version emphasizes the physical effects of the anticipated presence of Polynice, who lights the fires of Etéocle's hatred. The 1675–97 versions will place "il me semble odieux" in the second hemistich of line 1029 cited above, thus bringing the reader's attention more to the emotional effects created by the imminent arrival of the hated sibling. Spatial proximity influences the development of the identity of the character whose reactions and sentimental experience progressively take on more importance in the play. Over the years and through successive revisions, Racinian subjectivity progressively takes clearer shape, albeit in its unique ambiguity.[29]

A key aspect of the modernity of *La Thébaïde* develops between 1664 and 1697. The growing psychological complexity of characters entails a focus on emotions that are driven by biological and hereditary forces. According to Biet, the modernity of Racine's dramaturgy lies in an innovative representation of the passions: "In fact, Racine's attitude is much more modern than that of other authors. By directing our attentions to the area of human passions, and specifically to the individual experience of passions, he simultaneously takes our attention away from the world of politics."[30] The failure of the main characters' political strivings does not prevent them from taking on a psychological depth that forms an integral part of their modernity. This new form of subjectivity is an identity suspended and frustrated by circumstances, incapable of accomplishing objectives in the external world and equally unable, as Mitchell Greenberg explains, to find its own origins:

> Racinian tragedy [is] in essence a tragedy of origins, a tragedy that reflects the impossible quest of a subject, subjugated to the imperatives of the absolute. These imperatives demand that he or she be "one," integral, a "unified"

subject at the same time that the contrasting claims of the material body . . .
tell him/her that he or she is not one but two, not two, but many. In the
impossible desire to resolve their dilemma the Racinian heroes, and their
audience, are drawn on a labyrinthine journey to the origin: an origin that
alway entices because it holds out the prospect of recouping an initial (lost)
unity, but that also in its elusiveness proves to be chaotic, fragmentary, un-
seizable.[31]

The origins of the enemy brothers' hatred only mark the beginning of
the progressive destruction of their respective identities. Just as knowledge and power are fragmentary and on their way to destruction in *La
Thébaïde*, the complex identities of the play's characters only reveal
themselves, paradoxically, in their own progressive unraveling. A
throne that appears only to disappear as a site of legitimate power, characters who only develop in order to destroy themselves: these are the
political, spatial, and subjective paradoxes that structure the action and
esthetic composition of *La Thébaïde*.

Brought to the thresholds of power, of knowledge of divine will, of
death, and of the total realization of individual identity, often and significantly Racine's characters, like Orpheus, stay at this intermediary
position of indefinite becoming, without ever attaining what they want
to have or to know. Already in evidence in embryonic form in *La Thébaïde*, the interior life of the Racinian subject remains nonetheless subordinated in this play to the main plot of intersubjective relation,
dynamics dominated by the hatred that erupts in the midst of an ill-
fated family.[32] The struggle of the enemy brothers, which is at the center
neither of Euripides' *Phœnician Maidens* nor of Rotrou's *Antigone*, allows
Racine to begin elaborating a new figurative valorization of the conceptual space of the threshold. This ambiguous spatiality, which is also at
times a troubled temporality, constitutes the conceptual locus where the
characters must function and from which they speak. Occupying this
haunting in between space and time, the reader or spectator of Racine's
theater must interrogate the limits of her/his own knowledge of political
power, of the transcendent, of identity, and of the world. As they arrive
at the borders of the realm of the living, the enemy brothers discover
that this cosmos is not great enough to contain their animosity. The concept of the world, its boundaries, and the tragic subject's situation in
relation to those limits lies at the heart of Racine's next tragedy, *Alexandre le Grand*. Whereas in *La Thébaïde* the edges of the world become a
center of focus to the extent that they are defined by the struggles of an
ill-fated family, in *Alexandre le Grand* those cosmic margins play a central
role from the outset.

2

Alexandre le Grand or the Ends of the Earth

Il n'est rien qui puisse arrêter l'impétuosité de mes désirs: je me sens
un cœur à aimer toute la terre; et comme Alexandre, je souhaiterais
qu'il y eût d'autres mondes, pour y pouvoir étendre mes conquêtes
amoureuses.

—Molière, *Dom Juan*

There is nothing that can stop the impetuousness of my desires: I
feel I have a heart fit to love all the world; and like Alexander, I
wish that there were other worlds, so that I may extend my amorous
conquests there.

One world was not enough for young Alexander—his patience
wore thin; he fretted at earth's narrow limits, as though confined on
Gyara's rocks or Seriphos.

—Juvenal, *Satire X*

As HE EXTENDS HIS CONQUESTS INTO INDIA, ALEXANDRE LE GRAND
appears poised for world domination. This state of affairs disconcerts
rival sovereigns, such as the Indian kings Porus and Taxile, to no end.
Taxile prepares himself for collaboration with the seemingly unstoppa-
ble potentate. Influenced by his sister Cléofile, who enjoys a reciprocal
love with Alexandre, Taxile, who longs for the Indian queen Axiane,
opts for capitulation. By contrast, Porus, Taxile's rival for Axiane's affections, vows to fight to the end to preserve his autonomy as a ruler.
Axiane demands valor and courage in her suitors and thus favors Porus.
But word has it, throughout the fourth act, that Porus has perished in
battle. News arrives, however, in the play's major coup de théâtre, that
Porus remains alive. Taxile attacks him and dies in the process. The
dénouement stages a show of Alexandre's magnificent clemency: rather
than execute Porus, the great leader spares his life, thereby earning the
respect of the seditious Axiane and Porus and the enduring love of Cléofile, who will marry Alexandre once she has had time to mourn her
brother's death.

61

By the end of the play Alexandre's love and his power both gain strength and stability, and his influence over the world increases. Along with being a gallant hero—and this has drawn no small amount of criticism to *Alexandre le Grand*, often considered to be Racine's least worthy tragedy—Alexandre is also a dominating ruler. Particularly early in the play, he is characterized in terms of his control over the world and even the universe. His power reaches to the very ends of the earth and possibly beyond.

In this chapter I analyze representations of world(s) in the characterization of the omnipotent Alexandre. The concept of the ends of the earth and of the passage to regions beyond what is known to man takes part in an early development of Racine's dramaturgy of liminality.[1] Whereas in *La Thébaïde*, the border between the world of the living and the world of the dead was invoked in order to show the extremes to which the hatred of the enemy brothers drives them, in *Alexandre le Grand*, the theme of the limits of the known world contributes to heroic characterization.

The esthetic significance of the representation of Alexandre's military prowess remains an underappreciated aspect of the play. Partly as a result, *Alexandre le Grand* has suffered the disfavor of modern critics, whereas in 1665 and the years immediately following, the play achieved considerable popular success. Today, the play is known above all as a gallant, even romanesque work, a tragedy that due to the absence of a strong idea of fatality is perhaps not one. Antoine Adam's reading of the work offers a typical example of its underestimation. For Adam, in contrast to *La Thébaïde*, with *Alexandre le Grand* "[l]ove was no longer an accessory ornament. It was just about the only preoccupation of the characters, the only topic of their dialogues."[2] I contest this view by focusing on another major preoccupation in characters' discussions— Alexandre's military might and his potential to rule the entire world. The representation of Alexandre and of the world which he appears ready to control develops an esthetics of power and cosmic conceptualization that is unique to Racine's treatment of the Alexander myth.

Whereas Adam passes over the cosmic and military dimensions of the play, his comments on Le Brun's examination of *Alexandre le Grand* prove insightful. On the absence of local color—an aspect of the play which fell under Saint-Evremond's severely critical eye—Adam explains that, rather than conforming to the details of Indian culture described in Quintus Curtius, Racine's characters "appear in an atmosphere of extreme abstraction and generality."[3] Thus Porus did not arrive on the scene mounted atop an elephant, and as Adam explains, Le

Brun saw this to be for artistic reasons, "because the evocation of this exotic animal would have'shocked' the ear of the audience member and disrupted the subordination of details, and thus also the unity, the harmony of the work of art." Adam concludes that Racine was clearly working on new forms, and that with *Alexandre le Grand* we can hear the first strains of Racine's music.[4] But the artfulness of this play was intended not only to elaborate a love story and the image of an amorous leader, reminiscent of the gallant young Louis XIV; the drama also advances a representation of military might and potential for powers reaching to the ends of the earth. Louis XIV, the charming young host at Versailles, needed to be praised as a ruler and a leader of armies, even though in the 1660s before the War of Devolution with Spain (1667–68), he remained as yet untested.

The laudatory comparisons between Alexandre and Louis XIV, the ideological dimensions of this play, have received ample documentation.[5] *Alexandre le Grand* has thus been situated in the context of the early reign of Louis XIV and of Le Brun's series of paintings (1662–68) depicting the heroic exploits of Alexander the Great. Racine's second play thus took its place among numerous artistic and rhetorical endeavors aiming to announce and represent the heroic beginnings of a reign overflowing with potential (even though still not having accomplished much on the international level). Accordingly, characters discuss Alexandre not only in terms of his actual prowess but also with reference to his estimated capabilities.

POTENTIAL POWER

Setting the scene for the deliberations that will ensue among Indian kings and queens on the brink of losing their sovereign authority, Alexandre's ambassador Ephestion describes how troops wait at the ready to take over their lands, while Alexandre still holds back, offering a last chance at a peaceful resolution:

> Alexandre veut bien différer ses Exploits,
> Et vous offrir la Paix pour la dernière fois.
> Vos Peuples prévenus de l'espoir qui vous flatte,
> Prétendaient arrêter le Vainqueur de l'Euphrate;
> Mais l'Hydaspe malgré tant d'Escadrons épars,
> Voit enfin sur ses bords flotter nos Etendards.

(2.2.455–60)

[Alexander wishes to postpone his feats
And for the last time offers to you peace.
Your peoples, blinded by delusive hope,
Dreamt to withstand Euphrates' conqueror:
But Hydaspes, despite all these scattered squadrons,
Now sees our standards flapping on her banks]

The flags flying in the wind advance the idea of military might in a state of suspension, on the verge of unleashing Alexandre's fury on the hapless South Asian realm. Ephestion modulates from the multitudinous and colorful image of standards flying over the assembled troops to a picture of Alexandre's subjectivity, a kind of controlled anger: "Et lorsque son courroux demeure suspendu, / Princes, contentez-vous de l'avoir attendu" [And when his anger is still in abeyance, / Be satisfied with having called for it] (2.2.471–72). According to Ephestion's diplomatic rhetoric, there is a storm brewing, and the Indian kings still have a chance to find shelter before forces beyond their control overwhelm them.

In making an argument for conciliatory politics, Taxile reminds Porus that before being conquered by Alexandre Darius had had no idea what was going to be coming at him: "La valeur d'Alexandre à peine était connue, / Ce Foudre était encore enfermé dans la nue" [The might of Alexander was scarce known; / This thunderbolt was still veiled in the clouds] (1.2.173–74). The attribution to Alexandre of the thunderbolt as a metaphor for his power takes part in his deification. Figuratively he occupies the skies, in continuity with divinity, close to attaining a transcendent status through his prowess, while also on the verge of releasing the forces at his command, still locked within the storm cloud of his potential.

He holds the power to attack a given foe, like Darius or, in the current situation, Porus, and he also shows a more generalized kind of potential for world domination. In the opening scene, Cléofile, convincing Taxile not to fight the inevitable, stresses Alexandre's readiness for a quasi-transcendent status: "Quoi, vous allez combattre un Roi dont la puissance / Semble forcer le Ciel à prendre sa défense" [What! do you mean to fight a king whose power / Seems to force heaven to champion his defence?] (1.1.1–2). Taxile initially responds by reminding his sister that other kings like himself will not be so quick to grant virtual reality to Alexandre's promise of omnipotence:

En voyez-vous un seul, qui sans rien entreprendre
Se laisse terrasser au seul nom d'Alexandre,

Et le croyant déjà Maître de l'Univers,
Aille jusqu'en son camp lui demander des fers?

(1.1.17–20)

[Can you find one, who, lifting not a finger,
Faints at the mere mention of Alexander,
And, thinking him already lord of the world,
Runs slavishly to him entreating chains?]

Even in trying to refute Cléofile's assertion that Alexandre is already a kind of military demigod, Taxile only reaffirms the concept of Alexandre's potential for world domination by invoking this idea. As we will find out, Taxile's resistance does not hold for long, and he will indeed contribute to the glorification of his eventual ruler. Even the seditious Porus recognizes Alexandre's power in terms of quasi-divine status:

Oui je consens qu'au Ciel on élève Alexandre;
Mais si je puis, Seigneur, je l'en ferai descendre,
Et j'irai l'attaquer jusque sur les Autels
Que lui dresse en tremblant le reste des Mortels.

(1.2.161–64)

[Let Alexander to the skies be raised,
But if I can I'll see he is abased,
And on the very altars I'll attack him
That other trembling men erect to him.]

A Cornelian character who never flinches even in the face of superior strength, which he nonetheless has the perspicacity to recognize, Porus takes on increased heroic stature in this passage. Whereas Alexandre is raised to the skies, Porus accordingly elevates his ambition to set himself as his rival. He has courage to match and is prepared to accept the consequences of his refusal to bow down before the virtual master of the universe. And it is precisely at the altars that celebrate Alexandre that Porus will attack him. Porus thus chooses the site of transition between the terrestrial and the transcendent to contest the omnipotence of the apparent demigod.

   In the opposing direction, Alexandre recognizes Porus's indomitable spirit: "Votre fierté, Porus, ne se peut abaisser. / Jusqu'au dernier soupir vous m'osez menacer" [Porus, I see your pride must still defy: / You dare to threaten me with your last sigh] (5.3.1563–64). Porus and Alexandre are thus characterized in parallel. Porus distinguishes himself from other rulers, like Taxile, because he is ready to fight to the death. For Alexandre, by contrast, it is never a question of fighting to his death; it is a matter not of testing the limits of individual existence but rather of the known world. Safely distanced by his dominating strength from the thresholds to the world of the dead, Alexandre sounds out the known universe, interrogating its frontiers and raising the question of a world beyond what is known.

Pushing the World's Envelope

In all the speculation on Alexandre's imminent dominion of India, his influence seems to reach the limits of the known world. Porus complains of how natural barriers and the enormity of the world both threaten to become obsolete with the menace of Alexandre's imperialism:

> Faut-il que tant d'Etats, de Déserts, de Rivières,
> Soient entre nous et lui d'impuissantes barrières?
> Et ne saurait-on vivre au bout de l'Univers,
> Sans connaître son nom, et le poids de ses fers?
>
> (2.2.533–36)

> [Must all these realms, these deserts, these great rivers,
> Be brittle barriers between him and us?
> And may none live at the end of the world
> Without knowing his name or the weight of his chains?]

In the face of an expanding, seemingly limitless power, Porus posits the notion of the sites that remain for independent living. These hypothetical spaces are situated at the margins of conceivable geography. Deserts and rivers, formerly clear boundary lines, have vanished, and thus the defensive king on the run opens a speculation on the the borders of the world itself and on whether Alexandre will reach and traverse those zones.

Porus gives a hyperbolic criticism of the power-hungry Alexandre. The same idea appears later in the play in the words of Axiane: "Par quelle loi faut-il qu'aux deux bouts de la Terre / Vous cherchiez la Vertu pour lui faire la Guerre?" [By what law must you ferret courage out / And wage war on it to earth's farthest ends?] (4.2.1045–46). Thus the theme of world's ends functions to develop a figurative critique of Alexandre's excessive quest for power and domination. Timothy Reiss takes up this dimension of *Alexandre le Grand* and describes the play as an indictment of abuses of power: "*Alexandre* stood as a strong and complex warning on the dangers of excessive force and imperial pretension, on the nature of power and of passion. It did so through a complicated interplay between classical and modern writings on history, politics, and psychology, with its many commentators, its public and privy debates (within the Royal Council itself, as we know), and—above all— its steadily mounting tensions."[6] The anticipation of Alexandre's further conquests fuels a speculation on the extent of his powers that is both laudatory—he inspires awe—and critical—his unchecked advances throughout the world are deemed abusive.

In *De l'instruction de Monseigneur le Dauphin*, La Mothe Le Vayer warned against expansionist zeal and its potential for preventing a realm from enjoying any moments of peace:

> S'il y a quelque chose qui doive apparemment éloigner un Prince victorieux de faire jouir ses sujets du bonheur de la paix, c'est le désir d'accumuler conquête sur conquête . . . et d'étendre ses trophées jusques aux extrémités du monde, ou au delà. Si son ambition égale celle d'Alexandre.[7]

> [If there is something that seems to prevent a victorious sovereign from allowing his subjects to reap the benefits of peace, it is the desire for accumulating conquests . . . and for extending his dominion to the extreme limits of the world, or even beyond it. That is, if his ambition equals that of Alexander.]

Alexandre's greatest strength is also his greatest flaw. His limitless desire for new conquests prevents the greater good of peace from ever coming to fruition. Clearly, for the sovereign in training to whom La Mothe Le Vayer addressed his words of warning, the cultivation of peace needed to be taken every bit as seriously as military and political ambitions.

In Boileau's eighth *Satire*, Alexandre's lust for power renders the heroic figure almost ridiculous. He becomes no more than a madman with a god complex:

> Quoi donc? à vostre avis, fut-ce un fou qu'Alexandre?
> Qui? cet écervelé qui mit l'Asie en cendre?
> Ce fougueux l'Angely qui de sang altéré,
> Maistre du monde entier, s'y trouvait trop serré?
> L'enragé qu'il estoit, né Roi d'une province,
> Qu'il pouvoit gouverner en bon et sage prince,

S'en alla follement, et pensant estre Dieu,
Courir comme un Bandit qui n'a ni feu ni lieu,
Et traînant avec soi les horreurs de la guerre,
De sa vaste folie emplir toute la terre.[8]

[What then? in your opinion was this Alexander a madman? Who? this lu-
natic who burned all of Asia? This enraged visionary, who was so bloodthirsty that, even though he was master of the whole world, found it too
restricting. Born king of a province that he could have governed sagely, he
was so crazed that he went out, thinking himself a god, and ran wild like a
bandit with no home, bringing with him the horrors of war and filling the
earth with his vast folly.]

From Boileau's satirical perspective, the overpowering ruler, stretching
his conquests to the ends of the earth, becomes a crazed marauder.
Again, as in La Mothe Le Vayer, the lost prospect of peace takes its
place over against the terrible realities of war. The continuation of poin-
tless wars can only be construed as madness, as the sane world looks
on, seeing the ruined potential for peace, and condemns, through philosophical and satirical perspectives, the bloodlust of a ruler out of control.

And yet this is only one side to the story, the myth, and the figuration
of Alexander. In Racine's esthetic system, whereas Alexandre's future
vanquished enemies complain vociferously—and why would they not—
about his overpowering influence, they also envy his strength. Le
Brun's lionizing mythology of the ancient warlord, taking part in the
symbolism of the inauguration of Louis XIV's personal rule in the
1660s, finds a complementary idea of Alexandre's might in Racine's
dedication to the king:

Mais [Sa Majesté] me permettra de lui dire que devant Elle on n'a point vu
de Roi, qui à l'âge d'Alexandre ait fait paraître la conduite d'Auguste, qui
sans s'éloigner presque du centre de son Royaume, ait répandu sa lumière
jusqu'au bout du Monde, et qui ait commencé sa Carrière par où les plus
grand Princes ont tâché d'achever la leur.[9]

[But Your Majesty will permit me to say that no king has ever been seen
like you, who at Alexander's age has displayed the qualities of Augustus,
who, almost without stirring from the heart of his kingdom has spread his
light to the ends of the earth and who has begun his career where the greatest princes have sought to end theirs.]

In a masterful piece of rhetoric, Racine both associates Louis XIV with
Alexander and distances the young king from Alexander's excesses.

With the example of Augustus, Racine maintains the idea of global prestige while including also a notion of enduring rational peace in the kingdom and the world. Rather than spreading the fires of war, Louis XIV sheds the light of his influence, with the same force and to the same extent. Thus the global impact of Alexander's might becomes sublimated in Racine's rhetoric by means of the peaceful, rational counterexample of Augustus. The standard topos of the great ruler's influence extending to the limits of the earth thus comes to serve a new kind of figurative purpose in Racine.

Whereas in the play itself Alexandre's impact inspires fears and provokes complaints, the expansive potential of the image of world domination gives Porus an opportunity for rhetorical self-aggrandizement:

> Je vois d'un œil content trembler la Terre entière,
> Afin que par moi seul les Mortels secourus
> S'ils sont libres, le soient de la main de Porus,
> Et qu'on dise partout dans une paix profonde:
> *Alexandre vainqueur eût dompté tout le Monde,*
> *Mais un Roi l'attendait au bout de l'Univers,*
> *Par qui le Monde entier a vu briser ses fers.*
>
> (2.2.550–56)

> [In calm content I see the whole world tremble,
> In order that mankind, saved but by me,
> Should it be free, by Porus' hand be freed;
> And everywhere, in deep peace, men should say:
> "Alexander would have vanquished all one day;
> But at earth's corner on a king did stumble,
> Through whom the whole world saw its fetters crumble."]

As we saw earlier, Porus had used the idea of world's end to posit the possibility of free spaces for living outside Alexandre's dominion. In this passage, Porus uses the limits of the earth as a privileged site for a heroic struggle, a battle that establishes his own valor as self-proclaimed protector of the free world. He thus grafts his own heroic self-valorization onto Alexandre's established reputation as a global force. Thus while lamenting the effects of Alexandre's power, Porus does not fail to capitalize, in the dimension of figurative representations of military and political activity and of the situation of man in the universe, on the ideational potential of Alexandre's reputation for world domination. The standard story of Alexandre's armies as a force reaching to the ends of the earth thus becomes an object for rhetorical manipulation. In Racine's composition, the images created by reflection on this worldwide power serve a vivid depiction of world limits, a speculation on just how far Alexandre's power may go.

The poetic evocation of absolute boundaries reaches its highest point in the fifth act, when Cléofile extends the account of Alexandre's terrestrial might to a figurative representation of the thresholds to the otherworldly:

> Mais quoi, Seigneur? toujours guerre sur guerre?
> Cherchez-vous des sujets au delà de la Terre?
> Voulez-vous pour témoins de vos faits éclatants
> Des Pays inconnus même à leurs Habitants?
> Qu'espérez-vous combattre en des climats si rudes?
> Ils vous opposeront de vastes solitudes,
> Des déserts que le Ciel refuse d'éclairer,
> Où la Nature semble elle-même expirer.
>
> (5.1.1357–64)

> [What, my lord, forever wars on wars;
> Do you seek subjects even in the stars?
> Do you want as witness of your splendid show
> Regions their very peoples hardly know?
> What do you hope to fight in climes so rude?
> They will oppose to you vast solitude,
> Dim deserts never brightened by the sky,
> Where nature seems herself to droop and die.]

By reading this extraordinary passage as the culminating point of an art of world limits in *Alexandre le Grand*, I want to question what has become a received idea on this play in Racine criticism — namely, that military and political representations of Alexandre are only central to the first half of the play, in the talk about Alexandre while he is still offstage, and that these representations are entirely subordinated to the play's gallant love story.[10] As Cléofile's lament shows, the theme of the world's frontiers is a constant in *Alexandre le Grand*, from the beginning to the end of the tragedy.[11] In the final act, Cléofile forges farther into otherworldly speculation than other characters have done. The deserts that remain out of the reach of all sources of light; the lands where even nature withers away — these are places that still may be potentially accessible to Alexandre. Cléofile rhetorically evokes these atopical, paradoxical spaces on the threshold to the otherworldly in order to convince Alexandre to put an end to his career of accumulating military conquests. But the evocation is also artful. It is through a terrible kind of ethereal beauty that Cléofile attempts to sway the conqueror and to capture the imagination of the audience.

Racine found the conceptual basis for Cléofile's description in Quintus Curtius's *Life of Alexander*. The lamentations of the Macedonians open onto the idea of other, frightening worlds: "They were dragged beyond the sight of the sun and the stars, and they were forced to go to places that the gods have rendered inaccessible to men"; they were afraid of finding "fog, darkness, an eternal night . . . and stagnant waters where nature, coming to its end, came to utter her last gasps."[12] In Cléofile's rendering of the idea, we go from stagnant waters to dark deserts and from the notion of fear to that of solitude. Rather than focusing on the troops' apprehensions of the nether regions into which Alexandre would lead them, Cléofile describes for Alexandre's appreciation the "vastes solitudes" that the conqueror would encounter in the continuation of his exploits. At the threshold of world domination, thus at the ends of the earth, Cléofile predicts not only terrible sights of dying nature and a known world receding into darkness; she also focuses on an inner void that Alexandre will no doubt encounter at the end of his journey, beyond the crossing point to an outer space of nothingness and death. She places this profound loneliness in contradistinction to her offer of a life of shared love.

Thus the figurative construction of world and its limits, of the threshold to what is beyond, intersects with the well-known love plot in *Alexandre le Grand*. Rather than being merely a subordinate feature of the play, the representation of Alexandre's impact on the world, and of the world itself and its limits, remains at the center of the thematic objectives Racine pursued in his tragedy of 1665. One of the elements of the dramaturgy that Racine will continue to develop is the idea of ends of the known world, of potential points of access to regions of existence or experience that have not yet been reached by the individual in tragedy. The chaos, the invisible menace of these zones, but also the wonderment of their potential attainment, hover over the tragic world of the dramatic action in Racine's secular tragedies. Arguably the culmination of this scrutiny of the otherworldy will occur in *Phèdre*, at the shores of Trœzen, where Neptune's sea monster rises up from the unknown deep of the ocean to bring Hippolyte to the borderline between the world of the living and the world of the dead. But nowhere in the Racinian corpus does the idea of world itself, of the universe, and of what may lie beyond it, receive the kind of sustained treatment that it does in *Alexandre le Grand*. The conceptual exploration of world limits constitutes one of the strong points of a play that achieved popular success early in

Racine's career but that did not acquire the staying power of the later tragedies. Two years after *Alexandre*, Racine shifted his focus with *Andromaque* from the spatial speculation on global boundaries to a temporal meditation on the thresholds between present and past and between past and future time frames. From the inquiry into world limits and excesses of military power, Racine moved to a temporal reflection on mediocrity. The characters of *Andromaque*, who are nowhere near testing the limits of their world, as their forebears did, instead look obsessively both at the illustrious past of their parents and at their own disturbing future, while never fully finding their own identities in the present of dramatic action.

3

Generational Transition in *Andromaque*

IN THE OPENING SCENE OF *ANDROMAQUE*, WE LEARN THAT ORESTE HAS come to Epirus as a representative of the Greeks, who demand that the king Pyrrhus give them Astyanax. The child and his mother Andromaque, whom Pyrrhus holds captive, represent the last remnants of Troy. In the opening scene Oreste reveals to his friend Pylade that his official duties are no more than a pretext for the pursuit of his personal desires. He has actually come to Epirus to seek out his beloved Hermione, who has been betrothed by her father Ménélas to Pyrrhus.

Pyrrhus, for his part, loves Andromaque but cannot win her affections in return, as she unerringly cultivates her devotion to her deceased husband, the Trojan hero Hector. Pyrrhus resorts to blackmail. Having refused Oreste's request on behalf of the Greeks, he tells Andromaque that her son can remain in safety only if she will marry him. Should this marriage take place, says Hermione to Oreste, she will leave with him. Oreste is momentarily overjoyed, until he finds out that Pyrrhus, frustrated with Andromaque's resistance to his advances, has apparently decided to give up Astyanax to the Greeks.

Oreste then begins to plan the abduction of Hermione. Andromaque, who is greeted with indifference when she goes to Hermione for help, throws herself on the mercy of the king, who maintains that she must marry him to save her son. She then comes up with her "innocent stratagème" [innocent strategy], whereby she plans to wed Pyrrhus, thus saving her son's life, only to take her own immediately afterward. With this union once again becoming a possibility, the enraged Hermione demands that Oreste kill her fiancé. But Hermione has mixed feelings. In a veritable crisis of identity, she tries to figure out whether she really wants the death of Pyrrhus, whom she loves after all. When Oreste carries out her will, she greets him unexpectedly with a torrent of reproaches and insults. As the tragedy ends, the jilted Oreste descends into madness while Andromaque is being crowned sovereign of Epirus. So ends the infernal tangle of frustration and unrequited love that has

73

led, through a number of crises of identity, to the first moments of a shift in political power.

Andromaque stages an uncertain set of characters on the verge of self-actualization. They find themselves caught between two generations and must struggle to negotiate a passage from an illustrious past to an uncertain future, a temporality that poses an enigma for Racine's readers and spectators while facilitating an elaborate figuration of the threshold. This art of in-betweenness takes shape in a subjective and temporal context. Both historically and genealogically, Oreste, Hermione, Pyrrhus, and Andromaque are latecomers, uncomfortably occupying a dramatic time frame that stands as an epilogue to the Trojan War. Racine situates the dramatic action of the play that would be his first major success at a paradoxical point in time, both momentous and anticlimactic, a transitional moment at which the sons, daughters, and spouses of great heroes and heroines can only sift through the fallout of what once was Troy, while at the same time pursuing ill-fated amorous objectives and blindly speculating on what their future may hold.[1]

Racine's prefaces to *Andromaque* provide significant contextual clues for the study of the genealogical in-between space of generational transition and individual becoming in this play. In explaining his use of sources drawn from antiquity, Racine paid scrupulous attention to his literary forefathers. One gets a strong sense in reading the prefaces of 1668 and 1675–76 that, as was the case for the story of the house of Œdipus, the subject of *Andromaque* had already been thoroughly treated before the seventeenth-century playwright ever put pen to paper.[2] Racine showed in his paratextual prose a full awareness of his own situation as a latecomer, an imitator, not only in relation to Corneille's generation but also in regard to the ancients themselves: in the two prefaces combined, Racine cited Vergil, Euripides, Seneca, Horace, Aristotle, Herodotus, Homer, and Sophocles, in a painstaking attempt to respond to critics and to justify the creative uses he had made of classical models: "[I]l y a bien de la différence entre détruire le principal fondement d'une Fable et en altérer quelques incidents, qui changent presque de face dans toutes les mains qui les traitent" [There is a great difference between destroying the chief foundation of a fable and altering some incidents which change considerably in all the hands which deal with them] (298). Acknowledging that his creative efforts were in fact only a renewed exercise in the rhetorical technique of *dispositio*, Racine presented himself as merely the latest pair of hands to hold and pass on the myths and legends of antiquity. In justifying the changes that he made to his narrative inheritance before passing it on, Racine described his own dramaturgical practice as a paradoxical kind of imitation: he was true to the ancients in the very act of deviating selectively from their example. He imitated by not merely imitating. In this, paradoxically, lie both Racine's originality and his careful homage to his literary ancestors, an adherence that is closer for its inclusion of practices of deliberate variation. A strict imitation, by this logic, would actually have been a larger deviation than the kind of creative practice in which Racine engaged.

In his thinking on his own work of dramatic imitation and creation, then, Racine placed himself at a point of transition, between past and future, where the legacy passing through his hands would remain intact while also undergoing a number of purposeful changes. The prefatory explanation itself, the prose that justified his particular brand of dramaturgy, took its place in the quarrels of his times while also tacitly launching itself into an unknown future for the reception of Racine's works. I argue in this chapter that a similar dynamics of transition, from the examples of the past to the enigma of the future, pervades the dramatic action of *Andromaque*, elaborating a reflection on the relation of one generation to another, on the making of art, and on the temporality of human existence.

THE ABSENT PRESENT

Oreste's words in the very first lines of *Andromaque* situate the action of the play in a time frame caught between the past and the future: "Oui, puisque je retrouve un Ami si fidèle, / Ma Fortune va prendre une face nouvelle" [Since I have found my faithful friend again, / My Fortune now assumes a different face] (1.1.1–2). This beginning in medias res immediately refers us to the past, the idea of which is reinforced by the prefix "re-" in "retrouve" and the adjective "fidèle." Then, abruptly, the idea of "Fortune" directs us toward the near-future tense of "va prendre" and the unseen originality of the "face nouvelle" for which Oreste hopes. What is missing here is the present. The present-tense verbs he uses, "retrouve" and the auxiliary of "va prendre," refer to the past and the future respectively. We are faced with a present that barely exists, or the existence of which Oreste wishes to ignore, and that is traversed throughout by memories of the past and speculation on the future and by the connection or transition between these two time frames. The point of movement from past to future, the moment of transition, defines the temporality of *Andromaque* and the crisis of generational change that the play represents.[3]

The inheritors of the heroic deeds of Hector and Achilles, of Menelaus and Agamemnon, can only invoke the greatness of their parents, while struggling with the historically petty, amorous concerns of their own sparse present on the threshold to an unknown future. Latecomers, in a parasitically referential relationship to the accomplishments of those who preceded them, the characters in *Andromaque* stand on a void, the constantly vanishing temporality of their own lives, the slippage of their becoming. Their attachment to their forebears becomes manifest not only in the numerous retellings of events at Troy, but even within the intimate subjective space of naming. Ronald Tobin points out the significance of genealogical periphrasis, a practice of naming that "underscore[s] the 'generation gap' of which the main characters are acutely conscious."[4] Still an infant, without yet having had the chance to develop his own identity, Astyanax, "Fils d'Hector" [son of Hector], is named through this kind of circumlocution more often than any other character, in six different lines of verse (1.4.272, 3.6.904, 4.1.1092, 4.1.1108, 4.5.1330, 5.2.1461). Hector, the most influential ghost of the past in terms of naming, also serves to define Andromaque's identity as "la Veuve d'Hector" [Hector's widow] (3.4.864, 4.5.1328). Hermione appears as "Fille d'Hélène" [daughter of Helen] (1.4.342, 4.5.1328), Oreste as "Fils d'Agamemnon" [son of Agamemnon] (1.2.178, 1.4.274), and Pyrrhus as "Fils d'Achille" [son of Achilles] (1.2.146, 1.2.150, 3.3.847). Living in an epilogue to history, these characters circulate in a world of bygones and are thus left only with memories of the past, a present devoted to the pursuit of unrequited passions, and a future about which they can only hypothesize.

Oreste, fully aware that he represents a devolution from his noteworthy predecessors, has recourse to using genealogical periphrasis as a rhetorical tool against Pyrrhus. Oreste carries out his mission on behalf of his countrymen by reminding Pyrrhus twice that he is the son of Achilles:

> Avant que tous les Grecs vous parlent par ma voix,
> Souffrez que je me flatte en secret de leur choix,
> Et qu'à vos yeux, Seigneur, je montre quelque joie
> De voir le Fils d'Achille, et le Vainqueur de Troie.
> Oui: Comme ses exploits, nous admirons vos coups;
> Hector tomba sous lui; Troie expira sous vous;
> Et vous avez montré, par une heureuse audace,

Que le Fils seul d'Achille a pu remplir sa place.
Mais ce qu'il n'eût point fait, la Grèce avec douleur
Vous voit du Sang Troyen relever le malheur,
Et vous laissant toucher d'une pitié funeste,
D'une Guerre si longue entretenir le reste.

(1.2.143–54)

[Before all Greece speaks to you by my voice
Allow me first to say how pleased I am
To have been chosen for this task, my lord,
And let me show some joy that I behold
Achilles' son, the conquerer of Troy.
Yes, we admire your deeds as much as his.
Great Hector fell beneath him: Troy expired
Beneath you; and you showed by happy courage
That Achilles' son alone could fill his place.
But Greece with sorrow sees you, unlike him,
Relieve the luckless blood of Troy and, touched
With fatal pity, care for the survivor
Of that long war.]

Oreste at first creates a symmetry between Achilles and Pyrrhus with the term of comparison "Comme." Then, with the contrasting conjunction "Mais," placed after a period that marks a pause for reflection on the past, Oreste points out that Pyrrhus has strayed from his father's legacy, by conserving the "reste," the remnant of the Trojan War that prevents putting this event definitively to rest. The "reste" that Pyrrhus cultivates is a continuity with the past that Achilles strove to annihilate. Thus the only way for Pyrrhus to be perfectly faithful to the generation preceding him would be to render irrevocable the past in which this generation lived, to do away with this remainder of the Trojan War, and thus to make the transition to a new order. It is paradoxically only through a dynamics of discontinuity that Pyrrhus can maintain the generational continuity through which he would remain true to his father's legacy.

But Pyrrhus's erotic desire for Andromaque prevents him from making this definitive move, and a situation is preserved whereby the transition from the previous generation to a new one remains suspended, enigmatically suggested in the person of Astyanax. Pyrrhus proves incapable of closing accounts on the past precisely because he is unable and/or unwilling to remember that past. This is one of Pyrrhus's definitive character traits. Oreste, in transmitting the message of the Greeks, questions the accuracy of Pyrrhus's memory: "Ne vous souvient-il plus, Seigneur, quel fut Hector?" [Do you no more remember / What Hector was, my lord?] (1.2.155). Hermione looks back in frustration at "tant de bontés dont il perd la mémoire" [After so much affection—all forgotten (*Solomon translation*)] (2.1.414). Cléone describes Pyrrhus's forgetfulness as a blindness toward the past: "Madame, il ne voit rien. Son salut, et sa gloire / Semblent être avec vous sortis de sa mémoire" [He nothing sees: his safety and his glory / Seem to have vanished from his memory] (5.2.1457–58). Céphise remarks that Pyrrhus "ne se souvient plus qu'Achille était son Père" [who remembers / No longer that Achilles was his father] (3.8.994), and Andromaque sets her own capacity for remembering the deeds of Achilles over against Pyrrhus's negligence: "Dois-je les oublier, s'il ne s'en souvient plus?" [Should I forget, though he remembers not?] (3.8.996). Pyrrhus himself recognizes that his passion for Andromaque renders him oblivious to what has taken place in the past: "Un regard m'eût tout fait oublier" [One look would have thrown all aside (*Solomon translation*)] (2.5.644); "Mais enfin je consens d'oublier le passé" [But now at last / I can forget] (4.5.1352). As a result of his detachment from past time frames, Pyrrhus focuses only on winning over Andromaque and leaves open the question of the future of Hector's lineage.

Pyrrhus's lack of concern for the future complements his amnesic tendencies in guaranteeing the conditions for Astyanax's survival. Unlike the Greeks who have sent Oreste to Epirus, Pyrrhus shows no concern for what Astyanax may eventually become:

> On craint, qu'avec Hector Troie un jour ne renaisse:
> Son Fils peut me ravir le jour que je lui laisse:
> Seigneur, tant de prudence entraîne trop de soin.
> Je ne sais point prévoir les malheurs de si loin.
>
> (1.2.193–96)

> [But it is feared
> That Troy will be reborn; that Hector's son
> May rob me of the light I let him keep.
> My lord, excessive prudence must involve
> Too much of care. I can't anticipate
> Such distant ills.]

An unstable character who changes with the circumstances that surround him and who is defined by his desire for Andromaque, Pyrrhus shows an acute awareness of the uncertainty of the future. Taking the limits of his own knowledge, of past and future times alike, Pyrrhus simply concerns himself with how to woo or coerce the widow of Hector into marrying him.

Thus it would seem that Pyrrhus more than any other of the main characters in *Andromaque* manages to liberate himself from genealogical imperatives. Accordingly, he is not named, as is Astyanax, strictly by genealogical periphrasis. In a fit of fawning exaggeration, Phœnix gives the most striking alternative to conventionally generational naming: "C'est le Fils, et le Rival d'Achille" [The son and rival of Achilles] (2.5.634). Oreste calls Pyrrhus an "Enfant rebelle" [rebel child (*my translation*)] (1.2.237), and for Hermione he is simply "un Rebelle" (2.2.562). He claims that he wishes to love Hermione "sans être esclave de son Père" [without being her father's slave (*my translation*)] (1.2.242), but we well know that he cares little for Hermione. Still, his refusal to comply with the demands of Ménélas and the father figure constituted by the Greeks makes this character a catalyst for the generational transition that will maintain the intriguing possibility of a future for Astyanax.

It would be erroneous, however, to see in Pyrrhus a new kind of hero. When he suddenly changes his mind, telling Oreste that he has decided to obey the law of the fathers (2.4.609–12), only to reverse this decision after another amorous pang for Andromaque (2.5.644–75), it becomes clear that Pyrrhus is bereft of convictions or strength of will. When he sets himself up as a father figure for Astyanax, in an attempt to win Andromaque's affections, the result verges on the comical, and one wonders whether Pyrrhus might not have read seventeenth-century novels of gallantry after all:[5]

> Madame, dites-moi seulement que j'espère,
> Je vous rends votre Fils, et je lui sers de Père.
> Je l'instruirai moi-même à venger les Troyens.
> J'irai punir les Grecs de vos maux et des miens.
> Animé d'un regard, je puis tout entreprendre.
>
> (1.4.325–29)

> [Madam, if you would tell me but to hope,
> I'd give you back your son, and be his father;
> I will instruct him to avenge the Trojans,
> And I will go to punish all the Greeks
> For the wrongs we both have suffered. Fired by one glance
> I can do all.]

The love-struck sovereign's grandiose plans for Astyanax fall flat for
spectators and readers who know very well that Pyrrhus is only trying
desperately to seduce Hector's widow. In contrast to Barthes, who sees
in Pyrrhus the emancipated, forthright representative of a new individ-
ualism, Leo Bersani more aptly estimates that this character represents
"a rather shallow prophet of a new order."[6] Nevertheless, Pyrrhus plays
a significant role in unwittingly facilitating the generational shift that is
at the heart of *Andromaque.* In order to function in this capacity, as we
have seen, Pyrrhus must be as blind to the past as he is to the future.
He is not significant by reason of a greatness akin to that of Achilles —
that hero's valor seems in Racine's play to have been a recessive trait —
but rather, to the contrary, because of his utter emptiness. Caught in a
moment between the aftermath of an old history and the promise of a
new history, Pyrrhus does not even attempt to live up to his father's
legacy, for such an endeavor could only result in failure. Instead, he
abandons all hope of greatness and simply follows his erotic desires,
choosing to live by the laws of an unstable present.

Fully aware of the futility of filial striving, Pyrrhus mockingly questions the importance of Oreste's mission:

> La Grèce en ma faveur est trop inquiétée.
> De soins plus importants je l'ai crue agitée,
> Seigneur, et sur le nom de son Ambassadeur,
> J'avais dans ses projects conçu plus de grandeur.
> Qui croirait en effet, qu'une telle entreprise
> Du Fils d'Agamemnon méritât l'entremise,
> Qu'un Peuple tout entier, tant de fois triomphant,
> N'eût daigné conspirer que la mort d'un Enfant?
>
> (1.2.173–80)

> [Greece is too much concerned for me. I thought
> That greater cares were vexing her, my lord,
> That her ambassador had greater projects.
> Who would believe that such an enterprise
> Deserved the choice of Agamemnon's son
> To undertake it? That the people of Greece,
> So many times triumphant, should have stooped
> To plot the death of a child?]

The period following "grandeur" gives Oreste a painful pause in which
to measure fully the mediocrity of his situation. Indeed, for Oreste political duties are nothing more than a pretext for courting Hermione. In

contrast with the exploits of a legendary past ("tant de fois triom-phant"), which Pyrrhus recalls here for rhetorical reasons, Racine's characters must repeatedly take stock of the paltriness of their present. In his reply, Oreste points out the generational nature of the problem posed by Astyanax: "Oui, les Grecs sur le Fils persécutent le Père" [Yes, it is true, the Greeks are persecuting / The father in the son] (1.2.225). Regardless of how adamantly the Greeks try to identify Asty-anax with Hector, the fact remains that this infant is a mere substitute for their famous foe. Astyanax represents not only the promise of the future, but also the severe deficit marking the present and those who inhabit this temporality.

AN AWKWARD INHERITANCE

The shortcomings of Racine's characters become painfully apparent when, in a rush of amatory enthusiasm, Oreste places himself and his cousin at the level of their parents:

> Prenons, en signalant mon bras, et votre nom,
> Vous la place d'Hélène, et moi d'Agamemnon.
> De Troie en ce pays réveillons les misères,
> Et qu'on parle de nous, ainsi que de nos Pères.
>
> (4.3.1163–66)

> [In making my prowess and your name renowned,
> You shall be Helen and I Agamemnon.
> Let us revive the miseries of Troy
> Here in Epirus. Let men speak of us
> As of our fathers.]

This delusion of grandeur throws the eventual failures of Oreste and Hermione, two of the characters who burn themselves out in the strug-gle through generational transition, more sharply into relief. Oreste is clearly doomed when we see that he has lost a sense of who he is and who he is destined to be. A significant part of his emerging madness, then, comes to light in how he situates himself with reference to preced-ing generations.

Hermione herself reveals how far short she falls of Helen's example, but to her credit she does so not by deluding herself but rather by rec-ognizing her own inferiority:

Quoi? sans qu'elle employât une seule prière,
Ma Mère en sa faveur arma la Grèce entière?
Ses yeux pour leur querelle, en dix ans de combats,
Virent périr vingt Rois, qu'ils ne connaissaient pas?
Et moi je ne prétends que la mort d'un Parjure,
Et je charge un Amant du soin de mon injure,
Il peut me conquérir à ce prix, sans danger,
Je me livre moi-même, et ne puis me venger?

                                        (5.2.1485–92)

[My mother, without a single prayer,
Armed Greece to fight for her; her eyes beheld
In ten long years of battles twenty kings
Perish, who did not know her; while I who wish
Only a perjurer's death, and charge a lover
To recompense my wrong, with me as prize,
Without a risk, I who surrender myself,
Cannot avenge me?]

The plenitude of the adjective "entière" and the enumeration of events contained in the numbers "dix" and "vingt" produce an image of an expansive past, against the backdrop of which the singulars "un Parjure" and "un Amant" appear paltry. Gone is the grandeur of the collective and the multiple; Hermione is left only with the pettiness of the singular, the frustration of a jilted lover.

Although she is no Helen of Troy, Hermione does partially redeem herself, within the cynical value system of Racinian power struggles, by using genealogical discourses to her strategic advantage. She manages to turn her requisite statements of filial duty into rhetorical tools. In trying to gain leverage against Pyrrhus, Hermione plays on the expectations of Oreste by citing her obedience to her father: "J'ai passé dans l'Epire où j'étais reléguée. / Mon Père l'ordonnait. Mais qui sait si depuis, / Je n'ai point en secret partagé vos ennuis?" [I came into Epirus, / Where I was banished, by my father's orders. / But who knows if since then I have not shared / Your griefs in secret?] (2.2.522–24). She keeps Oreste's hopes alive by evoking this secret rebellion, thrown into relief by the reference point of Ménélas's wishes. Later in the same scene, Hermione demands that Oreste name her father to Pyrrhus, in an attempt to force the latter into marrying her: "Au nom de Ménélas allez lui faire entendre, / Que l'Ennemi des Grecs ne peut être son Gendre" [Go, tell him from my father, that the foe / Of Greece can never wed his daughter] (2.2.585–86). The father serves also as a useful pretext in Hermione's uncomfortable meeting with Andromaque, during which the invocation of filial duty facilitates conversational avoidance: "Je conçois vos douleurs. Mais un devoir austère, / Quand mon Père a parlé, m'ordonne de me taire" [I appreciate your griefs; but a strict duty, / When my father has spoken, bids me hold my peace] (3.4.885–86). Hermione is unique in her position at the point of generational transition in that she systematically uses her own filial obligations as a part of a strategic kind of rhetoric. To her, duty toward her father means nothing in itself; it simply provides the possibility of gaining more leverage in her struggle to win over Pyrrhus.

Hermione herself admits that she finds no inherent meaning in the genealogical prerogatives that have put her in her current situation: "L'Ingrat m'avait su plaire, / Soit qu'ainsi l'ordonnât mon amour, ou mon Père, / N'importe" [the traitor knew the art / Of pleasing me; it does not matter now / Whether my love, or my father, ordered it] (4.3.1197–99). In fact, she reveals that, before her father betrothed her to him, she already loved Pyrrhus "[à] qui même je m'étais destinée, / Avant qu'on eût conclu ce fatal hyménée" [to whom, in secret, even, / I once was destined before this fatal marriage / Had been arranged] (5.1.1433–34). Against Barthes's interpretation, according to which Hermione is a character firmly anchored in and representative of the past, I would emphasize here her similarity to Pyrrhus, for whom the past holds as little inherent value as the unknowable future.[7] Hermione goes even farther than the negligent Pyrrhus when she angrily breaks off ties with Oreste and her entire ancestry: "Je renonce à la Grèce, à Sparte, à son Empire, / A toute ma Famille. Et c'est assez pour moi, / Traître, qu'elle ait produit un monstre comme toi" [I renounce Greece and Sparta and its rule, / And all my family: it's enough for me, / That it produced a monster such as you] (5.3.1602–4). From a strong inferiority complex, to an art of discursive manipulation that is only moderately successful, Hermione arrives at a genealogical repudiation through which she vents her frustration with the present. Similarly to Pyrrhus, she cares not to see beyond the passions that consume her in the time frame of dramatic action.[8]

Andromaque is of an entirely different sort. She must deflect passionate advances in the present while she cultivates a love and devotion to Hector that is rooted, rather morbidly, in the past:

J'ai vu mon Père mort, et nos Murs embrasés,
J'ai vu trancher les jours de ma Famille entière,

Et mon Epoux sanglant traîné sur la poussière,
Son Fils seul avec moi réservé pour les fers.

(3.6.932–35)

[I've seen my father dead, our walls destroyed;
I've seen the days of all my family
Cut short, my bleeding husband dragged through the dust,
His son, alone with me, reserved for chains.]

The grieving widow constructs a procession of the past's ghosts, from her father to her entire family, from Hector to Astyanax, who, even though he is still alive, appears only through the possession ("Son Fils") of a dead hero, and who wears the chains, not only of Pyrrhus's power, but of history itself.[9]

Bound by a strong sense of historico-genealogical obligation, Andromaque repeatedly retells the story of her tragic past. In an attempt to summon her dead husband, to remind herself of her duty to him, she reports Hector's last words:

Hélas! il m'en souvient, le jour que son courage,
Lui fit chercher Achille, ou plutôt le trépas,
Il demanda son Fils, et le prit dans ses bras.
Chère Epouse, dit-il, en essuyant mes larmes,
J'ignore quel succès le sort garde à mes armes,
Je te laisse mon Fils, pour gage de ma foi;
S'il me perd, je prétends qu'il me retrouve en toi.
Si d'un heureux hymen la mémoire t'est chère,
Montre au Fils à quel point tu chérissais le Père.
Et puis-je voir répandre un sang si précieux?
Et je laisse avec lui périr tous ses Aïeux?

(3.8.1022–32)

[Alas! I remember now, the day his courage
Made him Achilles seek, or rather death,
He asked for his son and took him in his arms.
"Dear wife," said he, in wiping off my tears,
"I know not what result fate holds in store
For these my arms. I leave my son to you
As pledge of my true love. If he should lose me,
In you, I know, he'll find me once again.
And if the memory of a happy marriage
Is dear to you, then show the son how much
You would the father cherish." And can I see

A blood so precious shed? Can I allow
With him his ancestors to perish too?]

Hector's words, spoken on the cusp of battle, have a dramatic impact similar to the dying speeches of characters in *La Thébaïde*. In this passage, Andromaque sees Astyanax only through the memorializing lens of his attribution to Hector, his status as "gage." From this perspective, Astyanax's only inherent value is the child's continuity with the past that Andromaque feels obligated to relive, through her retellings, her recollections of Hector's dramatic statements, and her incantatory repetitions.[10]

Thus Andromaque is to a significant extent defined by her concerted faithfulness to the generations that preceded her and to the husband she has lost: "O cendres d'un Époux! ô Troyens! ô mon Père! / O mon Fils, que tes jours coûtent cher à ta Mère!" [O ashes of a husband! Trojans! Father! / O son! How costly are your days to me!] (3.8.1049–50). Andromaque struggles to ensure that the transition from her father's generation, through Hector's generation, to the future promised by Astyanax be in continuity with and true to the illustrious past of Troy. She must battle the hardships that Astyanax's continued existence and Pyrrhus's manipulation of that existence create for her and refuse the kind of perverse transition from Hector's legacy that Pyrrhus proposes: "Quoi? je lui donnerais Pyrrhus pour successeur?" [What! I would give him / Pyrrhus as his successor?] (3.8.988).

A FUTURE FOR ASTYANAX

In order to render possible the kind of generational transition that she wishes to effect, Andromaque must imagine a future for her son. To make this future a nonthreatening prospect, Andromaque proposes a radical distancing from the world of power relations and genealogical prerogatives in which Astyanax may be led to seek revenge: "Laissez-moi le cacher en quelque Ile déserte. / Sur les soins de sa Mère on peut s'en assurer, / Et mon Fils avec moi n'apprendra qu'à pleurer" [Let me conceal him / On a desert island. I'll look after him, / And he will only learn to weep with me] (3.4.882–84). She thus gives herself the role of guardian and affective mentor for her son, who will spend a life devoid of troublesome knowledge of the past: he will learn only to weep with his mother. This image of Astyanax as a purely affective being also plays a role in Andromaque's first entreaty to Pyrrhus: "Hélas! on ne

craint point qu'il venge un jour son Père. / On craint qu'il n'essuyât les
larmes de sa Mère" [They do not fear he will avenge his father / But
that he'll wipe his mother's tears] (1.4.277–78). But Andromaque's alternative visions of the future cannot replace the prevailing notion of
Astyanax, "[c]et enfant dont la vie alarme tant d'états" [this child
whose life / Makes many states afraid] (1.1.92), as the new generation
of defenders of Troy.[11]

   Reacting mistakenly to Andromaque's announcement of her "innocent stratagème," Céphise proposes a vision of the future whereby Astyanax will revive Troy: "C'est Hector qui produit ce miracle en votre
âme. / Il veut que Troie encor se puisse relever, / Avec cet heureux Fils,
qu'il vous fait conserver" ['Tis Hector who has worked this miracle /
Within your soul! He wants Troy to arise / With this happy son he's
made you to preserve] (4.1.1054–56). This future, entirely based on the
will of Hector, would merely constitute a repetition of past events, the
cycle of recurrences which the Greeks so adamantly wish to break. Envisioning this future scenario in the more intimate domain of the relationship between mother and son, Céphise rejoices at the prospect of a
young hero who would be both a loving child and a heroic sovereign:

> Vous lui pourrez bientôt prodiguer vos bontés,
> Et vos embrassements ne seront plus comptés.
> Quel plaisir! d'élever un Enfant qu'on voit croître,
> Non plus comme un Esclave élevé pour son Maître,
> Mais pour voir avec lui renaître tant de Rois.
>
>   (4.1.1071–75)

> [Soon you can lavish all your bounties on him.
> And your embraces will no more be numbered.
> What joy to raise a child whom one sees grow,
> No more a slave that's brought up for his master,
> But to see in him so many kings reborn!]

The evocation of infinitely repeated expressions of maternal love combines with the thematics of growth and rebirth in Céphise's words to
paint a rose-colored picture of Hector's son's life. This version of the
future is both conventional in its portrayal of Astyanax as the logical
successor to Troy and highly personal in its emphasis on the bond
between mother and child. But the possibility of Astyanax having an
independent identity is smothered, in Céphise's account, by maternal
affections and genealogical expectations.

   It is when Andromaque devises her "innocent stratagème" and anticipates her own death that Astyanax comes to hold the potential for an autonomous subjectivity. Faced with the prospect of being separated from her child, Andromaque attempts to influence Astyanax's future knowledge and identity through a didactic discourse on how to interpret the past and manage a future present. She leaves Céphise with instructions to impart to Astyanax:

> Fais connaître à mon Fils les Héros de sa Race;
> Autant que tu pourras, conduis-le sur leur trace.
> Dis-lui, par quels exploits leurs noms ont éclaté,
> Plutôt ce qu'ils ont fait, que ce qu'ils ont été.
> Parle-lui tous les jours des Vertus de son Père,
> Et quelquefois aussi parle-lui de sa Mère.
> Mais qu'il ne songe plus, Céphise, à nous venger,
> Nous lui laissons un Maître, il le doit ménager.
> Qu'il ait de ses Aïeux un souvenir modeste,
> Il est du sang d'Hector, mais il en est le reste.

> (4.1.1117–26)

> [Let my son hear of all
> The heroes of his race; and, if you can,
> Guide him to follow them. Tell him the deeds
> For which their names are famous—what they did
> Rather than what they were. Speak every day
> Of his father's virtues, and sometimes speak of me.
> But let him no more think of avenging us:
> We leave a master to him he should respect.
> Let him, with modesty, recall his forbears.
> His is of Hector's blood, all that remains.]

The word "reste" placed in rhyming position with "modeste" sets up the future as another small epilogue to Hector's heroic past. Andromaque passes on to the future a reading of this past, a method for Astyanax to follow in developing an awareness of the generations that have preceded him. In envisaging a future for her son, the protective mother emphasizes the importance of knowledge and also of restraint and moderation. Leaving Astyanax with the task designated by "ménager," Andromaque hopes to help her son break the cycle of violence through which she has lost the rest of her family. By means of this didactic discourse, Andromaque aims to place a rational set of guidelines on the uncertainty of her son's future.

What grounds the possibility of the historico-genealogical knowledge proposed by Andromaque for her son is Astyanax's epistemological status as a tabula rasa. While the adult characters simply do not know what the future will hold, Astyanax does not *yet* know. Just as he is on the threshold of life and identity formation, the child is also on the cusp of a future that will concern him more fully than the adults who surround him. He is "[u]n Enfant malheureux, qui ne sait pas encor / Que Pyrrhus est son Maître, et qu'il est Fils d'Hector" [A poor child / Who does not know yet Pyrrhus is his master / Or that he's Hector's son] (1.4.271–72). The degree zero of Astyanax's knowledge provides the possibility for inculcating him with a coherent vision of what has preceded him and with a method for interpreting what he will know. Andromaque sees in this a potential exit from the dead end of the vendetta. Andromaque's speculation on the future is thus partly a hypothesis on the nature of Astyanax's knowledge. What he will know and how he will interpret this knowledge and act on it may determine the shape of things to come.

Alongside the optimistic prediction of a sensible and moderate Astyanax lies the possibility, which tacitly motivates Andromaque's didactic speech, that the child's eventual character may elude all predictions concerning him. This is what Barthes calls Astyanax II, a sequel to Hector who will have his own identity as well, and who will have the potential to found a new future.[12] Barthes insightfully points out that Astyanax may eventually reject the total identification between him and Hector that those around him seem to take for granted.[13] In planning her own suicide, Andromaque must confront the fact that, regardless of all the speculation surrounding her son, she actually knows nothing of what Astyanax might eventually become. According to Bersani, "the play brings us only to the threshold of a new order for which no content is imagined."[14] This is not entirely true, since a number of possible versions are given for Astyanax's future, but the complete uncertainty of all of these visions highlights the radical instability of the endpoint of the generational transition that is being witnessed in *Andromaque*.

The character who is most attuned to the unpredictability of the future is Oreste, who points out early in the play that those looking forward in time can see only a void before them: "Hélas! qui peut savoir le Destin qui m'amène?" [Alas! / who knows / The fate which brings me now?] (1.1.25). Oreste contributes significantly to the elaboration of a poetics of uncertainty, an esthetic valorization of the temporal threshold to the future that counterbalances the repetitive thinking on the past in this play. Here I go against the grain of Horowitz's fine analysis, according to which "an essential anteriority conveys the dominance of the Racinian past over an always suspended present (there are only the times of pre-war and post-war, or prophecy and memory), and over a future wished desperately as transcendent, but which is finally depicted as merely a static reproduction."[15] If, however, the future as represented in *Andromaque* were to hold only the possibility of repetition, then the character Astyanax would not be presented as such a complete mystery. Unlike Etéocle and Polynice of *La Thébaïde*, who from their very infancy waged a "guerre intestine" in Jocaste's womb and thus already manifested the repetitive violence that would mark their adult lives, Astyanax himself shows no signs of who he will become. He is an absent center for the speculation of others, a negatively motivating force for conjecture about the future, the content of which remains shrouded in mystery and provides Racine with the opportunity for the esthetic forays descriptive of this future.

In his second preface, Racine admits to having been "obligé de faire vivre Astyanax un peu plus qu'il n'a vécu" [obliged to make Astyanax live a little longer than he did] (298). What is the length of the epilogue to the myth of Astyanax designated by "un peu plus"? Racine leaves the question suspended, just as the play does not reveal what the infant's character will eventually be. Unlike the hero of Ronsard's *Franciade* (1572), Astyanax, perhaps the most pivotal character of *Andromaque*, presents us only with a striking absence, a blank space for speculation on and figural evocation of an unknown future.

Oreste undertakes this task of premonition, in a self-conscious manner that foregrounds the strict limits of his knowledge:

> Et qui sait ce qu'un jour ce Fils peut entreprendre?
> Peut-être dans nos Ports nous le verrons descendre,
> Tel qu'on a vu son Père embraser nos Vaisseaux,
> Et la flamme à la main, les suivre sur les Eaux.
>
> (1.2.161–64)

> [And who knows what this son, when grown to manhood,
> Can undertake? Perhaps we shall behold him
> Descend upon our ports, as once his father
> Set fire to our ships, and torch in hand
> Follow them on the waters.]

The key term here is "peut-être," an ambiguous qualification that foreshadows the play's final scene, when Pylade fears becoming the victim of Andromaque's vengefulness: "Et peut-être qu'encor, / Elle poursuit sur nous la vengeance d'Hector" [perhaps on us / Wants to avenge Troy and her Hector still (*Solomon translation*)] (5.5.1635–36). Oreste's en-

tourage does not know at that point whether Andromaque will immediately take revenge upon them or not. The nature of the transition from
Pyrrhus's régime to Andromaque's remains just as ambiguous at the
play's end as the result of the generational transition from Hector to
Astyanax.

The unknown and the unknowable are domains to which Oreste is
uncomfortably sensitized. His developing insanity drives him toward a
fuller appreciation of the radical ambiguity of the future than that attained by any of the other characters of *Andromaque*. Oreste's visionary
approach to the future involves describing this time frame to Pyrrhus
in a threateningly figurative mode: "Et que dans votre sein ce Serpent
élevé / Ne vous punisse un jour de l'avoir conservé" [And that this serpent nurtured in your breast / Will punish you one day for having saved
it] (1.2.167–68). The double "s" of the subjunctive "punisse" represents
the threatening, hissing uncertainty of the future, a serpentine enigma
that hovers over the heads of characters in the present, whispering in
ambiguous signs the shape of things to come. The alliteration of the con-
sonant "s," centered on the metaphor "Serpent," resonates strongly
with Oreste's delirious words in the play's final scene: "Pour qui sont
ces Serpents qui sifflent sur vos têtes?" [For whom / Those serpents
which are hissing on your heads?] (5.5.1682). The darkness into which
Oreste falls, on the verge of irrationality, figures the indeterminate future with which Racine leaves us at the conclusion of *Andromaque*, a
temporal dimension that provides a philosophical and esthetic counterpoint to the weight of the past in this play.[16]

In this chapter I have studied the dynamics of generational transition
in *Andromaque* in order to highlight the complex temporal structure of
the play, which combines a mytho-historical past with a troubling future and an uncomfortable present. I have argued that Racine's esthetic
achievement in *Andromaque* is based in no small part on the balance between past and future time frames for the dramatic action and on the
sublimation of the present, charged with unrequited passions, defined
as deficient in regard to the past, and painfully bearing the seeds of the
future. While Racine's characters take stock of their unenviable status
as historico-genealogical latecomers, they experience their sparse present with an intensity that is truly the stuff of great tragedy, as they bring
us to the threshold of a future that is radically uncertain but that holds
rich potential for forays of characters' imagination and Racine's dramatic composition. In *Britannicus*, this future will be shrouded in fear
and darkness.

4

Life in an Antechamber:
Time, Space, and Power in *Britannicus*

L'on s'accoutume difficilement à une vie qui se passe dans une anti-
chambre, dans des cours, ou sur l'escalier.[1]

—La Bruyère, "De la cour"

It is difficult to grow accustomed to a life that takes place in an antechamber, in courtyards, or on a staircase.

Sᴇᴛ ɪɴ ᴀɴᴄɪᴇɴᴛ ʀᴏᴍᴇ ᴅᴜʀɪɴɢ ᴛʜᴇ ɪɴɪᴛɪᴀʟ ꜱᴛᴀɢᴇꜱ ᴏꜰ ɴᴇʀᴏ'ꜱ ʀᴇɪɢɴ
and appearing in the early modern France of 1669, Racine's *Britannicus*
dramatizes the changing nature of power through the ages. As they
struggle to position themselves advantageously near the seat of Roman
sovereignty, Néron, Agrippine, Junie, and Britannicus raise perennial
political questions: namely, who has the upper hand, over whom, and
why? The opening of the tragedy shows Agrippine, mother of the emperor Néron, pacing in an antechamber, in front of his closed door. Although it was she who placed Néron in power by disenfranchising his
half-brother Britannicus, the legitimate heir to the throne, Agrippine
now finds herself shut out. She no longer pulls the strings for a son who
seems to have come into his own by rejecting her authority. Néron has
also taken Britannicus's beloved Junie prisoner. The frustrated mother
seeks an explanation from Burrhus, one of Néron's closest advisors, but
all she gets is a set of rationalizations for the emperor's actions. Agrippine will not go quietly. She decides to support Britannicus in a new
bid for power, by means of the advancement of the freedman Pallas.

Narcisse, Néron's closest counselor, informs the emperor of what is
afoot, and Néron exiles Pallas. He also reveals his awkward affection
for Junie, who resists his advances out of her love for Britannicus. The
emperor then orders Junie to hold a conversation with Britannicus,
during which Néron will be a concealed observer. Either Junie rejects

91

her beloved or he dies. She has no choice but to obey, and Britannicus leaves the scene crestfallen. The next time he sees Junie, however, she explains her behavior to him and assures him of her continued devotion. But Néron has been informed of this exchange by Narcisse, so he confronts Britannicus and has him locked up in turn.

Agrippine pleads with Néron to reconcile with Britannicus, and the emperor pretends to concede to her demands, but it is no more than a ruse to bring about the ruin of his rival for love and power. Burrhus tries to talk his emperor out of this act of deceit, but his entreaties are effectively countered by the diabolical Narcisse. After the planned ceremony of reconciliation, Burrhus can only tell Agrippine sadly of the day's tragic event, the poisoning of Britannicus by Néron, Narcisse, and Locuste, an expert on poisons. The grief-stricken Junie runs to a convent of vestal virgins, and when Narcisse tries to stop her he is attacked and killed by an angry mob. Néron, who has received his mother's malediction, exits the scene as the play ends, with a somber countenance that announces the beginning of a career in high crimes.

A harbinger of things to come, the set of strategies deployed by Néron (with the Machiavellian help of Narcisse) constructs the threshold to absolute and abusive power, a state of political affairs not yet attained in Rome but threatening to materialize in a troublesome near-future time.[2] Both temporally and spatially, *Britannicus* dramatizes points of access to power, constructing a conceptual space that corresponds to the antechamber in which Agrippine paces anxiously at the opening of the tragedy. Strategies of position and influence take progressively clearer shape, in both spatial and temporal terms, as the dramatic action of *Britannicus* unfolds. Drawing on analyses of time and space in Michel Foucault's *Discipline and Punish*, this chapter gives an account of the places and moments of power in Néron's Rome. In stark contrast to the complex-ridden personae of *Andromaque*, Néron breaks from genealogical prerogatives by ignoring his mother Agrippine's wishes and usurping the highest position of privilege in Rome. While his disregard for his heritage never ceases to infuriate Agrippine and to confound the rightful heir Britannicus, Néron's awareness of the functioning of power allows him to maintain a position of strategic advantage throughout the play.

NERONIAN TIME

A manipulator of space and time, the emperor uses his station to delegate duties and set the schedules of those who depend on him. The opening scene of *Britannicus* foregrounds this temporality of power, facilitated by a spatiality of exclusion. As Agrippine waits with her confidante by Néron's closed door, she takes exacting stock of time's passage: "Albine, il ne faut pas s'éloigner un moment. / Je veux l'attendre ici. Les chagrins qu'il me cause / M'occuperont assez tout le temps qu'il repose" [I must not leave yet. / I wish to await him here: all the vexations / He causes me will occupy my time / While he reposes] (1.1.6–8). The emperor's restfulness obliges others to wait. The delay temporally represents his power, while his disenfranchised mother's agitated consciousness tracks every moment of time during the beginning of the drama. The period at the caesura following "Je veux l'attendre ici" breaks this line in half, figuring the fragmentation of the time designated by "moment." Agrippine's time is a disjunctive series of painful instants. The enjambment from "cause" to "M'occuperont" figures discontinuity in Agrippine's apprehension of time, while the emperor's tranquil temporal experience concludes the line with "tout le temps qu'il repose." Power here amounts to controlling one's own time as well as that of others.

In contrast to the frustrating schedules of Néron's subjects, the emperor's own time appears to be a continuous stream of calm, as Junie remarks later in the play:

> Vos jours toujours sereins coulent dans les plaisirs.
> L'Empire en est pour vous l'inépuisable source,
> Ou si quelque chagrin en interrompt la course,
> Tout l'Univers soigneux de les entretenir
> S'empresse à l'effacer de votre souvenir.
>
> (2.3.650–54)

> [Your halcyon days
> Glide by in pleasures. The Empire is for you
> Their inexhaustible source; or if some sorrow
> Should stop their course, the world, solicitous
> Your pleasures to maintain, hurries to wipe them
> From your remembrance.]

Néron's servants hover around him to rectify interruptions and discontinuities in imperial time. The empire brings a manageable rhythm of life to those who occupy positions of privilege, while those at the margins must adjust their actions to rapid changes. For Néron, being in power means counteracting the unpredictable temporality of accident in his own affairs, while throwing the schedules of others off balance.[3]

Agrippine expresses her fear of losing power to her son by imagining a quick succession of potential events, framed in a near future: "Je le craindrais bientôt, s'il ne me craignait plus" [I would fear him sooner / If he no more feared me] (1.1.74). Agrippine thus evokes a moment of reversal, during which Néron may gain the upper hand in a swift stroke of self-actualization. Although he will remain only an embryo of his future self in this play, momentarily halted in a process of tyrannical becoming, Néron justifies his mother's concern. With stichomythic abruptness, he threatens to effect rapid and dangerous changes, announcing the imminent erasure of Britannicus's claims to the throne: "Avant la fin du jour je ne le craindrai plus" [Before night falls, / I shall fear him no more] (4.3.1322). Racine's explicit reference to the play's time unity here underlines Néron's strategic uses of time, which shore up his own authority while destabilizing the actions of Britannicus, Junie, and Agrippine.

Néron's disenfranchised mother complains in the play's opening scene of the time constraints that her son's entourage imposes on her: "En public, à mon heure, on me donne audience" [In public, at my appointed hour, / I am given audience] (1.1.119). The predetermined schedule that mediates all approaches to the emperor casts all conversations in the impersonal mode designated by "on." Néron sees Agrippine at certain times, which are his times, and not hers, as is ironically indicated with "à mon heure." The diachrony of planned meetings is arranged in units, blocs of time, which are mirrored by the adverbial groups separated by commas in line 119. Thus the emperor keeps his mother in the temporal antechamber to power, an experiential space of frustration and suspension. Later, when Agrippine gets the chance to give voice to her demands, she asks "[q]ue vous me permettiez de vous voir à toute heure" [That you should let me see you any hour] (4.2.1292). She recognizes that the initial step in vying for power is to control the temporal playing field.

Agrippine tries to make headway in this domain by criticizing Néron's disjunctive use of time. Junie's sudden imprisonment, then, becomes a pretext for denouncing the emperor's hasty actions: "De quoi l'accuse-t-il? Et par quel attentat / Devient-elle en un jour criminelle d'Etat?" [Of what does he accuse her? And what crime / Makes her so suddenly a State offender? (*Solomon translation*)] (1.2.229–30). Agrippine's disbelief at Néron's quick acts of discipline exposes the strategy of doing things rapidly to throw others off balance. She sees clearly but remains powerless.

Although he is oblivious to the fact that Néron is eavesdropping on his conversation with Junie, Britannicus understands the importance of strategic time in counteracting the emperor's schemes: "Ménageons les moments de cette heureuse absence" [Let us employ / The moments of his lucky absence] (2.6.711). But, as is the case with Agrippine, Britannicus's awareness only highlights his impotence and vulnerability. Junie's unresponsive behavior will make Britannicus feel the bite of Néronian time:

> A peine je dérobe un moment favorable,
> Et ce moment si cher, Madame est consumé
> A louer l'ennemi dont je suis opprimé?
> Qui vous rend à vous-même en un jour si contraire?
>
> (2.6.732–35)

> [With much ado I snatch a lucky moment
> And now this precious moment is consumed
> Praising the foe by whom I am oppressed!
> Who in a day has made you contrary
> To what you were?]

The appearance of an abrupt reversal in Junie's emotions combines with the infiltration of Britannicus's precious "moment favorable" to impose temporal constraints on Néron's rival within the intimate subjective sphere of momentary temporality. The emperor, hidden and voyeuristically taking in the scene, exercises his influence by means of Junie's speech, silence, action, and inaction. As Suzanne Gearhart explains, in this scene "Junie becomes a product of power, a creation of Néron and an instrument he uses to torture Britannicus. It is not just that her every word, gesture, and expression are under Néron's control as she speaks with Britannicus. The destructive effect of Néron's power in this scene includes perhaps above all a violation of Junie's interiority, in which she is forced not only to do and say certain things but even to think and feel in terms of an interiorized image of Néron's cruel gaze."[4] It is specifically through his exacting use of time and through the creation of intersubjective temporalities of control and constraint that Néron extends his power to the private sphere of other characters' thoughts and emotions. In Racine's abstract esthetics of suspension, confinement takes the form not only of a locked room but also of a constrictive schedule. The closed door to the seat of sovereignty has its temporal analogue in the time of frustrated nonaccomplishment and disenfranchisement that characterizes the experience of the emperor's subjects.

The precision with which Néron determines other characters' time requires a concerted focus on small temporal units. Meticulous and rationalized, Néron's disciplinary chronometry aims for maximum temporal efficiency in the application of power. Narcisse revels in the rapidity with which the sorceress Locuste's poison will act on Britannicus: "Et le fer est moins prompt pour trancher une vie / Que le nouveau poison que sa main me confie" [And the new poison she has let me have / Is swifter than the sword to end a life] (4.4.1395–96). The ultimate moment the emperor wishes to control will be that of his rival's annihilation. As Barthes puts it, "Nero desires Britannicus' elimination, not his spectacular defeat. . . . [T]he Neronian poison, moreover, is a swift one, its advantage is not delay but nudity, the rejection of the bloodstained stage."[5] Foucault identifies the movement toward occulted practices of discipline in his description of a modern age that began taking shape in the seventeenth century, in part through the rationalization of penal procedures. The temporal minimization of capital punishment will culminate in the eighteenth century with the lightning stroke of the guillotine, while panoptic spatial arrangements will come increasingly to shape modern carceral institutions.[6] Racine's esthetic treatment of the functioning of power thus dramatizes the shift from the sanguinary spectacle to silent, systematic practices of domination. These modern methods of control are enacted meticulously in time and arranged systematically in space.

NERONIAN SPACE

Power develops in *Britannicus* along both temporal and spatial axes, through rapid movements at one extreme, through stasis and nonaccomplishment at the other. Néron deploys not only efficient temporal strategies but also panoptic control of space from strategic vantage points. This latter tactic he inherited from Agrippine, who wistfully recalls the days when she discretely dominated the senate: "Et que derrière un voile, invisible, et présente, / J'étais de ce grand Corps l'Ame toute-puissante" [Behind a veil, invisible and present, / I was the omnipotent soul of that great body] (1.1.95–96). In Foucaultian terms, Agrippine had held a panoptic perspective in her former seat of power. The all-seeing prison warden, in Jeremy Bentham's model of the Panopticon, must himself remain invisible to the prisoners whose evenly spaced cells surround the building's central tower. The tower itself is visible, but its occupants are not. Thus power is present but cannot be precisely located. Agrippine, "invisible et présente," exercised control without revealing her position, and thus for a time remained "toute-puissante," until her son dislodged her and took over her seat: "Il m'écarta du Trône où je m'allais placer" [He kept me from the throne I was about / To occupy] (1.1.110).

As Tacitus describes it, when senators were summoned to Nero's palace, Agrippina would "stand close to a hidden door behind them, screened by a curtain which was enough to shut her out of sight, but not out of hearing. When envoys from Armenia were pleading their nation's cause before Nero, she actually was on the point of mounting the emperor's tribunal and of presiding with him; but Seneca, when every one else was paralysed with alarm, motioned to the prince to go and meet his mother. Thus, by an apparently dutiful act, a scandalous scene was prevented."[7] Whereas Tacitus focuses on Agrippina's scandalous behaviors in pursuit of power, Racine maintains this focus while also developing a detailed account of her efforts at strategic spatial positioning. Agrippine's striving for the throne and her uncomfortable exclusion and subsequent situation at the margins of this site recall the mannerist geometry of power developed in *La Thébaïde*. But whereas in Racine's first play the enemy brothers remain evenly matched in their struggle for sovereignty, in the political moment dramatized by *Britannicus* Néron clearly holds the upper hand. He occupies the central seat of authority and constructs an uncomfortable in-between space for others to occupy. This interstitial zone is not the threshold to the throne, as it is in *La Thébaïde*, but rather the point of potential access to Néron himself, the possibility of speaking to the sovereign.[8]

At the opening of *Britannicus*, the emperor remains conspicuously inaccessible, even for a brief moment of consultation. Pacing in the antechamber to power, Agrippine can stare only at the door that conceals her son. David Maskell describes this point of impossible passage in terms of the staging of the play: "The door to Néron's apartment is the gateway to power. Agrippine makes to cross the threshold, hoping to regain the influence which is slipping from her grasp; but Burrhus stops her, a visual effect which echoes Léandre's 'No entry' barring the Comtesse in *Les Plaideurs*."[9] Both a powerful metaphor and a useful theatrical object, "[t]his door, loaded with significance, remains visible throughout the tragedy." According to Lucien Dubech, this object, this space becomes veritably personified in this tragedy: "One might say that the door is the principal character in *Britannicus* and that the play is a tragedy in front of a door."[10] In immediate proximity to this site, Néron's henchmen observe events and report conversations to him. Situated at the threshold between sovereignty and exclusion, they thus act as windows and walls of the central tower that he inhabits in his panoptic palace. Agrippine draws the conclusion, from her suspended spatial situation, that her influence over her son is decreasing with every passing moment:

> Et qui s'honorerait de l'appui d'Agrippine
> Lorsque Néron lui-même annonce sa ruine?
> Lorsque de sa présence il semble me bannir?
> Quand Burrhus à sa porte ose me retenir?

(1.2.275–78)

> [Who would be honored by my aid when Nero
> Himself proclaims my ruin; when he seems
> To banish me his presence; and when Burrhus
> Dares to withold me from his door?]

The pairing of "bannir" and "retenir" in rhyming position points to the exact nature of Agrippine's spatial subjection. Néron banishes her by having her held in place, trapped at a blocked point of approach to the sovereign. When she later demands access to her son at all times, she also insists on being released from her unbearable entrapment in the doorway: "Que ce même Burrhus, qui nous vient écouter, / A votre porte enfin n'ose plus m'arrêter" [That this same Burrhus, who comes to listen now, / Shall never dare to bar me from your door] (4.2.1293–94). She rages energetically but ineffectively against a practice of carefully calculated entrapment and frustrating stasis.

As he carefully wields his increasing power over Rome, Néron makes an exact science out of controlling the spatiotemporal structure of the threshold to power, of the antechamber in which he keeps Agrippine and Britannicus. Behind his walls and doors, invisible to those under his control, Néron uses his power to invest all of the spaces of his domain.[11] Junie tells Britannicus of Néron's capacity to occupy all that surrounds them: "Vous êtes en des lieux tout pleins de sa puissance. / Ces murs mêmes, Seigneur, peuvent avoir des yeux. / Et jamais l'Empereur n'est absent de ces lieux" [This place is full of his power. These very walls / Have eyes; and from this place the Emperor / Is never absent] (2.6.712–14). Imitating his mother's strategy of simultaneous presence and concealment, Néron lets Junie know that, though hidden, he will be more central to her conversation with Britannicus than the son of Claudius himself: "Caché près de ces lieux je vous verrai, Madame" [Hidden close by / I shall see you, madam] (2.3.679). Néron describes his own silent, discreet machinations in relation to "ces lieux," the places that he controls and uses to constrain others.

More precisely, Néron uses his power to create separate spaces for Junie and Britannicus to occupy during their tense conversation. In his reading of elements of panopticism in *Le Cid*, John D. Lyons discusses the importance of the separation between individual subjects for the functioning of panoptic power: "Panopticism prevents lateral interaction among the individuals who are juxtaposed in the system. Thus, in Bentham's ideal prison, the prisoners would not be able to see one another, to get into fights, or to pass on infectious diseases. This kind of separation is absent from the Castilian court in Corneille's play, and consequently individuation arises not only from the observation at a distance of the impersonal observer but also from the constant comparative observation of the courtiers themselves."[12] In the simultaneously modern and feudal world of *Le Cid*, mutual visibility and intelligibility among court members enables them to resist the panoptic power grounded in the universal visibility of all of their actions. *Le Cid*, then, is situated at a point of transition between the feudal exercise of power and an emerging modern panopticism. For Lyons, the modern individual theorized by Foucault as being subject to new systems of power is gradually in the process of being formed in the seventeenth century. One of the functions of Néron in *Britannicus* is to represent a stage in this development. Power in this tragedy operates one step closer to panopticism than it does in *Le Cid*, in that Néron calculatingly prevents lateral communication among those subjected to his invisible but oppressively ever-present gaze. He creates a barrier between Junie and Britannicus (as he also does between Agrippine and other characters) by means of his manipulation of space. The externalization of power in space, combined with the fact that the observer remains invisible, suggests another move toward panopticism, not yet fully accomplished but nonetheless strongly suggested in *Britannicus*—the transition to impersonal power. Spatial relations, rather than individual prerogatives, determine intersubjective dynamics of domination. It is not a single individual who holds power as a result of his or her identity or legitimacy. Both Agrippine and Britannicus try to formulate claims to the influence that Néron enjoys, but their words are futile in the face of Néron's understanding of the functional nature of power. The system is beginning to take precedence over the individual, and Néron is only too happy to maintain his observation post, in silence and invisibility.

As we have seen with Néron's temporal manipulation of Junie's and Britannicus's subjective experience, the emperor's exercise of power goes beyond the intentionality of a single, unified will; power circulates through a multiplicity of identities that are enlisted in its perpetuation. That the walls may have eyes attests to the spread of power throughout the subjectivities that are contiguous with the spaces of the palace. The panoptic gaze provides a case in point of this transsubjective ubiquity of silent forces of domination through surveillance. Gearhart analyzes these dynamics of power in her discussion of "the idea of a hidden spectator, who may be there or who may not be there, but who is in a sense ever-present precisely because his gaze is now *imagined* as being ever-present. The passage ["Ces murs mêmes, Seigneur, peuvent avoir des yeux"] suggests that in a situation such as this each individual watches him or herself. In this sense power becomes interiorized and its destructiveness is intensified insomuch as it comes not only from without but from within as well."[13] It is also from within that this power can be resisted, and Gearhart shows how Junie, in her final escape, manages to trump Neronian panopticism.[14]

Britannicus, however, fatally misunderstands the transsubjective flexibility and spatial mobility of the power Néron deploys. The disenfranchised prince expresses a misplaced, ineffectual outrage and claims to hold authority over the places he was to inherit and where Néron now imprisons Junie:

> Et l'aspect de ces lieux, où vous la retenez
> N'a rien dont mes regards doivent être étonnés.
> NERON
> Et que vous montrent-ils qui ne vous avertisse
> Qu'il faut qu'on me respecte, et que l'on m'obéisse?
> BRITANNICUS
> Ils ne nous ont pas vus l'un et l'autre élever,
> Moi pour vous obéir, et vous pour me braver
> Et ne s'attendaient pas, lorsqu'ils nous virent naître,
> Qu'un jour Domitius me dût parler en maître.

(3.8.1033–40)

> [and there's nothing here,
> Where you detain her, which should startle me.
> NERO
> Nothing to warn you that I must be respected
> And be obeyed?
> BRITANNICUS
> It has not seen us both
> Brought up together, myself at your command,
> And you to brave me; nor did it expect,

When we were born, that Domitius one day
Would speak to me as master.]

Britannicus rhetorically uses the stability of place and the temporal depth of childhood memory to discount Néron's claims to authority. Néron responds by referring simply to matters as they stand:

Ainsi par le destin nos vœux sont traversés,
J'obéissais alors, et vous obéissez.
Si vous n'avez appris à vous laisser conduire,
Vous êtes jeune encore, et l'on peut vous instruire.

(3.8.1041–44)

[So by fate
Our prayers are thwarted. I obeyed you then,
Now you obey. If you have not yet learnt
The art of obedience, you are still young,
And you can be instructed.]

The emperor understands that power changes hands according to the strategic positions one occupies. While Britannicus feels that the past gives him an investment in the spaces that surround him, Néron, as we have seen, infiltrates these places in the present. He thereby proposes a didactic discourse of power and obedience.

Derval Conroy's discussion of women's roles in Racine's theater raises the issue of Max Weber's differentiation between power and authority, a distinction that sheds light on Néron and Britannicus's competing claims: "Power, for Weber, 'is the probability that one actor within a social relationship will be in a position to carry out his own will despite resistance, regardless of the basis on which this probability rests.' Authority on the other hand hinges on concepts of legitimacy, i.e. when a person has the legitimate 'right' to carry out his/her will."[15] Britannicus's claim of legitimacy encounters Néron's enactment of power head-on. But the voice of authority becomes a voice of lamentation, while Néron's voice remains coolly descriptive and indeed incontrovertible. The genealogical depth and temporal stability of the notion of legitimacy loses out to the present-centered, functional temporality of the exercise of power. While Britannicus conceptualizes and rhetorically describes his legitimacy, Néron quietly maintains the upper hand on the throne and keeps his rival in an antechamber.

Through his functional ideation and application of power, Néron has dislodged both Britannicus and Agrippine, who laments the loss of identity that has resulted from a shift in position: "Ma place est occ-upée, et je ne suis plus rien" [My place is filled and I become a cipher (*Solomon translation*)] (3.4.882). Néron himself, however, is not much more than a ghost in the machine. This ineffectual would-be lover, who eavesdrops and delegates duties but rarely does anything himself, sim-ply holds the seat of authority in Rome, and only for the time being. Néron puts his spin on a network of forces that surpasses his individual agency but within which he manages for some time to occupy the most influential position.

POWER

Foucault insists on the strategic and systematic properties of modern power, which is located "not so much in a person as in a certain con-certed distribution of bodies, surfaces, lights, gazes; in an arrangement whose internal mechanisms produce the relation in which individuals are caught up."[16] Holding power becomes a question of skilfully manip-ulating the interplay of dispositions of bodies, spaces, and gazes, while always keeping oneself in an advantageous position.

Though he does not dispose of the modern technologies of discipline that Foucault discusses, Racine's Néron nonetheless exhibits a thor-ough understanding of a similar dynamics of power; Agrippine and Bri-tannicus cling to images of past privileges and lose the upper hand in the present. While these ill-fated characters look at the extended tempo-ral dimensions of memory and genealogical legitimacy, Néron pursues a micro-temporal focus, pertinent to what Foucault calls a microphysics of power: "Now, the study of this micro-physics presupposes that the power exercised on the body is conceived not as a property, but as a strategy, that its effects of domination are attributed not to 'appropria-tion,' but to dispositions, manœuvres, tactics, techniques, functionings; that one should decipher in it a network of relations, constantly in ten-sion, in activity, rather than a privilege that one might possess."[17] Néron understands the functional, impersonal nature of power better than those around him do. Racine's villain, in the early years of his reign, has little in common with the spectacularly cruel Nero of later years, during whose reign Rome burned and murders and forced suicides abounded. By contrast, Racine's "monstre naissant" [nascent monster] (372) is more an administrator of power than a memorable practitioner of pun-ishment. His calculating approach to maintaining political authority through acts of discipline serves to shape the zones that surround his throne. All points of access to power fall under his calculating eye and take part in Racine's dark poetics of authority, exclusion, and indefinite entrapment.

Reading Racine in the context of Foucault and Barthes reveals temporal and spatial elements of early modern conceptions of power while highlighting some of the contours of Racine's esthetics in this play. Unique in Racine's dramatic corpus, *Britannicus* enacts a poetics of power. The temporal situation of Néron's early years as emperor intersects with the spatial instability of Agrippine's positioning in the antechamber to sovereignty to create a tenuous tragic situation. Britannicus's exclusion and Junie's imprisonment locate these characters at the thresholds to the site occupied by Néron. These dramatic arrangements of space and time, with a Néron-in-the-making at the center, effectively poeticize the individual's suspended animation and implication in networks of power. Racine thus shows us the pains of the subject in the antechamber of an embryonic tyrant, where the excluded party can only look on, trapped in a vortex of failed striving, as power is exercised to reinforce his/her subjection. This kind of torture in suspension takes on a more lyrical form in *Bérénice*, where the eponymous heroine waits on the threshold, no so much of power, but rather of self-fulfillment through love. Behind the walls of the Roman senate and behind the conflicted countenance of the emperor Titus, her fate will slowly be decided, in an excruciating temporality of waiting. Whereas in *Britannicus* subjective suspension points to the systematic and impersonal nature of power, with *Bérénice* Racine creates a steadily mounting dramatic tension in order to explore the individual experience of duration.

5

The Tragic Time of Self in *Bérénice*

TIME TICKS AWAY WITH INCREASING PRECISION IN RACINE'S TRAGE-
dies of the late 1660s and early 1670s. From the hectic rush of a limited
present, constrained by a fiery past in *Andromaque*, to the calculated pu-
nitive temporalities of Néron's reign in *Britannicus*, Racine arrives with
Bérénice at a complex music of subjective time. Indeed time itself in *Bérénice* assumes the proportions of a virtual, invisible character.[1] In this
chapter, I examine the dramatic temporality of *Bérénice* through a close
reading the text of the play. I also examine the tragedy's preface, a significant document for understanding Racine's views on tragedy at a
time in his career when he experimented, more pointedly than any playwright before him, with minimalism as a dramaturgical principle.

Bérénice is unique within the Racinian dramatic corpus for its intensely subjective development of suspense and suspension.[2] Situated
in a meticulously described present on the threshold of a troubling future, the eponymous heroine marks a new phase in the construction of
the Racinian individual, a development that will culminate in the death
throes of Phèdre. But Bérénice even more than Phèdre gives a painstaking account of every moment of her experience of a tragic day, a
time frame constructed by Racine's most minimalist action. Titus loves
Bérénice, the Queen of Palestine. According to Roman law, Titus, as
emperor, cannot marry a foreign queen. Thus he must send her away,
after a period of deliberation that is painful not only to both of them,
but also to Antiochus, King of Commagene, who loves Bérénice but
cannot win her love in return. The plot is simple but artfully developed,
as Racine explains.

PARATEXTUAL TIME

In the preface to *Bérénice*, Racine sets out for himself a high dramaturgical goal: "attacher durant cinq Actes [les] Spectateurs, par une action

simple" [to hold the audience through five Acts, by a simple plot] (451). This preface, which makes frequent reference to the "Règles" [rules] governing the composition of tragedies, puts forth an exacting conception of theatrical time by foregrounding the formal ideal of a simple, unified action. Instead of developing a multitude of events and circumstances, Racine will endeavor to present to his readers and spectators one fundamental story that will unfold in all of its nuances during the five acts of this tragedy. The action is not empty or scant, however, by reason of its simplicity. In order to justify his choice of narratives, Racine points out that Vergil devoted a good portion of the *Æneid* to the tragic tale of Æneas and Dido: "Et qui doute, que ce qui a pu fournir assez de matière pour tout un Chant d'un Poème héroïque, où l'Action dure plusieurs jours et où la Narration occupe beaucoup de place, ne puisse suffire pour le sujet d'une Tragédie?" [And who can doubt that what could furnish enough matter for a whole book of an epic, in which the action lasts several days, may not suffice for the subject of a tragedy of which the span can only be a few hours?] (450).[3] The vocabulary that Racine uses — "fournir," "assez," "matière," "tout," "plusieurs," "beaucoup," "suffire" — makes clear that it is a question here of quantity. The playwright uses the idea of several days of narrational time to set up a contrast with the limited time frame of classical tragedy, so that there will be no question that the action he develops in *Bérénice* is largely sufficient. He arrives at this justification through a process of temporal quantification and comparison. The "plusieurs jours" of Vergil's narrative compared to the single tragic "journée" sketch out a rhetorical timeline that is to Racine's polemic advantage.[4]

The argumentation becomes more complicated further in the preface, when Racine takes the opposite direction and uses the criterion of *vraisemblance* [verisimilitude] to criticize the tendency to force too many events into the limited time frame of a single play: "Et quelle vraisemblance y a-t-il qu'il arrive en un jour une multitude de choses qui pourraient à peine arriver en plusieurs semaines?" [And what is there probable about a multitude of things happening in one day which could hardly happen in several weeks?] (451). Again we have a temporal comparison, but this time Racine sets it up differently, for a different rhetorical purpose. The unit of temporal plenitude, "plusieurs semaines," is considerably larger than "plusieurs jours," the term of comparison used in the discussion of Vergil. By distancing himself from dramatists who may have a tendency to cram too many events into a play, Racine makes the contrast stronger than in the passage sketching out the fullness of the plot of *Bérénice*. The two statements on temporal asymmetry differ also in the conception of narrational time that each represents. In the first, there is a significant story, well known in history, that occupies a considerable duration in an author of the stature of Vergil. In the second, the extreme multiplicity of gratuitous events corresponds to an uncontrolled, excessive time quantity, in stark disproportion to the classical time unity and in full infraction of the criterion of verisimilitude. Thus in the first case Racine conceives of time as duration, and in the second he presents time as a diachrony of multiple events. From the plenitude and coherence of duration, with reference to Vergil, we arrive at the fragmentation and excess of events diachronically disposed.

The difference between Racine's rhetorical uses of temporal disproportion points us to the importance of dramatic time in the preface to *Bérénice*. Strangely, although he uses the term "Règles" nine times in this preface, thus with more frequency than in any of the other prefaces to his tragedies, he never explicitly discusses the time unity. But the prominence of the question of time in Racine's argumentation (not to mention the extreme frequency of references to time in the play itself, which I discuss below) strongly suggests that the time unity is a significant part of what he accomplishes and justifies, in terms of his dramaturgy, with *Bérénice*.

Racine treads a thin line between the dramatic ideal of a unity for action on the one hand and the audience's expectation of events on the other. What will be the events which break up the single bloc of the tragic day, of the coherent Vergilian action of *Bérénice*, and how will it be possible to allow the fragmentation of multiple events without breaking up the solidity of an action chosen for its simplicity? I would propose that it is in the subjective experiences, emotions, and words of Racine's characters that this multiplicity will be developed. Racine chooses a sparse plot in *Bérénice* in order to concentrate the dynamics of tragic time within the intimate sphere of personal perceptions. The paradoxically simultaneous paucity and plenitude of external event in *Bérénice* allows for a concerted focus on individual conceptualizations of time. These temporal apprehensions contribute to an intensely subjective poetics of suspension between a painful present and a worrisome near future.

Instead of seeing subjects who live through numerous events organized by the author's narrational chronology, in *Bérénice* we see characters' multiple reactions to and interpretations of a single, incrementally developing event: Titus's reluctant rejection of Bérénice. These reactions and subjective experiences then become events in themselves and mark with precision the passage of dramatic time as the action unfolds. Within the sphere of individualized ideation of dramatic time, Racine elaborates a metatemporal level on which the characters themselves reflect on the time that organizes their common situation. At this metatemporal level, which constitutes a commentary within the fictional text on the structure of that very text, the play enters into continuity with the paratextual exploration of the preface, a complex metadramatic threshold to textuality and performance.[5]

THE TRAGIC TIME OF SELF

In the clearest moment of resonance between play and preface, Titus sets up a temporal asymmetry in his statement on the tragic nature of the present day, "[l]orsqu'un heureux hymen, joignant nos destinées / Peut payer en un jour les vœux de cinq années" [And a sweet marriage binding me to her / Can set seal on my five years' hopes at last] (2.2.443–44). The disproportion that Titus evokes, between the duration of five years and the intensity of a potential day of culmination, contributes to the development of tragic emotions by marking the present day as an eminent endpoint. The duration of five years subtends the single day of tragic time and infuses this smaller time unit with all the experiential significance of a lived past. It is through subjective experience of this temporal dynamics that the force of tragedy increases. Thus the rhetoric of temporal asymmetry that served Racine in justifying the action of the play contributes here to the thematic and structural coherence of paratext and text.

Antiochus experiences perhaps even more sharply the relation between the long duration of five years of waiting and the decisive time frame of the day of decision making, for he lives through the culminating day as the excluded third party, stuck at the threshold to interrelation, painfully witnessing Bérénice's enduring love for Titus:

> Aujourd'hui qu'il peut tout, que votre hymen s'avance,
> Exemple infortuné d'une longue constance,
> Après cinq ans d'amour, et d'espoir superflus,
> Je pars, fidèle encore quand je n'espère plus.
>
> (1.2.43–46)

> [Today when he is master and would wed you,
> I, sad example of long constancy,
> After five years of love and luckless longing,
> Depart, still loyal, when my hope is dead.]

Antiochus laments the uselessness of his past devotion in the context of a present that holds for him only renewed moments of frustration. As in the preface, the framing of the dramatic action by the extended duration of the past brings readers' and spectators' attention to the details of the present moments that characters observe in their passing.

Later in the play, Antiochus's suffering entails a heightened sensitivity to every instant of the tragic time that ticks away in the background: "Tous mes moments ne sont qu'un éternel passage / De la crainte à l'espoir, de l'espoir à la rage" [Throughout my days I'm being forever tossed / From fear to hope, from hope to desperation] (5.4.1311–12). Caught repeatedly in varying degrees of emotional disarray, Antiochus tracks the passage of time in a self-reflexive description of the intimate sphere of his own feelings and perceptions. The experience of time as a kind of torture of emotional in-between states is prevalent in Racine's tragedies, but rarely does the subjective perception of minimal units of time appear in such a detailed and emphatic form as it does here. The tragic individual's feeling of time as eternal passage constitutes the culmination of Racine's temporal threshold esthetics. From the opening lines of the play, Antiochus describes his tension-filled position, on the verge of departure yet hanging on as the moments of the action tick by. This anxiousness is expressed in the contrast between his desire for departure—"Retirons-nous, sortons, et sans nous découvrir, / Allons loin de ses yeux l'oublier, ou mourir" [Let me withdraw, depart, without a word, / And far away let me forget or die] (1.1.33–34)—and his inexorable stasis: "Arrêtons un moment" [Let's stay awhile] (1.1.1). Like Phèdre, Antiochus paradoxically advances the action by halting it at the cæsura of the first line of verse.[6] Stuck in a state of permanent becoming, Antiochus laments the indefinite temporality of an unaccomplished emotive transition.[7]

The focus on the "moment" as a unit of dramatic time and of subjective experience is a prominent characteristic of *Bérénice*, the play in which Racine had most frequent recourse to this term. In its singular and plural forms combined, the word "moment(s)" occurs forty times in *Bérénice*.[8] The prevalence in this play of the term "moment(s)" provides clear evidence that Racine sought to develop the representation of intimate, individual experiences of time in its smallest manifestations as a way of ornamenting and internally fragmenting the minimalistic action of the storyline. The many references to mere instants of characters' lives produce a diversity of subjective temporalities structuring the experience of suspension in the present, on the threshold to the future. As is evident in the case of Antiochus, the focus on the tragic moment can evoke the pain, frustration, and confusion that plague the speaking subject.

Ruth Sussman analyzes several instances of reference to the "tragic moment" in *Bérénice* and finds a spatial analogue to this unit of time in the space between Titus's and Bérénice's apartments: "[T]he antechamber is a concretization of the dramatic moment, suspended spatially as the heroes of the drama find themselves suspended temporally between past and future."[9] Whereas in *Britannicus* the antechamber figures the space between power and subjection, in *Bérénice* this transitional site exteriorizes the experiences of both Titus and Bérénice. In the opening lines of the tragedy, Antiochus observes their interaction through the doorways of these adjoining rooms:

> Souvent ce Cabinet superbe et solitaire,
> Des secrets de Titus est le dépositaire.
> C'est ici quelquefois qu'il se cache à sa Cour,
> Lorsqu'il vient à la Reine expliquer son amour.
> De son Appartement cette porte est prochaine,
> Et cette autre conduit dans celui de la Reine[.]
>
> (1.1.3–8)

> [Within this grand secluded chamber Titus
> Often unburdens his most secret thoughts.
> Here it is sometimes, stealing from his Court,
> He comes to whisper to the Queen his love.
> This door gives access to his private chamber
> And that door opens on the Queen's apartment.]

Titus and Bérénice oscillate between subjectivity and intersubjectivity, between one spatial situation, one temporal dimension and another, and, perhaps most poignantly, between uncertainty about how events will unfold and the inevitable knowledge of their respective destinies.[10] The questioning leading to this knowledge lies at the heart of what is tragic in *Bérénice*, and the eponymous heroine is, appropriately, the character most skilled in sounding the forces of destiny in the excruciating detail of subjective experience.

Even more sensitive to the passage of time than Antiochus, Bérénice interrogates her own desires and expectations in her famous monologue, during which she waits for Phénice to transmit a message from Titus:

> Phénice ne vient point? Moments trop rigoureux,
> Que vous paraissez lents à mes rapides vœux!

Je m'agite, je cours, languissante, abattue,
La force m'abandonne, et le repos me tue.
Phénice ne vient point. Ah que cette longueur
D'un présage funeste épouvante mon cœur!

(4.1.953–58)

[Will Phenice never come? O cruel moments,
How slow to my impatient need you seem!
Restless I run, in anguish all cast down;
Forsaken by my strength and killed by rest.
Will Phenice never come? How her delay
Affrights my heart with fatal premonitions!]

These excessive, expansive moments of time seem difficult and slow
against the backdrop of Bérénice's "rapides vœux." The verb "parais-
sez" makes it clear that Bérénice does not claim to observe this excess
objectively but rather that she endeavors to take stock of her own perceptions of the time that feels to her like a virtual death. Her wishes
("vœux") and the movements of her heart ("cœur") take center stage
in rhyming positions, as Bérénice describes her own emotional and
physical experience, a painful agitation that is out of sync with the time
that slowly ticks away under Titus's onerous deliberations. As Odette
de Mourgues points out, "this slowing down of the passing of time gives
to moments a cruel power of expansion and their dramatic intensity is
derived from their quality of never-ending suffering and the succession
of conflicting moods they contain."[11] It is not just dramatic time that has
slown down, however, but more specifically Bérénice's perceptions of
it. She constructs her own temporality, one that stands in sharp contrast
to the incremental unfurling of her destiny and to the patient rhythm of
Titus's decision making.

Bérénice represents the very principle of subjective time placed
against the calculating kind of time which Titus follows in examining
his duties as emperor. Perhaps the most moving expression of the personal experience of time comes when Bérénice laments the fading possibility of "un amour qui devait unir tous nos moments" [a love that was
to unite all of our moments (*my translation*)] (4.5.1106). Here she constructs a vision of the union of lovers as a perfect synchronicity, a temporality grounded in harmonious interrelation and independent of the
strictures of political obligations.[12] Bérénice achieves in her affective
rhetoric a kind of sublimation of time measurement, whereby she ar-
ranges time units with a meticulousness that is similar to a calculated

approach to time, but for which the end result is altogether different, grounded in emotions and passion.

Thus from within the constraints of her tragic situation, Bérénice succeeds in developing an alternative temporality based on her subjective experience of time. Bérénice brings to the fore the human tendency to construct temporalities that sharply clash with the rhythms of external events or the incremental unfolding of tragic fate. In this way she undertakes a subjective rebellion against the forces that constrain her, at the point of contact between her individual experience and the elements of social reality and destiny that determine her existence.

Little resistance is possible in *Britannicus*, where Néron uses his power not only to imprison other characters—Agrippine pacing outside his door, Junie locked up by his henchmen—but also to determine their schedules. In response, as we have seen, Agrippine complains that "En public, à mon heure, on me donne audience" [In public and at fixed times I have audience] (1.1.119), while she would like to have access to her son whenever she pleases. Britannicus, for his part, fails even to procure a single moment of intimacy with Junie, which would give him an advantage over Néron. Britannicus's invocation of genealogical prerogatives is as ineffective as Agrippine's nostalgic returns to her rather unsavory past privileges as these characters try to disrupt the Neronian present, a time frame dominated by the cold calculations of Néron and his advisors. In *Britannicus*, power shapes time.

By contrast, Titus experiences time ambivalently, torn as he is between the emotionally wrought temporality of passion and the necessary calculations of political duty.[13] In weighing the importance of both his affective life and his new role as a sovereign, Titus, alone on the stage, interrogates his own thoughts and feelings, trying to take stock of the time that has recently passed:

> Depuis huit jours je règne. Et jusques à ce jour
> Qu'ai-je fait pour l'honneur? J'ai tout fait pour l'amour.
> D'un temps si précieux, quel compte puis-je rendre?
> Où sont ces heureux jours que je faisais attendre?
>
> (4.4.1029–32)

> [I've reigned a week [*sic*]. My deeds till now will prove
> I've nothing done for honour, all for love.
> How to account for precious time deflected?
> Where is the happy epoch men expected?]

Counting the days that have gone by since the beginning of his reign, Titus then matches "jour" and "amour" in the rhyming position, indi-

cating how his passion has taken up the time that may have been devoted to his duties as emperor. From the interrogation of this recent
past leading to the present, Titus tries to account for what has taken
place in Rome on his watch. As the character who must closely follow
his duty and appeal to reason in order to resist the temptation of indulg-
ing his love for Bérénice, Titus takes a quantifying approach to time,
fighting the urge to give in to the frenetic temporalities of passion and
striving to place his days and moments in rational order.

Bérénice considers Titus's calculating methods to be utterly cruel,
and she sharply questions him about the exacting nature of his schedule
and his resulting emotional reticence: "Tous vos moments sont-ils dé-
voués à l'Empire? / Ce cœur depuis huit jours n'a-t-il rien à me dire?"
[Is all your time devoted to the State? / After a week [*sic*], you've nothing more to say?] (2.4.579–80). In her reference to the same lapse of
eight days, Bérénice produces an opposing conception of time, whereby
she criticizes the excessive precision in the disposition and use of Titus's
moments and demands a return to an affective, less premeditated kind
of duration. In other words, she inverts the values placed on the heart
and on duty. Sensing that she and Titus are experiencing incompatible
rhythms, she looks pessimistically into the future for confirmation of
this asynchronicity: "Daignera-t-il compter les jours de mon absence? /
Ces jours si longs pour moi lui sembleront trop courts" [He bids my
absent days untold remain? / These days so slow for me, will fly pell-
mell / For him!] (4.5.1120). Because he counts time in a way that mea-
sures his duty to the empire, Titus may not live through slowly passing
days in the manner of a frustrated lover. Bérénice and Titus will live
differently, and the passing of time provides a clear measure for this
dolorous discrepancy.[14]

Titus, for his part, turns to the diachronic structures of the past in
order to offer proof of his devotion. He refers to specific quantities of
time as evidence of his love for Bérénice:

> Comptez tous les moments, et toutes les journées
> Où, par plus de transports et par plus de soupirs,
> Je vous ai de mon cœur exprimé les désirs;
> Ce jour surpasse tout. Jamais, je le confesse,
> Vous ne fûtes aimée avec tant de tendresse.

(5.5.1352–56)

> [Think back on all the moments, all the days
> When I, by dint of passion and of sighs,
> Expressed to you the surgings of my heart.

Today caps all. Never, I must avow,
Were you so dear to me as you are now]

This, however, only adds fuel to the fire. Bérénice cannot be satisfied with such a calculating reminder in the light of the circumstances of her present, in which she and Titus are growing increasingly out of sync with one another, precisely because he insists on living by a rational temporality.

Bérénice's frustration with Titus's calculating attention to time recalls Hermione's exasperation with Pyrrhus, at the point where she realizes that he is preoccupied only with his strategy for winning Andromaque: "Perfide, je le vois, / Tu comptes les moments que tu perds avec moi" [Ah villain, I see clear / Each moment spent with me you count too dear!] (4.5.1383–84). Pyrrhus, who cares as little for the declarations of the past as he does for the ambiguities of the future, approaches time strategically, as he tries repeatedly to rid himself of Hermione and win Andromaque. While Hermione's heightened temporal awareness as a jilted lover leads to a jealous rage that will have catastrophic results, Bérénice is an entirely different kind of character, to whom Racine gives a uniquely plaintive voice. She meditates on her situation and cultivates a nuanced conception of time, a subjective temporality that is all her own. She is capable of doing this because Titus, caught between lover's time and the calculated temporality of the duties of the sovereign, leaves the temporal playing field open for a counterpoint to his plodding deliberations. Unlike the power-hungry Néron or the present-centered, flighty Pyrrhus, Titus opens up the possibility for the development of multiple temporalities in the perceptions of the characters of *Bérénice*, personae who thus live on the thresholds between individual ideations of time and the inexorable temporal structures of social obligation and transcendent determination of destiny. These subjective experiences of living in-between temporalities mark the specificity of Racine's most temporally nuanced play.

The concerted attention, in *Bérénice*, to mere moments of time as they are experienced by individual characters can be explained, as I have tried to do, as a method for respecting the time unity and the dramaturgical ideal of simplicity in action while at the same time keeping the audience's attention through five acts. A drama of subjectivity thus replaces the drama of external event, in a play that offers up a kind of action that takes place at the juncture between external event and interior realities. *Bérénice* puts forth a radical questioning of what constitutes actions and/or experiences on the classical stage.[15]

A consistently metatheatrical tragedy, *Bérénice* develops a subjective esthetics of interstitial time that refers systematically to the intermediary conceptual space of the paratext. The self-reflexive authorial argumentation of the preface frames the minimal action of the tragedy and places the reader between the text of the play and the theoretical reflection determining the playwright's construction of this same text. The esthetics of in-betweenness thus attains a metatextual level in *Bérénice* that serves to supplement the paucity of dramatic action with the richness not only of dramatic art but also of critical reflection on that art. The abstract nature of this dramaturgical theorizing is facilitated, then, by the simplicity of action. In turn, the theoretical inquiry brings detailed conceptual attention to the dynamics of subjective experience as they are represented onstage. This individual drama, as I have argued, is principally a tragedy of temporality.[16]

What emerges from a reading of time in *Bérénice* is a multiplicity of subjective time conceptions. From the calculations of Titus, to the exasperation of Antiochus, to the consciously subjective observations of Bérénice, time reveals itself to be a protean entity, taking varied forms against the backdrop of a regular rhythm of carefully planned dramatic time, a figural chronometry that tacitly governs the gradual, incremental unfolding of the action. A temporally detailed development of the esthetics of the threshold, *Bérénice* presents us with a minimal action that illuminates hitherto unexplored regions of the tragic time of the individual. While no one dies in this tragedy, the steady ticking of time in the subject's anguished experience amounts to a kind of slow emotional death, drawn out to the extreme in the subjective space of eternal passage.[17] The curtain falls on this undecided interstitial state, as Bérénice proclaims her imminent departure to Antiochus and Titus: "Tout est prêt. On m'attend. Ne suivez point mes pas. / Pour la dernière fois, Adieu, Seigneur" [All's ready. They await me. Let me pass. / For the last time, farewell, my lord] (5.7.1517–18). Bérénice's steadfast decision is punctuated by three periods, moments for pause, in the play's penultimate line. But these moments of stasis emerge in the text in tension with the anticipation of movement in space. To the end, action takes shape in tension with immobility. The frustrated Antiochus can only answer with a final "Hélas!" [Alas!] (5.7.1518).

6

Bajazet or the Dagger of Damocles

THE EARLY MODERN, ORIENTAL SETTING OF *BAJAZET* DIFFERENTIATES this work sharply from Racine's other tragedies. Flaws in dramatic composition, including the infamous "hecatomb" of an ending, set it apart as well.[1] Nonetheless, as Forestier points out, in *Bajazet* Racine succeeds in elaborating "a veritable poetry of the seraglio."[2] This poetic practice, which creates images of labyrinthine passages, closed doors, silent eunuchs, and a sultan's captives and sexual slaves, is entirely unique to *Bajazet* while at the same time developing elements of Racine's dramatic art that are observable in other tragedies. It is this esthetic dimension, contributing to common Racinian constructs — suspense and ontological suspension, the painful experience of in-between states and spaces, the thresholds to power and privileged places, to the other, to death — that I aim to analyze in this chapter, with a focus on the precarity of the eponymous character's situation. From the beginning to the end of the play, Bajazet's life, along with his political potential, hang in the balance. It is as if the sword of Damocles, in the form of a scimitar or dagger, were hanging over the head of this would-be sovereign, ever more closely approaching him, with each successive scene and line of verse, in the process of a detailed evocation of the dark corners of the Sultan Amurat's harem.[3]

Like *La Thébaïde*, *Bajazet* is at the outset a tragedy about the thresholds to power. Also similarly the play develops into a meditation, even more diabolical than in the case of the enemy brothers' story, on the passage to death. At the play's beginning, Bajazet is imprisoned in Constantinople, on the orders of his brother, Amurat, who is away laying siege to Babylon. In Amurat's absence, his wife Roxane has the power of life and death over Bajazet. The Vizir Acomat, who has his own plans for coming to power by toppling Amurat's reign, wishes to unite Roxane and Bajazet against Amurat and to rule from behind the scenes. This plan has the potential to come to fruition — Roxane, while she sadistically holds her dagger over Bajazet, nonetheless has feelings for the disenfranchised prince. A problem arises, however—Bajazet and Atal-ide love each other. This infernal tangle of passions, frustrations, and uneven power relations will result in a bloodbath that leaves few stand-ing (and includes the deaths of Atalide, Bajazet, and Roxane) at the fall of the curtain, an end that in political terms sees only an increase in the power of Amurat, whose campaign against the Babylonians will have turned out to be successful. Whereas Amurat succeeds, the other char-acters struggle and fail to achieve their desires in a claustrophobic, suf-focating dramatic space.

ENTERING THE SERAGLIO

In the opening scene, no sooner does the scheming vizir Acomat ex-press his desire to enter the harem than Osmin questions the feasibility of such a traversal:

> Viens, suis-moi. La Sultane en ce lieu se doit rendre.
> Je pourrai cependant te parler, et t'entendre.
> OSMIN
> Et depuis quand, Seigneur, entre-t-on en ces Lieux,
> Dont l'accès était même interdit à nos yeux?
> Jadis une mort prompte eût suivi cette audace.

> (1.1.1–5)

> [Follow me. The Sultana is due here.
> Yet I can speak to you and hear your news.
> OSMIN
> Since when, Sir, dare we set foot in this place
> Where access even to our eyes was banned?
> Such boldness would have once brought speedy death.]

Osmin's questioning holds us at the doorway to the serai and brings our attention to this liminary space, rather than to the interior of the sera-glio, which Acomat considers a potentially favorable site for negotiation with Roxane. Thus from the outset the act of crossing this threshold is privileged and highlighted in its danger and its tactical importance. The difference in the degree of agency exercised by each of the two charac-ters speaking in these opening lines takes shape in their respective ap-proaches to this place of passage. Acomat is ready to make the plunge into the dark, labyrinthine world of the harem; Osmin assumes a ques-tioning, analytical posture, focusing on the act of traversal itself. Even

short of that, he reminds the vizir that even the virtual traversal of looking into the serai, an act on the threshold of the threshold, as it were,
used to be punishable by death. From the outset, then, the prospect of
crossing into the seraglio constitutes a privileged object of discussion,
analysis, esthetic evocation, and, from Acomat's point of view, tactical
maneuvering.

Roxane's power takes the form of control over spaces of passage situated at the limits of the harem, between its dark interior and the world
outside. She reminds Bajazet of her status as gatekeeper: "Songez-vous
que je tiens les portes du Palais, / Que je puis vous l'ouvrir, ou fermer
pour jamais" [Do you not know I hold the palace gates, / That I may
open or forever shut them] (2.1.507–08). With Amurat's orders threatening him at every moment, and with Roxane's noose tightening around
his neck, Bajazet precariously occupies the space between the inside of
his prison and the externality of his potential freedom and political
power. The tragedy takes place on the verge of death and in the dim,
partial light of a doorway.[4]

The promise of Bajazet's liberation from imprisonment in the harem
goes hand in hand with the promise of the throne. There is only one
way to get through the doorway, by accepting Roxane's love and the
possibility for political legitimization that the liaison would entail. Acomat rhetorically evokes this door, in the form of the Adrianople Gate,
as he tries to persuade the young prince to take the power that is offered
to him:

> Tout ce qui reste ici de braves Janissaires,
> De la Religion les saints Dépositaires,
> Du Peuple Byzantin ceux qui plus respectés
> Par leur exemple seul règlent ses volontés,
> Sont prêts de vous conduire à la Porte sacrée
> D'où les nouveaux Sultans font leur première entrée.
>
> (2.3.621–26)

> [All the fine Janissaries still left here,
> The holy guardians of our great religion,
> The most respected men of Istanbul,
> Who rule the people by their high example,
> Are there to take you to the sacred Gate
> Through which our Sultans make their sovereign entry.]

The key image framing the situation suggests the Janissaries' readiness.
In addition to evoking the transitional space of the gate to sovereignty,

Acomat paints a picture of a military collectivity at the ready, on the verge of effectively advancing Bajazet's interests.

The idea of readiness and imminent political transformation has been prepared by statements on the will of the collectivity in Bajazet's favor: "Le superbe Amurat est toujours inquiet, / Et toujours les cœurs penchent vers Bajazet. / D'une commune voix il l'appellent au Trône" [Proud Murat is still uneasy; / And every heart inclines to Bajazet: / With one voice they are calling him to rule] (1.2.215–17); "Osmin a vu l'armée, elle penche pour vous" [Osmin has seen the army leaning in your favor (*my translation*)] (2.1.431). The use of the verb "pencher" sets a scene of suspense and anticipation, further developing the precariousness of Bajazet's situation, but this time in a positive light. Just as the sword of Damocles hangs over his head throughout this tragedy, so does the possibility of gaining sovereignty float in the near future realm of possibility and potential.

In the passage describing the Janissaries' readiness, the locution "sont prêts de vous conduire" takes the place of the verb "pencher" in the other passages cited above, all of which contribute to Acomat's strategic rhetoric, part of his scheme for taking power from Amurat. Bajazet, however, is not seduced by these visions of grandeur and takes self-deprecating stock of his situation: "Infortuné, proscrit, incertain de régner" [Ill-starred, proscribed, uncertain of the throne] (2.1.483). He does not accept the means for acquiring power that are offered to him. If, as Barthes claims, Bajazet is a "prostituted male," he plays this role unwillingly and continues, albeit unsuccessfully, to offer up resistance.[5] He cannot follow Acomat in cynically embracing the possibility for sovereignty by means of feigned affection for Roxane. Rather, in response to Acomat's claim that the Janissaries are prepared to lead him through the hallowed gates of power, Bajazet counters with a different view on the doors to freedom:

> Hé bien, brave Acomat, si je leur suis si cher,
> Que des mains de Roxane ils viennent m'arracher.
> Du Sérail, s'il le faut, venez forcer la porte.
> Entrez accompagné de leur vaillante escorte.
> J'aime mieux en sortir sanglant, couvert de coups,
> Que chargé, malgré moi, du nom de son Epoux.
>
> (2.3.627–32)

> [Good Ahmet, if indeed I'm dear to them,
> Let them all come and snatch me from Roxana.
> If it must be, force the Seraglio's gate:

Enter, together with their valiant escort.
I would prefer to leave, with bloody blows,
Than bear her husband's name against my will.]

Situated as he is in the painful space of the in-between, Bajazet would rather see this site destroyed entirely, so that interior and exterior may become violently conflated and so that the threshold may lose its privileged status in the perceptions of the play's characters. In other words, this character has tired of others trying to prepare entries and exits for him—he wishes to do away with this spatial dynamics entirely, for he is aware that, by being situated in liminary spaces, he is merely being manipulated.

Roxane's remarks on how she has opened a potential passage to power for her captive are typical in this regard: "Commencez maintenant. C'est à vous de courir / Dans le champ glorieux que j'ai su vous ouvrir" [Then stand forth now; for you will have to take / The field of glory I have opened you] (2.1.439–40). Roxane directs him toward a threshold she has prepared. Traversal must be an act of will ("C'est à vous de courir"). In trying to elevate him to the throne, Roxane seeks not only Bajazet's acquiescence; she also requires his active, subjective engagement in the process that she wishes to initiate. In a gesture both affectionate and coercive, Roxane constructs an intersubjective circumstance requiring Bajazet's initiative as a recognition of her power. Paradoxically, she wishes to see agency in the form of its own relinquishment, of its subordination to her will.

Bajazet responds by demanding that Roxane make a choice: "Madame, encore un coup, c'est à vous de choisir. / Daignez m'ouvrir au Trône un chemin légitime, / Ou bien, me voilà prêt, prenez votre victime" [Madam, once more, it is for you to choose. / Please clear for me a just way to the throne, / Or else I am prepared: sacrifice me] (2.1.564–66). If he is to be placed at a threshold prepared by another, he must have a say in what this place of passage will be like. Disempowered as he is, however, the threat of suicide gives him his only (meager) leverage in trying to determine the nature of the transition he will make. As a result, Roxane will continue modifying her own plans for preparing either Bajazet's passage to power or to death.

Roxane includes herself in the scheme that she develops for Bajazet and Atalide. She envisions the space of the throne not as a place of occupation but rather of precarious passage, even after she will have placed Bajazet there. The sultana intends to see what the results of this political ascension will be in the personal arena—whether Bajazet will betray her for Atalide:

Laissons de leur amour la recherche importune.
Poussons à bout l'Ingrat, et tentons la fortune.
Voyons, si par mes soins sur le Trône élevé,
Il osera trahir l'amour qui l'a sauvé.
Et si de mes bienfaits lâchement libérale
Sa main en osera couronner ma Rivale.
Je saurai bien toujours retrouver le moment
De punir, s'il le faut, la Rivale, et l'Amant.
Dans ma juste fureur observant le Perfide,
Je saurai le surprendre avec son Atalide.
Et d'un même poignard les unissant tous deux,
Les percer l'un et l'autre, et moi-même après eux.

(4.4.1237–48)

[I'll leave aside whether they love or hate;
I'll haunt him to the end, and hasard fate.
I'll see if, placed upon the throne by me,
He dare betray my love that sets him free,
If basely lavish of what I bestow,
His hand will dare to crown my rival's brow.
I shall be always able to discover
The time to strike my rival and her lover.
In righteous rage I'll spy upon the traitor;
I will surprise him with his Athalida;
And stabbing both of them with the same dagger,
Will stab myself and from their union stagger.]

Roxane has meticulously prepared this scenario. She includes several elements that comprise the specificity of the esthetic evocation of the threshold in *Bajazet*. Firstly, she extends the intermediary potential of the throne to the occupation of the throne itself. It is a mark of her power (at least in Amurat's absence) that she can carry out this kind of experiment, in which Bajazet, already on the throne, will unwittingly still straddle the blurry boundaries of potential power. Drawing out the intermediary status of the apparently definitive political situation, the jilted and calculating Roxane will observe, like Néron, Racine's other great preparer of thresholds.[6] Roxane's observations are strategic, and she will maintain in them a careful sense of timing ("Je saurai bien toujours retrouver le moment"; "Je saurai le surprendre avec son Atalide"). At this threshold to Bajazet's power and to his love for either her or for Atalide, Roxane foresees a decisive moment of potential violence.

Earlier in the play, Roxane rendered explicit her strategy of prepar-

ing the site of passage to the throne. Her words place this kind of strategic intermediary space at the conceptual center of the tragedy:

> Bajazet touche presque au Trône des Sultans.
> Il ne faut plus qu'un pas. Mais c'est où je l'attends.
> Quel que soit mon amour, si dans cette journée
> Il ne m'attache à lui par un juste hyménée,
> S'il ose m'alléguer une odieuse loi,
> Quand je fais tout pour lui, s'il ne fait tout pour moi;
> Dès le même moment sans songer si je l'aime,
> Sans consulter enfin si je me perds moi-même,
> J'abandonne l'ingrat, et le laisse rentrer
> Dans l'état malheureux, d'où je l'ai su tirer.
>
> (1.3.315–24)

> [Bajazet almost mounts the Sultan's throne:
> But one step more is needed. This I await.
> In spite of all my love, if, still to-day,
> He does not bind me to him by strict wedlock,
> If he dare cite to me a hateful law,
> When I do all for him, if he does not all for me,
> From that same moment, heedless of my love,
> Or whether I myself am doomed to die,
> I'll cast the wretch away and let him slip
> Into the dreadful doom from which I saved him.]

Both the place and time of this tragedy take on highly specific forms in
Roxane's statement of purpose and strategy. It will be during this tragic
day (a metatheatrical reference to the time unity) and at this site, one
step from the throne, that Bajazet's fate will be decided. Racine's punctuation plays a significant role here. Lines 315–16 include three periods,
offering considerable time for pause and reflection. The period at the
caesura of line 316 temporally expands the dimensions of the intermediary space still separating Bajazet from the throne. The vertical metaphor of Bajazet's potential fall into previous misery, all at the hands,
indeed at the whim of Roxane, is framed by reference to a strategic
moment of condemnation, a card Roxane will hold for herself and that
signifies her absolute power in the sultan's absence.[7] Within the claustrophobic space and limited time of the dramatic action, the eponymous
character appears with Roxane's dagger hanging over his head. He still
lives and still holds the potential to cause a political upheaval, but he is
making his way to his own death.

ROXANE'S DAGGER

In the play's first scene, Acomat describes how Amurat, who was still without an heir, had let his brother live, although the custom was for sovereigns to kill their rivals in blood:

> Ainsi donc pour un temps Amurat désarmé
> Laissa dans le Sérail Bajazet enfermé.
> Il partit, et voulut que fidèle à sa haine,
> Et des jours de son Frère arbitre souveraine,
> Roxane au moindre bruit, et sans autres raisons,
> Le fît sacrifier à ses moindres soupçons.

>   (1.1.127–32)

> [Thus Murat held his hand a little while,
> With Bajazet imprisoned in the palace.
> On his departure, he assigned Roxana
> Supreme control over his brother's life,
> Directing, loyal to his hate, she should,
> At the least rumble, without other cause,
> Put him to death upon the least suspicion.]

The repetition of the adjective "moindre" highlights the extremely thin thread by which Bajazet's life hangs, the minimal distance beteen the potential and the actuality of his murder. From the very outset, Roxane's power over him defines his situation. From this point on, aspects of her development as a character contribute to the spectator's and reader's understanding of the danger in which Bajazet finds himself.

Acomat tries to capitalize on the urgency of Bajazet's circumstances by incorporating his understanding of them into his rhetoric. Driven by the ambitions that are served by the proposed union between Bajazet and Roxane, Acomat uses a language of imminent danger to manipulate the people in Bajazet's favor: "Déclarons le péril dont son Frère est pressé" [His brother's peril let us loud proclaim] (1.2.247). Like Pylade in *Andromaque*, Acomat claims to be prepared for immediate departure, hoping up until the very last moment to save his associate.[8] But the self-centered Acomat also wishes to preserve his own chances for wresting power away from Amurat. Thus he capitalizes rhetorically and strategically on Bajazet's potential victimhood.

By contrast, Atalide sees these dangers through the optic of her love for Bajazet and her fears for his safety. She tries to impress on Roxane the perils surrounding the young man they both love:

Bajazet vous est cher. Savez-vous si demain
Sa liberté, ses jours, seront en votre main?
Peut-être en ce moment Amurat en furie
S'approche pour trancher une si belle vie.

(1.3.263–66)

[Bajazet is dear to you. Who knows tomorrow
If in your hands his life or freedom rest?
Perhaps the furious Murat, at this moment,
Is hurrying here to cut short his dear days.]

It is ironic that Atalide would be telling Roxane of the dangers Bajazet faces, since Roxane metaphorically holds her dagger so closely over his head. But Atalide accomplishes an ingenious maneuver, by which she recontextualizes the intersubjective circumstances, envisioning a situation in which it is not Roxane's but Amurat's power that threatens to move the action across the threshold of Bajazet's life/death. Knowing what it is like to love him herself, Atalide plays on Roxane's emotions, using a rhetoric of urgency, complete with two consecutive enjambments, to try and sway the tyrannical sultana. Predictably, the plea fails, and Roxane will only continue to mull over her confused thoughts and feelings, becoming more dangerous with every passing scene.

Bajazet's uncertain situation hinges on Roxane's confused emotions. Like Hermione, she lives on the indivisible borderline between love and hate. Her language, accordingly, intensifies:

Dans ton perfide sang je puis tout expier,
Et ta mort suffira pour me justifier.
N'en doute point, j'y cours, et dès ce moment même.
Bajazet, écoutez, je sens que je vous aime.
Vous vous perdez. Gardez de me laisser sortir.
Le chemin est encore ouvert au repentir.
Ne désepérez point une Amante en furie.
S'il m'échappait un mot, c'est fait de votre vie.

(2.1.535–42)

[I can wash all in your perfidious blood;
Your murder will suffice to prove my faith.
Be sure of it, I run to see it done.
Bajazet, listen: I ache with love for you.
You doom yourself. Take care I do not leave you.
The way to penitence is open still.

Do not drive desperate my frenzied love.
If one word slipped from me, you would be dead.]

These verses highlight the verbal nature of the predicament. The mark
of Roxane's strength is the power of her words, a single one of which
would bring about Bajazet's death. Once again, with "dès ce moment
même," Roxane points to the extremely limited temporality of the circumstances still staving off Bajazet's demise. And it is precisely at this
moment, hovering over the dramatic action in the form of the final period of line 537, that Roxane feels her love for Bajazet with full force.
Unlike Hermione, who finds her passion for Pyrrhus growing as a result of the hatred inspired by her frustration and neglect, Roxane redis-
covers her love, with a new intensity, in the process of exercizing a
sadistic kind of domination over her beloved. Her arousal resembles
Néron's experience of taking pleasure at the tears he caused Junie to
shed (2.2.402). Far beyond Néron's maladroit expressions of frustrated
attraction, Roxane, as we will see, develops proto-Sadean torture sce-
narios that give expression to these desires.

TORTURE AND DEATH: ROXANE'S NOOSE

The character Roxane plays a metatheatrical role in *Bajazet,* for she
acts as a kind of diabolical director for those under her power. Just as
she prepared scenes for Bajazet's potential accession to the throne,
when in the end her wishes remain unfulfilled she constructs frightening visions of pain and slow death for Bajazet. In contrast to Néron and
Narcisse, who favor immediate, silent death for their victim Britannicus, Roxane tells Acomat that she intends to prolong the ontologically
intermediary status of her victim, in an imagined scene of arousal by
torture:

> Laissez-moi le plaisir de confondre l'Ingrat.
> Je veux voir son désordre, et jouir de sa honte.
> Je perdrais ma vengeance en la rendant si prompte.
> Je vais tout préparer. Vous cependant allez
> Disperser promptement vos Amis assemblés.
>
> (4.6.1364–68)

> [Leave me the pleasure of confounding him.
> I wish to watch his woe, relish his shame.
> I'd waste my vengeance if I made it swift.

I'll go to make all ready. You, too, go
And scatter swiftly your assembled friends.]

The terms "plaisir" and "jouir" and the triple anaphoric repetition of
the first-person singular pronoun point to the self-centered attitude of
the perpetrator of torture. With no possibility of intersubjective com-
munion, Roxane decides that the only avenue for fulfillment available
to her is the maximization of her pleasure through the production of
pain in her victim. In temporal terms, Roxane wishes to extend the duration of Bajazet's experience on the verge of death. In order to avoid
rapidity, she aims to prepare the scene of her domination of Bajazet.
She proposes a carefully prepared scenario that directly anticipates
Sade.[9]

For Barthes, the specificity of the kind of violent power that oppresses all characters in *Bajazet* lies in the respiratory constraints that
structure the harem, "the most asphyxiating milieu known to Racinian
tragedy": "[T]he Seraglio is literally the smothering caress, the death-
dealing embrace. In *Britannicus* the funereal substance of this caress was
poison; in *Bajazet* it is strangling; perhaps because Nero's thematics is of
an incendiary order, his weapon is logically the gelid; since Amurath's
thematics (or Roxanne's, who represents him) is of a respiratory order,
with his countermanded and reissued orders, his weapon is the cord."[10]
In her plans for Bajazet, Roxane figuratively tightens a noose around
him, desperately attempting to increase her level of arousal, when her
desire for him remains unrequited: "Like those geese stuffed to make
their livers succulent, Bajazet is imprisoned in the shadows, set apart,
ripened for the pleasure of the Sultana, who moreover will manipulate
his murder as one controls an orgasm."[11] Thus the threshold takes a
particular, eroticized form in *Bajazet*. The tragedy stages a tense interplay between suffering and pleasure in a scenario that figures both Roxane's power over Bajazet and her frustration at not having her love
returned.

The gender roles according to which Néron torments Junie and Pyrrhus blackmails Andromaque have been reversed in *Bajazet*. Although
she only has her privileges because of the absent Amurat's orders,
within the power economy of the dramatic action of *Bajazet*, Roxane is
a formidable female character, unique in her authority and the lengths
to which she will go to use and abuse it. In tragic fashion, when this
potency proves not to be effective in the emotional sphere, it is deployed
in order to bring the objects of Roxane's wrath to the verge of death,
the final element in this drama of ontological in-betweenness.

The tragedy concludes with Atalide killing herself, her confidante Zaïre observing the tragic scene: "Elle expire" [She is dying (*my translation*)] (5.12.1755). To the very end, the esthetic evocation of the ontological space between life and death is exploited to heighten the emotive effect of the action. Contrary to Roxane's expectations, in the end Bajazet dies quickly. Roxane, for her part, dies a slower death, for she is still alive when Orcan delivers Amurat's message of victory and continued power. Osmin describes the death scene:

> Oui, j'ai vu l'Assassin
> Retirer son poignard tout fumant de son sein.
> Orcan, qui méditait ce cruel stratagème,
> La servait, à dessein de la perdre elle-même,
> Et le Sultan l'avait chargé secrètement,
> De lui sacrifier l'Amante après l'Amant.
> Lui-même d'aussi loin qu'il nous a vus paraître,
> *Connaissez*, a-t-il dit, *l'ordre de votre Maître,*
> *Perfides, et voyant le sang que j'ai versé,*
> *Voyez ce que m'enjoint son amour offensé.*
> A ce discours, laissant la Sultane expirante,
> Il a marché vers nous, et d'une main sanglante
> Il nous a déployé l'ordre, dont Amurat
> Autorise ce Monstre à ce double attentat.
>
> (5.11.1683–1700)

> [Yes, I saw the assassin
> Draw out his dagger steaming from her breast.
> Orhan, premeditating this foul blow,
> Served her, with the intent of killing her;
> The Sultan had adjured him secretly
> To sacrifice both lover and his mistress.
> He, himself, catching sight of us from far:
> "Bow down," he said, "before your master's order;
> Obey the signal of his sovereign seal,
> Traitors, and leave at once this sacred palace."
> With these words, leaving the Sultana dying
> He strode towards us; and with a bloody hand
> He flaunted in our faces Murat's order,
> That authorised this monster's double murder.]

The dénouement, which Racine himself recognized as being overly sanguinary, esthetically valorizes (to a fault) the ontologically intermediary status of the dying victims of Amurat's power.

Flawed in its excesses, *Bajazet* occupies a unique place in Racine's oeuvre. Unlike the other secular tragedies, *Bajazet* puts forth a poetics of deferred death, violence, and suffocation in an setting that is exceptional, both for its spatial and temporal parameters. *Bajazet* goes beyond the euphemistic recreation of the exotic Orient to foreground the figuration of sexual violence and torture. From the threshold to political power to the space between life and death, the eponymous character, an ineffectual being albeit with strong principles, experiences an intense set of passages that contribute to a poetry of the seraglio. This dark labyrinth constitutes the most tightly confined space in Racine's secular tragedies. In *Mithridate*, to which we now turn, the imaginary spaces evoked in characters' dialogues are expansive by comparison. Traveling by sea and land to wage war, evade potential captors, and pursue his desires, the King of Pontus undertakes a different and yet related exploration of the passage between life and death. Both a success and a failure at both living and dying, Mithridate manages in his words, silences, deeds, and misdeeds to question the very nature of dramatic action.

7

Not Going Out to Meet Destiny in *Mithridate*

> The Pursuit of Mithridates, who had thrown himself among the
> tribes inhabiting Bosphorus and the shores of the Mæotian Sea, pre-
> sented great difficulties.
>
> —Plutarch, *Life of Pompey*

MITHRIDATE, KING OF PONTUS AND ILLUSTRIOUS ENEMY OF ROME, IS
away, and everyone believes him dead. His son Pharnace, an ally to the
Romans, pursues Monime, who had been promised to his father. So
does Xipharès, Mithridate's more beloved son, and Monime loves Xipharès in return. In a surprise turn of events, Mithridate arrives on the
scene, his death having been a mere rumor that he himself has circu-
lated for strategic purposes. The king now wishes to find out which of
his sons is trying to steal his fiancée. When Pharnace is accused, he
gives away his brother. Mithridate then tricks Monime into revealing
the love between her and Xipharès, who is only saved from his father's
vengeance by a sudden Roman attack, in which the traitor Pharnace
participates. Mithridate has sent Monime a poison, and she is ready to
take it, because she believes that Xipharès has died in battle. At the last
moment, Mithridate's interlocutor Arbate arrives to discard the poison
and announce that Mithridate is dying. He has attempted to commit
suicide, but, being the quintessentially immune sovereign, he has trouble giving up the ghost. During his slow death, Mithridate announces
that Xipharès has heroically routed Pharnace and the Roman troops,
and he gives his loyal son the hand of Monime, bequeathing to him his
military legacy as supreme enemy of Rome.

A reflection on processes of representation, a tragedy of politics and
subjectivities, *Mithridate* advances an esthetic system based on a poetics
of suspension. As John Campbell has argued, this tragedy foregrounds
"not suspense but a kind of suspension. . . . Throughout the play, however frantic the external action may at times appear, characters are as
though suspended between life and death, without being able to live or

die."[1] It seems fitting that the legendary sovereign who had taken pains to immunize himself against poisons, thus to live along the borderline between life and death, should be the eponymous character of this tragedy of unsettled in-betweenness. It is also a tragedy of ontological ambiguity, at the limits of life, also of the world, the boundaries between earth and sea, the thresholds to utterance and to self-actualization, to interaction and to self-examination. Finally, in its metatextual and paratextual dimensions, *Mithridate* examines points of entry into discourse and the work of theater itself while questioning the very nature of dramatic action—do these characters ever actually do anything?[2]

A Breach in Etiquette

At the start of the second act, interaction and communication (or lack thereof) take center stage. A specific question of civility comes under examination when Monime shocks those around her by refusing to go out and greet Mithridate, who, in a coup de théâtre, has returned from the sea, as if back from the dead. Why then won't his fiancée go out and meet him? Whereas in *Phèdre* Thésée's return is a veritable eruption onto the scene, in *Mithridate* the sovereign's unexpected arrival is deferred, and as a result the energy seeps out of what might have been a resounding moment but what fizzles into anticlimax.

Phœdime announces Mithridate's return to Monime:

> Princes, toute la Mer est de vaisseaux couverte,
> Et bientôt démentant le faux bruit de sa mort
> Mithridate lui-même arrive dans le Port.
> MONIME
> Mithridate!
> XIPHARES
> Mon Père!
> PHARNACE
> Ah! Que viens-je d'entendre?
> PHŒDIME
> Quelques Vaisseaux légers sont venus nous l'apprendre,
> C'est lui-même. Et déjà pressé de son devoir
> Arbate loin du bord l'est allé recevoir.
>
> (1.4.328–34)

> [Princes, the sea is all alive with ships;
> And soon, despite the false news of his death,

The King himself drops anchor in the port.
MONIMA
Mithridates!
XIPHARES
My father!
PHARNACES
What do I hear!
PHAEDIMA
Some light ships are at hand to tell the news;
The King, himself! Already, spurred by duty,
Arbates left the shore to welcome him.]

A dutiful friend and servant, Arbate conspicuously goes out to greet
Mithridate, far from the coastline, meeting him more than halfway in a
gesture that is observed by the collectivity in the interstitial space of
shores and shallows. Phœdime paints a colorful, baroque image of the
sea as an in-between space, populated by ships and the light vessels
serving as intermediaries between water and land. These messenger
boats freely traverse this area to bring news. They operate at the margins of the state, at those geographical limits where the freshest news of
what is coming from the sea and from other states arrives, and where
this dramatic surprise develops.[3] Amid these light ships, Arbate stands
out in his eagerness and good will toward his king.

By contrast, Monime stays behind, sulking in her chambers: "Quoi,
vous êtes ici, quand Mithridate arrive, / Quand pour le recevoir chacun
court sur la rive?" [What? You stay here when Mithridates comes, /
When all run to the shore to welcome him?] (2.1.375–76). Act 2 thus
begins with a remark on the location of Monime, who insists that she is
not yet married to Mithridate, and that she will wait for him where she
is. The situation underlines Monime's merely potential identity, as the
betrothed but not yet instated queen.[4] She stands at the threshold to
marriage and to power, but she is not keen on crossing it. She thus
hangs willfully in limbo and, as Forestier points out, her intermediary
status provokes the debate on etiquette that stalls dramatic action and
dooms the wedding plans from the outset.[5]

Her publicly visible lack of support or enthusiasm for the marriage
proposal arouses Mithridate's frustration: "N'était-il pas plus noble, et
plus digne de vous, / De joindre à ce devoir votre propre suffrage, /
D'opposer votre estime au destin qui m'outrage" [Was it not nobler,
worthier of you, / To add your own free choice to duty's voice, / [And
to] [m]eet my injurious fate with your esteem] (2.4.574–76). In a sense,
here he is also asking her to come out and engage him, to meet his des-

tiny, but she refuses once again, staying in a personal space of concealment by remaining between utterance and silence: "Je vois malgré vos
soins vos pleurs prêts à couler" [I see your tears about to flow, despite
you] (2.4.582). Monime has earlier commented on the difficulty with
which she has stifled her urges for self-expression:

> Les Dieux m'ont secourue, et mon cœur affermi
> N'a rien dit ou du moins n'a parlé qu'à demi.
> Hélas! si tu savais, pour garder le silence,
> Combien ce triste cœur s'est fait de violence!
>
> (2.1.409–12)

> [The Gods have saved me, and my rallying heart
> Said nothing, or at least betrayed but half.
> Alas! if you knew how I had to force
> My sorrowing heart to keep its silence still!]

Monime strains in suspension, on the verge of expression. She stands
paralyzed in the world of sociability and sinks into withdrawal. Phœdime's "montrez-vous" [show yourself] (2.1.387) only provokes a flat
refusal: "Regarde en quel état tu veux que je me montre. / Vois ce visage
en pleurs, et loin de le chercher, / Dis-moi plutôt, dis-moi que je m'aille
cacher" [See in what state you would I show myself, / My face in tears;
and far from seeking him, / Ah, tell me rather where to hide myself]
(2.1.388–90); "Je ne paraîtrai point dans le trouble où je suis" [I will
not show myself in my present discomfiture (*my translation*)] (2.1.422).
Monime's breaches in civility result from a more generalized misan-
thropy. Her intractable situation, being in love with the son of her
husband-to-be, has placed her in this state of indecision, paralysis, and
suspension. Unable to speak, to decipher her destiny, or to show herself
without apprehension, Monime refuses to go out and meet this shadowy
fate, just as she declines to emerge from her privacy to greet a husband
who has figuratively returned from the grave. In her state of suspended
animation, the queen-to-be is on the verge of knowledge, of power, and,
as we will see, of love and fulfillment, but she stays there, just as she
will eventually be brought to the brink of death without ever making
that crossing.

Potential Unfulfilled

Later in act 2, in one of Racine's most poignant scenes of frustrated
love, Monime laments her predicament to Xipharès:

Ah! Par quel soin cruel le Ciel avait-il joint
Deux cœurs, que l'un pour l'autre il ne destinait point!
Car quel que soit vers vous le penchant qui m'attire,
Je vous le dis, Seigneur, pour ne plus vous le dire.
Ma gloire me rappelle, et m'entraîne à l'Autel
Où je vais vous jurer un silence éternel.

(2.6.693–98)

[Alas! how harshly Heaven, in its spite,
Joined our two hearts not fated to unite!
For despite all the love my heart may pour,
(I tell it now, my lord, to tell no more)
My honour holds me back. At the altar due,
I'll swear myself for ever dead to you.]

Monime undergoes physical forces of attraction and repulsion that determine her social situation and her modalities of communication. A strong tension, between "penchant qui m'attire" and "m'entraîne à l'Autel," figures the torn subjective status of the play's would-be heroine, who repeatedly sinks into inaction and moves paradoxically toward nonaccomplishment. The internal conflict takes shape on the level of language in the paradoxical mode of enunciation through which she announces the cessation of communication: "Je vous le dis, Seigneur, pour ne plus vous le dire." Like Romeo and Juliet, the frustrated lovers speak with an urgency created by the sense that every conversation could be their last. Hushed tones sound out the language of suspended animation in anticipation of the dénouement.

The suspension between interrelation and irrevocable separation is mirrored, within the complex dynamics of Monime's erotic and emotive experience, by a balance between pleasure and pain and between titillation and shame. In a remarkable passage, Monime alludes to these conflicting feelings:

Je sais qu'en vous voyant, un tendre souvenir,
Peut m'arracher du cœur quelque indigne soupir,
Que je verrai mon âme en secret déchirée
Revoler vers le bien, dont elle est séparée.
Mais je sais bien aussi, que s'il dépend de vous,
De me faire chérir un souvenir si doux;
Vous n'empêcherez pas que ma gloire offensée
N'en punisse aussitôt la coupable pensée,
Que ma main dans mon cœur ne vous aille chercher,
Pour y laver ma honte, et vous en arracher.

Que dis-je? En ce moment, le dernier qui nous reste,
Je me sens arrêter par un plaisir funeste.
Plus je vous parle, et plus, trop faible que je suis,
Je cherche à prolonger le péril que je fuis.
Il faut pourtant, il faut se faire violence.
Et sans perdre en adieux un reste de constance,
Je fuis. Souvenez-vous, Prince, de m'éviter,
Et méritez les pleurs que vous m'allez coûter.

                                          (2.7.729–46)

[I know on seeing you, my loving eye
May draw from my heart some unworthy sigh;
That I should see my soul, in secret riven,
Toward its forbidden sweets for ever driven.
But I know too, though it depend on you,
To stir up memories so sweet and true,
You shall not stop my honour, all distraught,
From punishing at once my guilty thought;
Nor my hand, seeking in my heart your name,
Plunging to pluck it out and purge my shame.
Why, at this very moment, our love's last,
I feel a fatal pleasure hold me fast:
The more I speak to you—ah! woe is me!—
The more I seek to fan the flames I flee!
And yet I must, I must tear me away;
Before my dwindling firmness I betray,
I flee. Remember, Prince, to shun me. Keep
Away, and earn the tears you'll make me weep.]

Monime reveals that her love has taken a masochistic turn. She has learned to inhabit the agony of unsatisfied anticipation, and she has managed even to enjoy it at moments. After giving a nod to Cornelian sensibilities of honor and duty, Monime quickly descends into the tangle of her conflicted passions and discovers a perverse kind of arousal that becomes her only form of solace in her suspended state of becoming.

When, later in the day, tricked by Mithridate, she believes that her union with Xipharès will finally take place, she recalls the two years of waiting that have preceded the events of the tragic day at hand:

Après deux ans d'ennuis, dont tu sais tout le poids,
Quoi je puis respirer pour la première fois?
Quoi, cher Prince, avec toi je me verrais unie?

Et loin que ma tendresse eût exposé ta vie,
Tu verrais ton devoir, je verrais ma vertu
Approuver un amour si longtemps combattu?
Je pourrais tous les jours t'assurer que je t'aime?
Que ne viens-tu . . .

(4.1.1173–80)

[After two years of cares, you know their strain,
What? I may, for the first time, breathe again?
What? dearest Prince, I, free to be your wife!
And far from my love having risked your life.
You, free in duty, I, in virtue, free
To crown a love so long in jeopardy!
To tell you every day how much I love you!
· Why do you not come?]

After all this time, she has reached the threshold to happiness and fulfillment of self through interaction with the other. It is to this site of
personal passage that Mithridate, the master of passages, escapes, and
machinations, has brought her, only to stop her there and punish his
beloved son. Monime's "Que ne viens-tu" casts the whole scene as yet
another missed encounter, an inability to venture out to meet destiny,
whether it be personal, as in the case of the frustrated love shared by
Monime and Xipharès, or political, as in the case of her potential to
become queen.

ON THE VERGE OF POWER

Once Monime has confessed her love to Xipharès, the king's more
valiant son urges her to embrace her fate by stepping to the marriage
altar:

Que voudrais-je de plus? Glorieux, et fidèle,
Je meurs. Un autre sort au trône vous appelle.
Consentez-y, Madame. Et sans plus résister
Achevez un hymen, qui vous y fait monter.

(4.2.1247–50)

[What more could I want? Gloriously your own,
I die, while destiny gives you a throne.
Resist no more, my lady, please agree.
Accept this bond that crowns your dignity.]

All she has left to do is to climb upon this throne, by way of marriage, and fulfill her destiny. According to Phœdime, she recently showed a willingness to make this transition: "Sans murmure, à l'Autel vous l'alliez devancer" [You hastened to the altar uncomplaining] (4.1.1150). But Phœdime's statement may be more rhetorical than descriptive, as she tries to convince Monime to go through with her marriage to Mithridate. It would be hard to believe that Monime was going to hurry to the altar, after waiting for Mithridate sullenly in her room while the rest of the city was at port.

Monime's refusal to approach the altar echoes her refusal to go out to the shores to take part in Mithridate's destiny. At these shores now, and in the liminary space of the sea's shallows, Mithridate's ships are filling and waiting at the ready for a new departure:

> Tandis que mes soldats prêts à suivre leur Roi
> Rentrent dans mes vaisseaux, pour partir avec moi;
> Venez, et qu'à l'Autel ma promesse accomplie
> Par des nœuds éternels l'un à l'autre nous lie.
>
> (4.4.1273–76)

> [While all my troops, ready to follow me,
> Are re-embarking on my ships to sail,
> Come, let me crown my promise at the altar
> And bind you to me by eternal ties.]

Just as she has proven intransigent with Phœdime and elliptical in her exchanges with Xipharès regarding her political future, Monime hesitates to appease Mithridate. Instead, she deliberates—the key terms in Racine's text are "balancer" [hesitate] and "penser" [think] (4.4.1277–78)—and, pursuing her own avoidance strategy, she declines to participate in the latest of Mithridate's great escapes. Refusing to enter that liminal zone of sea and shore where new departures take place, she also refuses to meet her destiny as Mithridate's queen. She therefore remains *en-deçà* [on this side] in respect to her fate, at the thresholds to love and self-actualization, to political power, and to departure (and it all started to become visible through a breach in etiquette). The final threshold she will have trouble crossing will be that of death. This site of ontological transition is a privileged one in the story of Mithridate, who was known among sovereigns of antiquity for his skill in controlling the borderlines between the world of the living and the world of the dead.

Mithridate and the Thresholds of Death

As Plutarch tells it, the King of Pontus made an entire military career
out of dancing at death's door. When his nemesis Pompey once came
close to Mithridates' forces on the banks of the Euphrates, his concern
with his enemy's knack for evasion forced him to fight in the dark:
"[F]earing lest he should pass over the river and give him the slip there
too, he drew up his army to attack him at midnight."[6] That very night,
Mithridates dreamt that he was alone and in limbo, in the middle of a
vast ocean, floating on a scrap from a sunken ship. He paid attention to
his dreams and at times made an effort to interpret them.[7] At the end of
this one, his men awoke him with news of Pompey's imminent assault.
Racine's Mithridate recounts this episode to Arbate as a way of lamenting his lost powers of resistance against Rome:

> Je suis vaincu. Pompée a saisi l'avantage
> D'une nuit, qui laissait peu de place au courage.
> Mes Soldats presque nus dans l'ombre intimidés,
> Les rangs de toutes parts mal pris, et mal gardés;
> Le désordre partout redoublant les alarmes,
> Nous-mêmes contre nous tournant nos propres armes,
> Les cris, que les rochers renvoyaient plus affreux,
> Enfin toute l'horreur d'un combat ténébreux;
> Que pouvait la valeur dans ce trouble funeste?
>
> (2.3.439–47)

> [I am defeated. Pompey seized the advantage
> Of a night allowing little room for courage.
> My half-clad soldiers, threatened in the dark,
> Scarce anywhere retrieving their formations,
> Disorder doubling everywhere their doubts,
> Ourselves, turning our own arms on ourselves,
> Harsh cries retorting harsher from the rocks,
> The endless horror of a midnight fight;
> What use was valour in this foul affright?]

What Judd Hubert calls the "défaite nocturne" [nocturnal defeat]
throws the notion of heroism sharply into question and casts its shadow
over the rest of the play.[8] In sketchy circumstances, it does no good to
stand up and fight—better to act tactically, escape, and fight another
day, rather than on this night, with its tricky effects of light and darkness.

With the moon at their backs, casting long shadows before them, Pompey's forces confused Mithridate's soldiers, who as Plutarch tells it lunged and "threw their darts at the shadows without the least execution."[9] In Cassius Dio,

> When the moon rose, the barbarians rejoiced, thinking that in the light they would certainly beat back some of the foe. And they would have been benefited somewhat if the Romans had not had the moon behind them and as they assailed them, now on this side and now on that, cause much confusion both to the eyes and hands of the others. For the assailants, being very numerous, and all of them together casting the deepest shadow, baffled their opponents before they had yet come into conflict with them. The barbarians, thinking them near, would strike vainly into the air, and when they did come to close quarters in the shadow, they would be wounded when not expecting it. Thus many of them were killed and no fewer taken captives. A considerable number also escaped, among them Mithridates.[10]

In a battle where there could be no clear heroes, where the distinction between advantage and disadvantage could at any moment be blurred beyond recognition, only the most cunning could survive. Pompey triumphed, but capitalizing on the visual ambiguity of this shadowy battle setting, Mithridates and a group of his men broke through enemy lines and escaped.

After fleeing the battle scene and arriving at the castle of Inora, Mithridates, always the tactician in the face of adversity, bestowed a dangerous gift on his men: "[T]o every one of his friends he gave a deadly poison, that they might not fall into the power of the enemy."[11] The king who was known for his practice of immunizing himself to poisons aimed to give his soldiers control over the border between life and death. In the absence of heroism, they were thus assured of an exit strategy that questioned the limits of benevolence and self-preservation.

In Racine's tragedy, Mithridate provides poison for Monime once he has discovered her love for Xipharès. Both punishment and balm, this poison promises to liberate Monime from her intractable situation and finally put an end to her state of suspended animation:

> Et toi, qui de ce cœur, dont tu fus adoré,
> Par un jaloux destin fus toujours séparé,
> Héros, avec qui même, en terminant ma vie,
> Je n'ose en un tombeau demander d'être unie,
> Reçois ce sacrifice, et puisse en ce moment
> Ce Poison expier le sang de mon Amant.

(5.2.1537–42)

[And you, my love, for ever separate
From this adoring heart through jealous fate,
Hero, with whom I dare not even crave,
At death's door, to be one within the grave,
Accept this sacrifice; let, with my moan,
This poison for my lover's blood atone!]

This toxin has the added advantage of potentially absolving Xipharès
of his virtual crime of stealing his father's bride. In the next major coup
de théâtre, however, Monime's suicide will be interrupted, as Arbate
arrives on the scene to fling the poison to the ground and report Mithridate's impending death:

> Le Roi touche à son heure dernière,
> Madame, et ne voit plus qu'un reste de lumière.
> Je l'ai laissé sanglant, porté par des soldats,
> Et Xipharès en pleurs accompagne leurs pas.
>
> (5.4.1555–58)

> [The King's life is near its term,
> My lady, and, his dying eyes are closing.
> I left him bleeding, carried by his soldiers;
> And Xiphares in tears is following them.]

He goes on to describe how Mithridate has finally come the closest he
has ever been to death's door, although like Monime he has trouble
exiting the world of the living and remains entrenched at the crucial
point of passage:

> Enfin las, et couvert de sang et de poussière,
> Il s'était fait de morts une noble barrière.
> Un autre Bataillon s'est avancé vers nous.
> Les Romains, pour le joindre, on suspendu leurs coups.
> Ils voulaient tous ensemble accabler Mithridate.
> Mais lui, *C'en est assez,* m'a-t-il dit, *cher Arbate.*
> *Le sang, et la fureur m'emportent trop avant.*
> *Ne livrons pas surtout Mithridate vivant.*
> Aussitôt dans son sein il plonge son épée.
> Mais la mort fuit encor sa grande Ame trompée.
> Ce Héros dans mes bras est tombé tout sanglant,
> Faible, et qui s'irritait contre un trépas si lent.
> Et se plaignant à moi de ce reste de vie,
> Il soulevait encor sa main appesantie,

Et marquant à mon bras la place de son cœur,
Semblait d'un coup plus sûr implorer la faveur.

(5.4.1599–1614)

[Tired at last, and steeped in blood and dust,
He had piled up a noble wall of corpses.
A fresh battalion then advanced on us;
To link with it, the Romans held their blows.
They wished to fall, as one, on Mithridates.
But he: "It is enough, Arbates," said he,
"My blood and rage are pushing me too forward.
Your Mithridates must not fall alive."
With this he plunged his sword into his breast.
But death eluded still his lion-heart.
The hero fell, all bleeding in my arms,
Feeble and fretful at so slow an end;
And moaning at me he was not yet dead,
He raised once more his great and heavy hand
And, pointing in the region of his heart,
Seemed to beg me to strike a surer blow.]

From his heroic fighting behind a wall of corpses, Mithridate wears a mantle of blood and dust and thus carries corporeal signs of the crossing to the world of the dead. Spent as he is, however, the king has difficulty dying and insists that he does not want the Romans to take him alive.[12] In the absence of poison, he calls on Arbate to aid him in suicide.

In the end, Mithridate tells Xipharès and Monime to flee and continue the war against the Romans, rather than waiting for them to regroup. As the king lives out his final moments before his last escape, this time from life itself, the curtain falls on the final scene:

Mais je sens affaiblir ma force, et mes esprits.
Je sens que je meurs. Approchez-vous, mon Fils.
Dans cet embrassement, dont la douceur me flatte,
Venez, et recevez l'âme de Mithridate.
MONIME
Il expire!
XIPHARES
Ah, Madame! Unissons nos douleurs,
Et par tout l'Univers cherchons-lui des Vengeurs.

(5.5.1705–10)

[But I feel my strength is ebbing with my heart.
I feel I am dying. Closer, son,

With this embrace whose sweetness gladdens me,
Come and inherit Mithridates' spirit.
MONIMA
He's dead.
XIPHARES
Ah, let us now our sorrows blend
And rouse the whole world to avenge his end.]

As is the case with Créon at the end of *La Thébaïde*, the play concludes by describing death throes in the present tense. Thus the action ends temporally at the very moment of transition from life to death. In a sense both Monime and Xipharès occupy this in-between space as well, each of them just having come back from death's door to find a new destiny to decipher. They may go out to meet this fate, somewhere beyond the fall of the curtain that marks the moment of Mithridate's passing on.

Just as Mithridate rendered himself immune to poisons, Monime in her brooding subjectivity has kept herself safe and separate from the ill-fated king's destiny. This inconstant lover and escape artist now must go it alone. His final evasion occurs behind the curtain, and he dies, appropriately, while passing the buck, bequeathing his legacy and his destiny during an unfinished war. He has answered the question he had asked himself in the fourth act, when he drew a contrast between his immunity to poison and his vulnerability to a dangerous love:

> J'ai pris soin de m'armer contre tous les poisons;
> J'ai su par une longue et pénible industrie
> Des plus mortels venins prévenir la furie.
> Ah! qu'il eût mieux valu, plus sage, et plus heureux,
> Et repoussant les traits d'un amour dangereux,
> Ne pas laisser remplir d'ardeurs empoisonnées
> Un cœur déjà glacé par le froid des années?
> De ce trouble fatal par où dois-je sortir?

> (4.5.1418–25)

> [I trained myself to guard against all venoms:
> I learnt, by long and painful industry,
> To be immune against the deadliest poisons.
> Ah! how much better, had I, wiser, happier,
> Repulsing all the slings of perilous love,
> Not let these poisoned passions fill my heart,
> Already frozen by my winter years!
> Then how am I to cut this fatal knot?]

By the end of the fith act, the exit has been located, in death combined with the bequest of a military legacy. Read from a metadramatic or met-adiegetic perspective, Mithridate's question pertains to the structure of the play's plot. In other words, how will the tragic knot become untied at the end? Along with being a schemer, womanizer, and escape artist, Mithridate is also a thinker. His penchant for rational examination of ideas and situations appears in the famous line "Voyons, examinons. Mais par où commencer?" [Let's see, examine. But where make a start?] (3.4.1022). Nearer the end it is a matter of "par où . . . sortir." At the metadramatic level, then, Mithridate reflects on the process of dramatic creation itself.

Mithridate, with its eponymous character's self-reflexive observations and complex maneuverings, brings us to the thresholds of self-actual-ization, of power, of death, and, in the metatextual space of Mithridate's commentaries, of the very processes of dramatic representation that give him a fictional life, and death, that are equally, irreducibly com-plex. As Michael O'Regan puts it, "Racine's aim is not to describe what Mithridates did or what happened to him, but to show him as the figure of the anti-Roman hero, the opponent of tyranny. This is Racine's *idée*, which he chooses to illustrate under the name of Mithridates. . . . [Ra-cine manages] to create in this way something more 'philosophical' than a mere historical portrait."[13] Although Racine is far from presenting us with an "anti-Roman hero" in *Mithridate*, O'Regan's distinction between the philosophical and the historical usefully underlines the complexity of the protagonist. What is the philosophical content of this portrait of an anti-Roman antihero, and how does Mithridate's failed self-actualization affect our understanding of the play's potential meanings? Far from being an unequivocal celebration of sovereignty, as Goldmann would have it, *Mithridate* poses irreducible contradictions in its pro-tracted temporality of suspension and nonaccomplishment.[14] In its met-atextual dimensions, *Mithridate* examines points of entry into and exit out of narrative.

The questioning of diegetic conditions extends to an interrogation of the nature of dramatic action. Self-reflexive stasis, difficulty of utter-ance, and the entropic transformation of action into inaction implicitly counteract the positivistic tendency to see the theatrical text as some-thing that above all is doing or accomplishing something. Time and again the text of *Mithridate* represents unfulfilled promises, with the energies that drive dramatic action gradually dissipating. Campbell calls the play "a symphony of negation," a work "driven by . . . a truly tragic sense of loss and waste that permeates the human condition itself."[15] Hubert also uses a musical analogy to describe the tragedy's entropic concluding rhythms: "There is thus a kind of *diminuendo* in this respect, as the events unfold: a grand departure (but toward the Romans), a strategic evasion (toward misfortune), and a complete disappearance (into unfettered love)."[16] According to Nina Ekstein, the shores that lie ambiguously between land and sea give way in the fifth act to the blood that marks the borderline separating life from death; ultimately, "[t]he tragedy ends in a liquid dissolve."[17] For Henry Phillips, it is a question of spatial contraction, from a vast figurative geography of deserts and seas to "a king [who is] impotent in his own house."[18] The imaginary spaces evoked throughout the tragedy thus mirror the entropic process whereby action fuses with its opposite as the meaning of the work consistently evades our grasp in its fundamental metadramatic ambiguity, just as its characters disappear in an unresolved situation. While *Mithridate* examines complex individuals in terms of their metadramatically significant action and inaction, *Iphigénie* further explores the limits of the strained self that cannot immediately exit the destabilizing space of the threshold. As we will see in the following chapter, the subject's reckoning with ontological in-betweenness can, disturbingly, lead not only to failures and stasis but ultimately to disintegration.

8

Subjective Dispersion in *Iphigénie* or the Unbearable Fullness of Being

Racine's *IPHIGÉNIE* (1674) IS A DRAMA OF ANTICIPATION IN EXCESS. With the gods' all-powerful yet undisclosed will hanging over them, this tragedy's characters stumble in the dark, interrogating their destinies in a present moment overfilled with potential, on the cusp of the future. As in a number of Racine's tragedies, characters find their circumstances unbearable, so filled are they with a strong yet vague sense of what is to come. As tensions mount, the waiting leads to confusion, to experiential saturation, and eventually to the dispersion of identities. Among Racine's secular tragedies, *Iphigénie* evokes most vividly the human predicament of being caught between knowledge and ignorance, between awareness of the weight of the gods' wishes and obliviousness to what will become of the situation at hand.

The Greek fleet, ready to embark on the war against Troy, is held in check by an inert sea and sky. An oracular pronouncement has informed the Greek nation and their king Agamemnon that the blood of Hélène must be spilled, in the person of Iphigénie, in order for the spell that has stilled the bay of Aulis to be broken. While the oracle seems to require the sacrifice of Agamemnon's daughter Iphigénie, it will eventually be revealed that Eriphile, daughter of Hélène and Thésée and thus a kind of substitute Iphigénie, will serve as the sacrificial lamb. Her death will appease the gods and set the war machine in motion. But this revelation occurs only in the final scene of the tragedy. In the events leading up to this sacrifice, everyone onstage is equally in the dark about what the gods have decreed.

Pregnant with a vague but strong sense of what is to come, Agamemnon, Clytemnestre, Achille, Eriphile, and Iphigénie desperately try to articulate their experience through language and, when language fails them, to project elements of themselves into the world around them. Blindly grasping for answers and sounding their future, Racine's dramatis personae function as vessels for the heavy burden of human responsibility in a world dominated by invisible, transcendent forces. Filled to overflowing with their tragic situation, they perform a drama of human pain and radical uncertainty at the threshold between the terrestrial and the transcendent, between self and others, between responsibility and powerlessness, and between knowledge and its absence.

WANDERING IN THE DARK

Iphigénie starts on a note of ambiguity, in a crepuscular scene of two characters, Agamemnon and Arcas, searching themselves and for each other. From the outset, nothing is self-evident, and Arcas must make an effort to recognize his king:

> C'est vous-même, Seigneur! Quel important besoin
> Vous a fait devancer l'Aurore de si loin?
> A peine un faible jour vous éclaire et me guide.
> Vos yeux seuls et les miens sont ouverts dans l'Aulide.
>
> (1.1.3–6)

> [My lord, it's you! What pressing need has made
> You rise so long before the break of day?
> There's but the faintest glimmer of the dawn;
> Our eyes alone are open now in Aulis.]

Dialogue and action begin at the liminal moment of dawn, a transitional temporality that stretches the time unity, raising the question of whether it is the day before or the fatal day at hand. Arcas and his sovereign converse at the outset of the play in an in-between state from which they interrogate their own situations and destinies. As Arcas points out, they occupy a privileged position in comparison to the rest of their community: they are out and about while the entire city, and even Neptune (1.1.9), the god who is keeping the Greek army at port, sleeps peacefully, unaware of the thoughts that trouble Agamemnon. In spite of the vigilance that distinguishes them from their fellow citizens, these characters undergo the pain and uncertainty of talking about and examining their lives during this shadowy break of day.[1]

Still, at this stage of events, language is working reasonably well for Agamemnon, who as we find out later has not always had such an easy time giving voice to his thoughts and emotions. Upon hearing Calchas pronounce the oracle that calls for the blood of (an) Iphigénie, "Je demeurai sans voix, et n'en repris l'usage, / Que par mille sanglots qui se firent passage" [I was struck dumb, and no word could I say / Until a thousand sobs had cleared the way] (1.1.65–66). He remembers a time when he was bereft of a voice, on the borderline between speaking and simply making noise. He sobbed profusely in the face of destiny, uttering thousands of sounds that carried a strong meaning but did not allow him for all his expressive prolixity to enter the symbolic order of reasoned speech.[2] The final image of the king at the end of the play has him withdrawing from all communication, hiding his face to conceal his tears (5.5.1708–10).

In this respect the king resembles Eriphile, who also deals in a half-accomplished kind of utterance representing a scattered self.[3] In her attempts to communicate with others, Eriphile experiences the same kind of vocal frustration as the king himself. Although she is most often considered to be an excluded party, having nothing to do with the familial and/or political/military ties that bind together the rest of the characters in this tragedy, Eriphile in fact shares a good deal in common with the ostensible center of social and political legitimacy, Agamemnon. While Eriphile is a kind of half-heroine, half an Iphigénie—and this is enough for her to function as the sacrificial lamb (or black sheep) in the play's tragicomic dénouement—Agamemnon, with the weight of the gods' will hanging over his love for his daughter, feels like only half the man he used to be.

For Barthes, Agamemnon's underlying weaknesses are revealed in his uses and misuses of language: "Like every weak person, Agamemnon lives abusively in language; it is by language that he is attacked: he fears and flees Clytemnestra's speeches; and it is by language that he protects himself, nebulously swathing himself in aphorisms, bitter reflections on human nature."[4] In the same way that he wanders under cover of night, in the ambiguous moments between yesterday and today, Agamemnon shrouds himself in the vagaries of his practices of utterance. His sobs, his clichés, and his attempted acts of benevolent deception all reveal the clouded mind of the king in a play in which confusion reigns supreme.[5]

Agamemnon's uncertain uses of language—both his painful bleats of terror and frustration and his all-too-comfortable banalities—point to the king's inability to communicate with others. The difficulty in the opening scene of entering into conversational contact with Arcas is in this sense revealing. Felix Freudmann provides a compelling argument for the meaning of this murky exchange: "With the play's opening lines, Agamemnon's isolation rises before us out of the night. The lonely king

stumbles through the darkness among his sleeping people and wishes
to be heard; very much as he will move blindly among sundry schemes
which will come to naught, schemes rooted in instincts as ancient and
obscure as the night's shadows and which relate of necessity to other
individuals in dreamy pursuit of their own visions. Few tragic heroes
suffer so clearly from a breakdown in communication with others and
even from the lack of a clear perception of their own motives."[6] Agamemnon is detached from the world around him, by the very reason
that he was attached to it, through his concern for his kingdom and his
love for his daughter. When military objectives and paternal love come
into direct conflict, the individual subject begins to break down. In contrast to Corneille's Horace, who without hesitation kills his kin in order
to preserve the social order, Racine's beleaguered leader in *Iphigénie*
cannot come to a decision. He thus takes part, along with Eriphile, in
developing a motif central to this work—the confusion, alienation, isolation, and subjective disintegration that result from the quintessentially
tragic predicament of the direct conflict between public obligation and
private desire. Standing at this crossroads, the king undergoes a series
of communicational and cognitive lapses that hamper his interactions
with others in his family and in his immediate military and political cir-
cles.

Clear thinking and consciousness are absent when the gods visit Agamemnon at night, further aggravating his unease by means of carefully
timed reproaches that strike their object in the state between wakeful-
ness and sleep:

> Pour comble de malheur, les Dieux toutes les nuits,
> Dès qu'un léger sommeil suspendait mes ennuis,
> Vengeant de leurs Autels le sanglant privilège,
> Me venaient reprocher ma pitié sacrilège,
> Et présentant la foudre à mon esprit confus,
> Le bras déjà levé menaçaient mes refus.

$$(1.1.83\text{--}88)$$

> [To crown my misery, the Gods each night,
> The moment a light slumber calmed my cares,
> Avenging adamant their altar's rights
> And frowning on my sacrilegious pity,
> Would threaten my dazed mind with thunderbolts,
> Their arms already raised, dared I refuse.]

The predicament of this tragedy's most developed character takes on
the extended dimensions of duration, constructed in his recent memory,

in this description of sleepless nights and supernatural encounters. It was during such nocturnal bouts that he started, over time ("toutes les nuits"), to get the sense that the sword of Damocles was hanging over his head, in the form of the menacing raised arms of the gods, who stood before him and brought the thunder and lightning of utter disapproval.

Frightening and imposing though the gods may be, Agamemnon has trouble understanding their message. His mind is confused and his perceptions clouded in the liminal state of consciousness in which they find him. Like Charlemagne's dreams, the gods' oneiric appearances offer insights but demand further exegesis and interpretation, in anxious anticipation of events to come.[7] These visions become the object of narrative and fuel the desire to recount the situation to another character. It is in that difficult space, where one tries to understand what is being handed down from above, or where one aims to enter into contact and communication with another, that narrative desire comes into play. The attempt to tell others what is taking place, as a means to ease the pervasive tension, only highlights the fact that the characters in *Iphigénie* at key moments have a difficult time finding themselves and one another.

Before Clytemnestre and Iphigénie can come into contact with Agamemnon during the course of the dramatic action, they err for a few moments in a forest. Eurybate's account of a relatively brief time of confused wandering in the woods introduces the arrival of the mother and daughter on the scene:

> La Reine, dont ma course a devancé les pas,
> Va remettre bientôt sa Fille entre vos bras.
> Elle approche. Elle s'est quelque temps égarée
> Dans ces bois, qui du Camp semblent cacher l'entrée.
> A peine nous avons dans leur obscurité
> Retrouvé le chemin que nous avions quitté.
>
> (1.4.339–44)

> [The Queen—I have just come ahead of her—
> Will soon arrive here with your loving daughter.
> She is approaching. She had lost her way]
> [In woods that seemed to hide the camp's entrance. (*my translation*)]
> [In their Dark depths we found it difficult
> To find again the path that we had left.]

These woods are a dark and uncertain space, offering difficult access to the tent of the sovereign and the fatal shores that lie in the background. Like the coast of Aulis, the forest is a place of passage and a momentary obstacle, though not nearly as serious an impediment as the inert sea that prevents the Greeks' departure under Neptune's iron hand. The woods cause only a momentary "égarement," but it is a kind of wandering that is by no means insignificant. Why should Iphigénie pass through this forest before speaking to Agamemnon? Was she subconsciously avoiding this meeting with her father and with destiny?

As a result of this momentary detour, a lapse in communication occurs — the letter that Agamemnon wanted to use to trick Iphigénie into thinking that Achille had changed his mind about marrying her never reaches Clytemnestre. The ruse by which Agamemnon attempted to keep his wife and daughter from coming to Aulis, for the planned marriage of Iphigénie to Achille, has failed. Figuring the confusion that ensues, the dark woods play optical tricks as Clytemnestre stumbles through them. The wanderers are barely able to set themselves back on the right path again once they have strayed from it. Strangely, the woods somehow do not fully hide the entry to the camp, but rather "semblent cacher l'entrée." The curious compound verb describes a quizzical illusion: how can a forest only *seem* to hide an army camp? The combined verb form is pregnant with the overdetermination of this woodland as an in-between space of confusion, a temporary obstacle to the further progression of the action. This "quelque temps" is a time of deferral that facilitates the mounting of Agamemnon's confusion and the perplexity of his entire family in the face of destiny. Paradoxically, the delay in the mother and daughter's arrival is precisely the circumstance that allowed them to come to Aulis. They thus unwittingly stumble toward their (apparent) fate, which will still elude them in the end. The metaphor of the woods can be extended to the entire play: thus throughout *Iphigénie* the dramatis personae all wander in the forest in the hope of finding the clearing that might show them an unequivocal meaning for the will of the gods and an indication of what their future holds.

FULL TO OVERFLOWING

Suspense clearly constitutes one of the key elements of *Iphigénie.* The action is temporally situated in anticipation of a major mytho-historical event. As Nina Ekstein has explained, unlike a number of other plays in which the past ostensibly exerts much greater pressure than the future, in *Iphigénie* the future hangs over characters as the predominant temporal dimension structuring dramatic action.[8] For Ekstein, the radi-

cal instability of the future contributes to the characters' general confusion. Suspense and interrogation of the future are motivated by the
oracles to which the personae on numerous occasions refer, the central
oracle being the one that announces the necessity of Iphigénie/
Ériphile's eventual death. As a result of the pronouncements and predictions that structure their understanding of the world, the characters
in this tragedy, rather than carrying around just the baggage of the past,
are also filled to overflowing with the future, with the possibilities of
their own actions and of the situations in which they find themselves.

Although we may see him, following Barthes, as a character of limited means and initiative, Agamemnon is close to the gods and in communication with them, maintaining a kind of continuity with divinity
but still dominated by its invisible forces. Agamemnon wants no part of
this high station or the fame and fortune that accompany it. Arcas has
to remind his king of the great import of the circumstances at hand and
of the immense potential of the Greek fleet aligned on the shore:

> Quelle gloire, Seigneur, quels triomphes égalent
> Le spectacle pompeux que ces bords vous étalent,
> Tous ces mille Vaisseaux, qui chargés de vingt Rois
> N'attendent que les vents pour partir sous vos lois?
>
> (1.1.25–28)

> [What glory, Sire, what triumphs could be more
> Than the splendid sight extended on this shore;
> These thousand ships, bearing a score of kings,
> That need but winds to sail at your command?]

The adjectival group "chargés de vingt Rois" weighs on the noun "Vaisseaux," which it modifies with the burdensome force of the gods' will
on Agamemnon's worried mind. The shores of Aulis set up a transitional space, on the cusp of departure toward Troy, that fills to overflowing with the potential of war. The positive value that Arcas sees in
the unequaled pomp and sprawl of this maritime scene is precisely what
Agamemnon finds unbearable, for he stands on the uncomfortable
thresholds between human endeavor and transcendent will, between
public and private life, between duty and desire. Thus he uses a bitter
rhetoric to describe the burden of sovereignty:

> Triste destin des Rois! Esclaves que nous sommes
> Et des rigueurs du Sort, et des discours des Hommes,

Nous nous voyons sans cesse assiégés de témoins,
Et les plus malheureux osent pleurer le moins.

(1.5.365–68)

[Sad destiny of kings! To be the sport
Of Fortune's stings, and every man's report,
So that, always by witnesses besieged,
The most unhappy dare to weep the least!]

He finds himself in a paradoxical position, an intermediary state between mortality and immortality. As we have seen, Agamemnon does indeed dare to cry, rather copiously, to overflow with the tears of his terrible responsibility.

Agamemnon's brimming eyes provide one of the images of saturation that serve in *Iphigénie* to give form to the pregnancy of the tragic moment at Aulis.[9] While the shores are full to overflowing, the sails of the Greek ships are flat and devoid of the winds that would carry them to Troy. Their absent volume is displaced in different, individual human spaces. Eriphile, bereft though she may be of socially approved identity, seethes with anger, frustration, and unrequited love. She states quite clearly to Achille that she holds more knowledge of her destiny than she is willing to divulge:

Souffrez que loin du Camp, et loin de votre vue,
Toujours infortunée, et toujours inconnue;
J'aille cacher un sort si digne de pitié,
Et dont mes pleurs encor vous taisent la moitié.

(3.4.889–92)

[Far from the camp and far from you, alone,
Ever unhappy and ever unknown,
Let me my piteous destiny bewail
With tears that tell you only half the tale.]

In the absence of the desired state of affairs, she opts to harbor the sorrow that she will not in the current scenario fully express. It is as if she, like Andromaque, were offering to take an unwanted child off to a deserted land to cry in peace and isolation.[10] With the resolution of the crisis still on the horizon, Eriphile is filled with the forces that she cannot currently unleash.

Near the play's end, Calchas, the vehicle for the gods' oracular pronouncements, inspires awe as he stands on the threshold between present and future:

Déjà de traits en l'air s'élevait un nuage.
Déjà coulait le sang prémices du carnage.
Entre les deux partis Calchas s'est avancé,
L'œil farouche, l'air sombre, et le poil hérissé,
Terrible, et plein du Dieu, qui l'agitait sans doute.

(5.6.1741–45)

[Already a cloud of arrows dimmed the sky;
Already blood flowed, presaging the slaughter.
Between the two sides Calchas took his stand,
With fierce eye, fearful mien and hair on end,
Demoniac-drunk with the God possessing him.]

The double "Déjà" places us on the verge of seeing a change in the circumstances holding back the Greek armada. Situated in the intermediary space between Achille's followers and the rest of the army, Calchas serves as a vessel for the transcendent will that hangs over the destinies of the play's characters. What agitates him is the very same force that, with the catalyzing action of Eriphile's spilling blood, will fill the sails of the motionless fleet and send them off to Troy.

In anticipation of this scene, after Calchas's initial announcement that he will make the necessary sacrifice, Achille observes the ships that are otherwise ready for departure by the Grecian shores and projects his impatience onto these vessels, conjuring up the image of their imminent deployment:

Les Dieux vont s'apaiser. Du moins Calchas publie
Qu'avec eux dans une heure il nous réconcilie,
Que Neptune et les Vents, prêts à nous exaucer,
N'attendent que le sang que sa main va verser.
Déjà dans les Vaisseaux la voile se déploie.
Déjà sur sa parole ils se tournent vers Troie.

(3.3.837–42)

[The Gods will be appeased. Calchas, at least,
Announces they'll be gracious in an hour;
That waves and winds, ready to hear our prayer,
Only await the blood he'll sacrifice.
Already in the fleet they're hoisting sails,
His word already turns the ships to Troy.]

The period after "s'apaiser" is what one might call a pregnant pause. "Dans une heure," "prêts," and the anaphoric "Déjà" combine to construct one of the predominant temporalities of *Iphigénie,* the overfilled moment of anticipation, the time of imminence that takes in Achille's observations the clear conceptual shape of the final hour, a temporal notion that assumes the imaginary form of the ships' unfurling sails on the shores of Aulis.[11] The vessels turn toward Troy and their sails start to fill, in this pregnant moment of potential, taking us to the brink, going forward but not yet there, still agonizingly interrogating the near future that will be even more closely approached in the final scene.

The repetition of "Déjà," a poetic and rhetorical device employed by Racine, both reveals Achille's strong desire for the continuation of the campaign and his inability to pursue actively the emerging Greek nation's objectives. He remains trapped in a pattern of repetition for emphasis because, contrary to the dynamic image he attempts to conjure, nothing is yet in motion. The intransitivity of the repetition emerges in tension with the successful act of utterance. We are, after all, in the domain of language, at least one step ahead of Agamemnon and Eriphile's inarticulate tears of rage and sobs of grief.

The response to the unbearable fullness of being in this play is initially to put things into words, to exteriorize parts of what is taking (or not taking) place in symbolic form. The weight of external circumstances simultaneously threatens to crush the characters and prompts them to speak. Paradoxically, they are both paralyzed and incited to utterance by the overdetermination of their tragic situations. Confronted with a daunting externality, characters find that they have simply interiorized too much. Desperately trying to ease the burden of existence, they use language to represent and project elements of their experience outward into the world around them. As we will see in the following section, this process of exteriorization is extended on an ontological level to a veritable projection of self into the external world. But the first step is simply to speak. Arcas, burdened with the knowledge that Iphigénie is to be sacrificed, finally says that he cannot hold out any longer, that he must reveal Agamemnon's plan and enlist the aid of Achille:

> Autant que je l'ai pu, j'ai gardé son secret.
> Mais le fer, le bandeau, la flamme est toute prête,
> Dût tout cet appareil retomber sur ma tête,
> Il faut parler.
> CLYTEMNESTRE
> Je tremble. Expliquez-vous, Arcas.

ACHILLE
Qui que ce soit, parlez, et ne le craignez pas.

(3.5.904–8)

[As far as I could, I have kept his secret.
But sword, fire, blindfold, all are ready now.
Were all these instruments on me to fall,
I must speak!
CLYTEMNESTRA
I am trembling. Speak, Arcas.
ACHILLES
Whoever it may be, speak, do not fear.]

The comma at the hemistich after "pu" in line 904 denotes Arcas's moment of decision. At the limit of individual ability and capacity, Arcas reflects on the recent past during which he has served as the keeper of the truth of Agamemnon's secret travails. But the situation has changed, and the hard fact of external necessity drives the impersonal expression stating the need for disclosure: "Il faut parler." Clytemnestre's reaction, in anticipation of Arcas's announcement, is visceral. Achille, in his practically minded posture, always ready for action, expands the call for utterance into a more generalized kind of disclosure—somebody, anybody, speak!

Yet there remains something unsaid that language is trying to say, some blockage, something just beyond what characters can think of or say, the unimaginable, the unspeakable, just beyond their reach; to be human is to continue interrogating this void, to continue gazing into the abyss of what cannot currently and perhaps never will be said. The anguished questioning takes place on the threshold to a region of language that is both beyond language and at the heart of it. Heidegger pursues the inquiry in terms of the being of language itself: "But when does language speak itself as language? Curiously enough, when we cannot find the right word for something that concerns us, carries us away, oppresses or encourages us. Then we leave unspoken what we have in mind and, without rightly giving it thought, undergo moments in which language itself has distantly and fleetingly touched us with its essential being."[12] Paradoxically, at the same time that characters arrive at the limits of what language can express for them, they unwittingly engage in an encounter with language *qua* language. Racine's theater thus brings us also, as readers and spectators, to the question of the very nature of poetic language. Far from degenerating into meaninglessness or articulating an unambiguous national ideology, the minimalism and insistent limitations of Racinian language point beyond merely referential language to the fundamental question of humanity's relationship to language. What can we say about what we live and perceive? What remains that cannot be said? For Racine's characters, this questioning is born of an intense pain and frustration that also leads in another direction beyond language—it is as if language were not enough, as if Racine's characters were arriving at the threshold between their pained speech and other, even more dolorous forms of self-expression.

Selves in Dispersion

When the self is full to overflowing, Racine's characters react by casting parts of that subjectivity into the world of interpersonal relations, through communication in the form of language, and, in an ontological sense, into the physical world around them. *Iphigénie* includes strong images of identities attempting to project themselves physically into material reality. These subjective constructs suggest one way of reading Iphigénie's statement of desire to make contact with Achille:

> Je l'attendais partout, et d'un regard timide
> Sans cesse parcourant les chemins de l'Aulide,
> Mon cœur pour le chercher volait loin devant moi,
> Et je demande Achille à tout ce que je vois.
>
> (2.3.605–8)

> [I everywhere expected him; with modest eyes
> Forever scouring every road from Aulis,
> My heart to seek him winged ahead of me,
> While I asked all who passed for my Achilles.]

Iphigénie describes a projection of self into space and of the other onto people and objects in space. Her interpolation of everything and everyone she sees places Achille into contact, in Iphigénie's view of the world, with everything that surrounds her.[13] The spatial separation she describes between her heart and her identity in "volait loin devant moi" is doubled by the distance between the first-person possessive "Mon" and the first-person tonic pronoun "moi," at the beginning and end of line 607 respectively. This line thus represents in verse form a distended subjectivity, coming to grips with the pain of a love that is in conflict with external circumstances. The difficulties of the advancement of action toward war with Troy and the weighty decisions that must be made impregnate characters with a critical mass of responsibility. Their reaction is first to speak and then, in the case of Iphigénie, who is under the most pressure, to throw a privileged portion of herself, her heart, out into the world, in the desperate hope of being able to reintegrate this externalized part of self into a whole and healed identity. Selves in *Iphigénie* are disarticulated, nowhere at home with themselves.[14]

Iphigénie points to the crux of this tragedy by referring to Agamemnon's difficult choice as a dispersion of self through blood: "Quel Père de son sang se plaît à se priver?" [What father enjoys spilling his own blood? (*my translation*)] (3.6.1015). Agamemnon is being asked to throw a portion of himself and his family to the gods so that the nation, to which he is also intimately attached, may reconstitute itself in an organized assault on Troy.[15] As is indicated by the strong alliteration of "Père," "plaît," and "priver" (also carried into the following line's "pourquoi," "perdrait," and "pouvait"), this loss of self results from a violent and painful process that must be initiated masochistically by that very self. Iphigénie shows a greater ability than her own father to make this kind of sacrifice:

> Je saurai, s'il le faut, Victime obéissante,
> Tendre au fer de Calchas une tête innocente,
> Et respectant le coup par vous-même ordonné,
> Vous rendre tout le sang que vous m'avez donné.
>
> (4.3.1181–84)

> [I shall, obedient victim, on your word,
> Offer my innocent head to Calchas' sword,
> And, saluting the blow that you decree,
> Return you all the blood you've given me.]

Ironically, although the daughter acknowledges the debt of ancestral blood, an identity that she owes her father and the ill-fated house of Atreus, she is far more capable than Agamemnon of spilling that blood out into a world that supposedly needs it. As in the scene where she showed her heart flying forth in search of Achille, here again Iphigénie articulates a desire to offer up parts of herself as a reaction against the unbearable weight of being that this tragic situation has created.

Eriphile, of course, will top them all and actually spill the blood at Diana's altar that the gods and the Greeks have in fact been demanding all along.[16] Eriphile had foreshadowed her capacity for self-disarticulating masochism when she expressed her sadistic desire to project a portion of herself onto others:

Une secrète voix m'ordonna de partir,
Me dit qu'offrant ici ma présence importune,
Peut-être j'y pourrais porter mon infortune,
Que peut-être approchant ces Amants trop heureux,
Quelqu'un de mes malheurs se répandrait sur eux.

                                                                    (2.1.516–20)

[A secret voice commanded me to come,
Saying to me, in thrusting here my presence,
I might perhaps bring my bad luck with me;
That perhaps, in contact with these happy lovers,
I might infect them with my misery.]

She has come to Aulis so that, like a disease, her pain and frustration might spread to the happy couple. Barthes sees in this passage a light that Eriphile wishes to shed on Achille and Iphigénie. In an opposing direction, Charles Mauron offers the more appropriate image of a shadow being cast on the happiness of the would-be lovers.[17] I would propose to identify in this statement the more visceral metaphor of disease, a kind of germ warfare practiced by Eriphile, whose proximity to and contact with others is intended to sow seeds of pain and despair.[18]

As numerous critics have remarked, selves and society are in a state of precarious order verging on disorder during the moment preceding the Greek fleet's departure for Troy. Eriphile describes one form that this feverish sense of self takes—it is a question of a heightened sensitivity to external forces, a visceral reaction to the world that takes the form of an agitation of the blood:

Tout le Camp n'en sait rien. Doris, à ce silence
Ne reconnais-tu pas un Père qui balance?
Et que fera-t-il donc? Quel courage endurci
Soutiendrait les assauts qu'on lui prépare ici.
Une Mère en fureur, les larmes d'une Fille,
Les cris, le désespoir de toute une famille,
Le sang à ces objets facile à s'ébranler,
Achille menaçant tout prêt à l'accabler.

                                                                    (4.1.1117–24)

[The whole camp has no hint. Do you not find
In this silence a father's shifting mind?
And what else can he do? What heart so staunch
Would brave the onslaughts they prepare to launch:
A raging mother, and a daughter's sighs,

An entire family's despairing cries,
His very blood, all ready to relent,
Achilles rampant, on his ruin bent?]

The familial situation takes a disturbing, disorderly shape that sets the blood in uncomfortable motion. From silence to tears, to cries, to the impending threat of Achille's bad temper, all of these factors create a kind of agitation that thoroughly destabilizes Eriphile's sense of self. She who will finally undergo an actual dispersion of self at her own hands is emblematic of the predicament that all characters share in the midst of the suspense of *Iphigénie*.

Even Calchas, who seems all-powerful not only as a religious figure but also in a sociopolitical sense (5.3.1625), is hampered by his own set of limitations. We find out that "Il sait tout ce qui fut et tout ce qui doit être" [He knows whatever was and what must be] (2.1.458). In addition to the kind of knowledge we would usually associate with the seer—Calchas has intimate familiarity with what is to come—the soothsayer also knows the past, in an analogous way, as is indicated by the symmetrical repetition of "tout ce qui." In regard to the present, however, the verse reveals nothing. Calchas stands on a void in the present, impregnated with a sense of what is to come, but equally at pains as other characters are with the hyperbolically distended final hour before the departure of the Greek fleet.

In the essay "Nos affections s'emportent au-delà de nous," Montaigne gives an account of what he considers to be the inescapable human relation to the present:

Ceux qui accusent les hommes d'aller tousjours béant après les choses futures, et nous apprennent à nous saisir des biens presens et nous rassoir en ceux-là, comme n'ayant aucune prise sur ce qui est à venir, voire assez moins que nous n'avons sur ce qui est passé, touchent la plus commune des humaines erreurs, s'ils osent appeler erreur chose à quoy nature mesme nous achemine, pour le service de la continuation de son ouvrage, nous imprimant, comme assez d'autres, cette imagination fausse, plus jalouse de nostre action que de nostre science. Nous ne sommes jamais chez nous, nous sommes tousjours au delà. La crainte, le desir, l'esperance nous eslancent vers l'advenir, et nous desrobent le sentiment et la consideration de ce qui est, pour nous amuser à ce qui sera, voire quand nous ne serons plus. *"Calamitosus est animus futuri anxius."*[19]

[Such as accuse mankind of the folly of gaping after future things, and advise us to make our benefit of those which are present, and to set up our rest upon them, as having no grasp upon that which is to come, even less than that which we have upon what is past, have hit upon the most universal of human errors, if that may be called an error to which nature herself has disposed us, in order to the continuation of her own work, prepossessing us, amongst several others, with this deceiving imagination, as being more jealous of our action than afraid of our knowledge.

We are never present with, but always beyond ourselves: fear, desire, hope, still push us on towards the future, depriving us, in the meantime, of the sense and consideration of that which is to amuse us with the thought of what shall be, even when we shall be no more. *Mind anxious about the future is unhappy.*][20]

Iphigénie is the dramatic realization, in the age of French classicism, of this universal human predicament. Awaiting a future that weighs on their present, distending their experience of the final hour of the tragic day, Racine's dramatis personae in this play grope their way through a world whose driving principles elude them and oppress them at the same time. As a result, they are doomed (as perhaps we all are) to exist outside of themselves and thus never to be at home with themselves. Their struggles take the form of language and, when utterance falls short, of projections of self into external reality. While the sails of the Greek fleet remain flat and still, the individuals coming to grips with the situation created by an inexorable oracle are filled to overflowing with their responsibility to live the present on the threshold of the future, to undergo the private experiences that lead to the renown of public, historical record.

Standing on numerous thresholds, between self and others, between present and future, between duty and desire, knowledge and ignorance, immanence and transcendence, Agamemnon, his family, and his emerging nation strike a theatrical pose that is both unique and wholly characteristic of Racine's highest art, a dramaturgy and a kind of poetry that examines who we are, how we live in the world, and how we might better understand our relationship to language. The fundamental difficulties of utterance and of movement in space that define Racine's characters receive their final secular treatment in *Phèdre*, where possibilities for self-actualization through speech and action present themselves, only to recede from view again and again.

make] (1.3.226). When Œnone presses her, Phèdre foresees a physical reaction to what she is about to say: "Tu frémiras d'horreur si je romps le silence" [You would be horror-struck if I should tell you] (1.3.238). In her reluctance to speak, Phèdre has recourse to interpolating the gods and, like Mithridate, to asking herself questions that pertain to the act of telling: "Ciel! que lui vais-je dire! Et par où commencer?" [What shall I say? And where shall I begin?] (1.3.247). The difficulty of confessing thus leads to metacommentary, to a level of discourse that examines the conditions of possibility of discourse itself. The tragedy of the thresholds of utterance folds back on itself to open up a reflection that develops at the thresholds of tragedy.[3]

Ultimately the truth comes out in a painful and truncated manner:

> J'aime . . . à ce nom fatal je tremble, je frissonne.
> J'aime . . .
> ŒNONE
> Qui?
> PHEDRE
> Tu connais ce Fils de l'Amazone,
> Ce Prince si longtemps par moi-même opprimé.
> ŒNONE
> Hippolyte? Grands Dieux!
> PHEDRE
> C'est toi qui l'as nommé.
>
> (1.3.261–64)

> [I love . . . I shudder at the fatal name . . .
> I love . . .
> OENONE
> Whom do you love?
> PHAEDRA
> You know the son
> Of the Amazon—the prince I've harshly used.
> OENONE
> Hippolytus! Great Gods!
> PHAEDRA
> 'Tis you have named him.]

Phèdre thus manages to confess without naming the name that she cannot bear to sound out. Proceeding first by means of the genealogical periphrasis that refers to Hippolyte's mother, then to the title carried by Thésée's son, Phèdre insists in the end on the fact that Œnone has pronounced the "nom fatal" that she herself could not bear to say aloud.

Even after the confession, Phèdre remains only on the verge of confessing. The connection between the threshold of avowal and the threshold of death, the mark of which appears in the fear and trembling that accompany this painful act of speech, foreshadows the importance that other ontological in-between states will have for the dénouement of the tragedy, a play that initially stages the transition from silence to self-expression.

This drama of difficult naming recurs later in the play, when Aricie has to name Phèdre but cannot bring herself to do so. As Aricie speaks to Thésée about the monsters he has slain, she cannot bear to name one monstrous being who continues to exist, uncomfortably close to Thésée without his knowing it: "Mais tout n'est pas détruit. Et vous en laissez vivre / Un . . . Votre Fils, Seigneur, me défend de poursuivre" [But all are not destroyed, and you have left / One still alive. . . . Your son, my lord, forbids me / To tell you more] (5.3.1445–46). Phèdre, who was initially the subject of difficult utterance, has now become the unnameable object.

The void left in Aricie's report to Thésée produces some nervous questioning: "Quelle est donc sa pensée? Et que cache un discours / Commencé tant de fois, interrompu toujours?" [What is in her mind? / What does it hide, this speech of hers, begun / So many times, and always interrupted?] (5.4.1451–52) The question marks in Thésée's speech point to the uncertainty that weighs on him as he finds himself on the cusp of knowing but still in the dark. From others he hears only interrupted speech. Unable to attain the referent, he remains at the level of the sign. When others fail him, he sounds out the voices of his innermost self, in an attempt to arrive at the truth of what is taking place in his family: "Mais moi-même, malgré ma sévère rigueur, / Quelle plaintive voix crie au fond de mon cœur?" [But I myself, in spite of my stern rigor, / What plaintive voice within my heart cried out?] (5.4.1455–56). A voice inside Thésée is close to becoming audible, but, to the family's detriment, it cannot in the end be heard.

This dynamics of interruption and suspension of communication extends also to writing, as in Thésée's observation about Phèdre, who seems to be trying to write something down but cannot bring herself to accomplish this act:

> Elle porte au hasard ses pas irrésolus.
> Son œil tout égaré ne nous reconnaît plus.
> Elle a trois fois écrit, et changeant de pensée
> Trois fois elle a rompu sa lettre commencée.

> (5.5.1475–78)

[Then here and there she walks irresolute,
Her wandering eyes no longer knowing us.
Thrice she has written; then, with change of mind,
Thrice she has torn the letter she began.]

The failure of writing takes part in an overall disintegration of self. Phèdre's progressive loss of self-control, her difficulty walking and her inability to recognize others, visually frames the failed act of writing.

Similarly to speech and writing, movement through space takes place only with great difficulty. Just as the characters have trouble projecting their thoughts out into the world of communication, they also struggle to set themselves in motion and languish on the verge of departure. From the opening scene to the dénouement, embarkations are announced, but, significantly, never take place.

ON THE VERGE OF DEPARTURE

From the beginning of the play, Hippolyte's actions are framed by an imminent exit: "Le dessein en est pris, je pars, cher Théramène, / Et quitte le séjour de l'aimable Trézène" [It is decided, dear Theramenes. / I'm leaving now, and cutting short my stay / In pleasant Troezen] (1.1.1–2). Two present-tense verbs describe Hippolyte's stated desire to leave the scene, but as we well know, he will remain tragically present through all five acts, and the play will conclude with another attempted departure on the shores of a dangerous sea. In the midst of the action of the play, the possibility of Hippolyte leaving is brought up by Panope, when she announces Thésée's supposed death and the ensuing contestation for the throne of Trœzen. Above all, she fears that the young prince may take some of the people with him: "Déjà même Hippolyte est tout prêt à partir, / Et l'on craint, s'il paraît dans ce nouvel orage, / Qu'il n'entraîne après lui tout un Peuple volage" [Hippolytus / Is ready to depart, and it is feared, / If he becomes involved in this new storm, / Lest he draw to him all the fickle mob] (1.4.332–34). But once again the exit remains no more than a concept for characters to invoke as a part of the dramatic dialogue.

Rather than operating on a literal level, the notion of departure functions as a part of the esthetic construction of the play. In addressing "the question of unrealized departures" in Racine, Richard Parish uses the metaphor of magnetism to describe the tragic nature of the theatrical space that frames projected travels: "[S]uch intentions . . . become less and less likely to be realized as the play progresses. This is the case because the place in which the characters find themselves behaves as a magnet, and progressively underlines the inability of those within it to escape. In other words, the stage increasingly reflects the protagonists' tragic destiny in spatial terms."[4] Trapped though they may be, many of Racine's characters continuously strain to find an exit. Anne Ubersfeld argues that these tense strivings contribute to determining the (negative) nature of dramatic space: "The imaginary scenic space is . . . to be defined by this movement of perpetually frustrated flight, like that of a bound animal at the end of its chain or a bird tugging at the string which keeps it prisoner."[5] Their actions and thoughts thus emerge against the backdrop of a fundamental tension between movement and stasis, between utterance and silence, an anguish that ultimately questions the nature of dramatic representation by staging paradoxically static actions that are undermined by longings for an exit from the very scene of action.

Similarly to failed acts of speech, indefinitely deferred movements through geographical space contribute to the construction of a system of interlocking situations of suspension, of individual subjectivities on the verge of acts that are never accomplished. As we have discussed, in Jean-Louis Barrault's directorial conception of the play, what characters see and deal with onstage is always framed by an imagined elsewhere, an idea of alternative space that has its psychological importance but remains unattainable.[6] In her opening scene (1.3), when Œnone questions her suicidal tendencies, Barrault has Phèdre looking longingly and far away before she responds to her nurse's concerns. Her next line sketches out the spatial contours of her imaginary wanderings: "Dieux! Que ne suis-je assise à l'ombre des forêts! / Quand pourrai-je au travers d'une noble poussière / Suivre de l'œil un char fuyant dans la carrière?" [O that I were seated / In the forest shade, where through a cloud of dust / I could behold a chariot racing by!] (1.3.176–78). In her thoughts she has placed herself in the liminal zone of the shadows cast by the forest's edge. Both the shade and the dust she envisions forge a figurative connection to the passage to the underworld that increasingly dominates the spatial imaginary evoked by characters througout the play. The verb "fuyant" points to the fleeting nature of the imagined alternative spaces that she is conjuring while ironically underlining the impossibility of leaving the scene of the tragedy at hand.

Racine's protagonists are on the verge of a number of critical actions: utterance, departure, and death. Before addressing the best-known of these esthetic elements — Phèdre's incrementally approaching death and

Théramène's account of Hippolyte's final gasps—we now turn to the play's conceptual geography of in-between spaces, a less commonly recognized aspect. These sites correspond figuratively to the situation of the individual on the verge of action, of speech, or, as we will see later, of exiting the space of the terrestrial world and entering the world of the dead. In complementarity with the "geometry of the void" that structures scenic space, geographical space in *Phèdre* remains ever liminal and uncertain.[7]

THE FIGURATIVE GEOGRAPHY OF IN-BETWEEN SPACES

Corresponding to the individual's positioning between stasis and departure, geographical spaces in *Phèdre* are represented as intermediary sites, uncertain zones that heroes like Thésée navigate while others wonder whether they will ever come back alive. At the opening of the play, Théramène describes how he has searched for Thésée in areas of transition, all the way to where the world of the living disappears into the underworld:

> J'ai couru les deux Mers que sépare Corinthe.
> J'ai demandé Thésée aux Peuples de ces bords
> Où l'on voit l'Achéron se perdre chez les Morts.
> J'ai visité l'Elide, et laissant le Ténare,
> Passé jusqu'à la Mer, qui vit tomber Icare.
> Sur quel espoir nouveau, dans quels heureux climats
> Croyez-vous découvrir la trace de ses pas?
>
> (1.1.10–16)

> [I have already,
> My lord, to satisfy your natural fears,
> Crossed the Corinthian sea, and asked for Theseus
> Upon those distant shores where Acheron
> Is lost among the dead. I went to Elidos
> And sailed from Tenaros upon the sea
> Where Icarus once fell. By what new hope,
> Or in what lucky region will you find
> His footprints now?]

As Forestier points out, Théramène has traveled on an isthmus, a narrow zone separating larger areas of open water:

The isthmus of Corinthia, which connects the Peloponnesian peninsula to the rest of Greece, separates the Ionian Sea from the Aegean Sea. In order to suggest that Théramène's investigation has led him to all of the Greek coasts that border these two seas, Racine has us follow the journey of his character in the form of an arc that starts in the northwest part of Greece (Epirus, through which the river Acheron flowed on its way to Hades), descends the western coast of Pelopponesis (Elidos) all the way to its southernmost point (the promontory of Tenaros, which was also a point of entry to the underworld), and goes all the way to the easternmost part of the Aegean Sea (the Icarian Sea, which borders Asia Minor).[8]

According to Forestier, the geographical account given by Théramène foreshadows the significance for the tragedy of the points of entry of rivers like the Achéron into the world of the dead. Traveling along borderlands and testing geographical limits in his search for Thésée, Théramène has also reached the ends of the world of the living, and we will later find out that Thésée has truly tested those limits (he exceeds even Alexandre) by actually crossing over into the world of the dead only to reemerge in the midst of a family catastrophe.[9]

In-between spaces in the topography of *Phèдre* also serve to give figurative form to characters' sentiments. Thus the conceptual geography mapped out in characters' accounts operates at times an exteriorization of self, as in the passage where Phèdre describes how her desperate desire for Hippolyte took the external form of hatred and aversion: "Aux bords que j'habitais je n'ai pu vous souffrir. / En public, en secret contre vous déclarée, / J'ai voulu par des mers en être séparée" [(I) could not bear your presence where I dwelt. / In public, and in private, you known foe, / I've wished the seas to part us] (2.5.600–602). She situates herself metonymically on the shores of a larger place and invokes the sea as an agent of definitive separation. The notion of "bords" is thus that of the possibility of intersubjective contact, which in Phèdre's terms can prove treacherous. Rather than being separated by oceans, if one shares the same shores with the feared other, contact becomes dangerously possible. The seashore thus figures the possibility of interaction, as in the passage where Hippolyte reminds Thésée of how he had brought Aricie and, what is more troubling, Phèdre, to their present location:

> Je ne la cherchais pas,
> C'est vous qui sur ces bords conduisîtes ses pas.
> Vous daignâtes, Seigneur, aux rives de Trézène
> Confier en partant Aricie, et la Reine.

> (3.5.927–30)

[I sought her not: you brought her to these shores,
And when you left entrusted to the banks
Of Troezen, Aricia and the Queen.]

The use of the terms "bords" and "rives" in consecutive lines of verse
indicates a strong figuration of angles of intersubjective approach in the
limits of land masses. The shore is a place of transition and a site of
possibilities for future action and interaction. These tragic places spatially frame the beginnings of fatal actions and attractions.[10]

Seashores function as privileged sites for the exteriorization of self.
Thésée's valor as a slayer of monsters takes the concrete form of the
safe shores his exploits have created: "Vous avez des deux Mers assuré
les rivages. / Le libre voyageur ne craignait plus d'outrages" [already
you, / Chastiser of insolence, had secured the shores / Of the two seas;
the private traveler feared / Outrage no more] (3.5.941–42).[11] Because
Thésée has left the mark of his heroic subjectivity on these seashores,
the traveler need not fear the possibilities for danger that these liminal
spaces hold.

In a different sense, Thésée's geographical influence can also become
an instrument of domination. When he describes Hippolyte's alleged
sullying of space in Trœzen, Thésée points Hippolyte toward areas external to his own power and influence. These as-yet-unconquered zones
are the only places where the accused son will be able to take refuge:
"Tu parais dans des lieux pleins de ton infamie, / Et ne vas pas chercher
sous un Ciel inconnu / Des Pays, où mon nom ne soit point parvenu"
[You would appear / In places full of your own infamy, / And do not
seek, under an unknown sky / A country which my name has not yet
reached] (4.2.1050–52). Thésée's power over space is so great that only
the unknown has not yet been conquered by him. He thus banishes his
son beyond the limits of the knowable world, into the hypothetical
fringes of the known earth.

Thésée refers to geographical space hyperbolically in order to express absolute hatred for his son: "Fusses-tu par-delà les Colonnes
d'Alcide, / Je me croirais encore trop voisin d'un Perfide" [Even if you
should go beyond the pillars / Of Hercules, I still would be too near
you] (4.2.1141–42). Thus he organizes geographical space according to
his self-definition as a hero and according to his sentiments. In this last
example, his loathing for Hippolyte takes the topographical form of a
vast range of separation between father and son that proposes a solution to the current predicament.

Whether it is to give figural form to emotions or to evoke potential interactions and/or dangers, the conceptual geography of in-between spaces functions in *Phèdre* to advance the play's inquiries into subjectivity. Just as the evocations of space test the limits of the known geographical world—and the pillars of Hercules, or the Straits of Gibraltar, designate the very limits of the known world of the Greeks—statements about self test the limits of subjectivity. Perhaps in no other classical tragedy is space so intimately linked with the personalities and passions of characters. As Ubersfeld has argued,

> Trœzen is an infernal threshold, a gateway to evil and death, a crossroads where all the ways leading from Epirus to Attica, from Crete to the Land of the Dead, meet and cross each other; a border region where forest (Hippolyte) and "furrow" (Aricie), land and sea, life and death, innocence and sin, touch each other. The "impossible" place where the horses of the forest have their deadly encounter with the monsters of the wave.
>
> An ambiguous space, the ambivalence of which extends to the very characters who inhabit it.[12]

While this analysis of in-between spaces effectively points up the significance of transitions, passages, and meetings for the dramatic action, it remains only cryptically evocative of exactly how the ambivalence of space extends to characters' identities. In order to delineate more clearly the contours of selfhood, which gain conceptual and esthetic specificity within the frame of Racine's figurative geography, I propose in what follows the metaphor of the shores of self.

SUBJECTIVE INSTABILITY OR LEAVING THE SHORES OF SELF

Taking stock of profound changes in his own self-definition, Hippolyte admits to Aricie that he is not as immune to love as he had once thought:

> Moi, qui contre l'Amour fièrement révolté,
> Aux fers de ses Captifs ai longtemps insulté,
> Qui des faibles mortels déplorant les naufrages,
> Pensais toujours du bord contempler les orages,
> Asservi maintenant sous la commune loi,
> Par quel trouble me vois-je emporté loin de moi!
>
> (2.2.531–36)

> [I, rebel against love,
> For long have scorned its captives. I deplored

The shipwreck of weak mortals, and proposed
To contemplate the tempests from the shore.
But now enslaved under the common law,
I see myself transported.]

In the past he had looked on from the shore as others fell victim to the forces of love. In this context the sea coast provides a haven of nonengagement from which one can safely contemplate that which remains completely other. But now Hippolyte has entered this threshold space and as a result has stretched the boundaries of his selfhood. He has figuratively left the shores of a former, coherent pattern of identity formation. As Goodkin describes this process, "Hippolyte's movement is purely centrifugal, going away from his center, and toward nothing."[13]

In complementarity with Phèdre's *fureurs,* Hippolyte's subjective destabilization advances one of this tragedy's core concepts. His confusion runs as deep as that of the eponymous character: "Moi-même pour tout fruit de mes soins superflus, / Maintenant je me cherche, et ne me trouve plus" [Now for all fruit of my superfluous cares, / I seek but do not find myself] (2.2.547–48). Along with not being able to find himself, Hippolyte experiences a profound confusion between self-reflexive acts of recognition on the one hand and intersubjective interaction (with Aricie) on the other: "Je n'ai pu vous cacher, jugez si je vous aime, / Tout ce que je voulais me cacher à moi-même" [I could not hide from you—by this / Judge if I love you—all I would conceal / Even from myself] (5.1.1345–46). Here the outer limits of selfhood are redefined in the intermediary zone of contact with the other, who through love has come as close to the self as the same self. In all of these cases, Hippolyte tests the limits of his identity and reflects on the fact that the dramatic action has obliged him to leave the shores of his subjectivity in a search for a new autodefinition inspired by his love for Aricie. The departure that has proven impossible in the tragically magnetic, claustrophobic space of Racine's stage has become internalized in a process of profound subjective change. Unable to leave the coast of Greece, Hippolyte departs instead from his former self.

This interior shift projects itself topographically and intersubjectively in the (ultimately failed) plan to meet at the outskirts of Trœzen, at the very limits of this geographical entity: "Aux portes de Trézène, et parmi ces Tombeaux, / Des Princes de ma race antiques sépultures, / Est un Temple sacré formidable aux Parjures" [At the gates of Troezen, / Among the tombs, the ancient sepulchers / Of the princes of my line, is a holy temple / Dreadful to perjurers] (5.1.1392–94). The temple he has chosen for this rendez-vous (which tragically will never occur) is also significantly located at the threshold between the world of the living and the world of the dead. The straying away from self leads to a kind of death for the former identity, which no longer exists as it did previously. Throughout this play, death goes hand in hand with radical changes in identity, as the example of Phèdre's subjective instability shows most clearly.

Phèdre takes account of the fact that she also is in the process of exiting the parameters of her former selfhood. As early as her first appearance onstage, she experiences a profound subjective uncertainty: "Insensée, où suis-je? et qu'ai-je dit? / Où laissé-je égarer mes vœux, et mon esprit?" [Fool! Where am I? What have I said? / Where have my wits been wandering?] (1.3.179–80).[14] She knows that she has crossed important boundaries and that this crossing will have irrevocable effects on her relationship to Hippolyte: "Il n'est plus temps. Il sait mes ardeurs insensées. / De l'austère pudeur les bornes sont passées" [Too late. He knows of my mad passion. / I've crossed the bounds of rigid modesty] (3.1.765–66). This profound change in interrelation and identity causes the complete subjective instability that oppresses Phèdre from her very first entry into the tragic action, in scene 3 of act 1, a moment when she feels her knees buckling beneath her, shrinks from the bright sun of the tragic day, loses her strength, and feels that she has reached the moment of her death:

> N'allons point plus avant. Demeurons, chère Œnone.
> Je ne me soutiens plus. Ma force m'abandonne.
> Mes yeux sont éblouis du jour que je revois,
> Et mes genoux tremblants se dérobent sous moi.
>
>   (1.3.153–56)

> [Let's go no further, dear Œnone, stay.
> I've reached the limit of my strength; my eyes
> Are blinded by the daylight, and my knees
> Give way beneath me.]

Phèdre's reaction to daylight figures the extent of her disorientation. As Œnone notices, Phèdre rejects the very light of the day that oppresses her: "Vous la voyez, Madame, et prête à vous cacher, / Vous haïssez le jour que vous veniez chercher?" [But now you see it, ready to hide yourself, / You hate the day you sought] (1.3.167–68) Since she is the daughter of Helios himself, her rejection applies equally to her ancestors, to whom she is ashamed to remain visible. Unlike *Iphigénie* and *La*

Thébaïde, where the action opens in the uncertain shadows of daybreak, at the beginning of *Phèdre,* at the main character's entry onto the scene, the sun shines all too brightly.

The darkness and shadow of the previous night are by no means absent from the construction of the tragic time frame, however; in *Phèdre* the crepuscular has been interiorized. In spite of what she sees before her, Phèdre extends the time of night in her own emotions. External, meteorological conditions appear to be stable—the sun is shining; but the refusal to see the light, the desire to live between night and day determines Phèdre's experience of time. A chronic insomniac of late, this character is a nocturnal being:

> Les ombres par trois fois ont obscurci les Cieux,
> Depuis que le sommeil n'est entré dans vos yeux,
> Et le jour a trois fois chassé la nuit obscure,
> Depuis que votre corps languit sans nourriture.
>
> (1.3.191–94)

> [Three nights have come and gone
> Since sleep last entered in your eyes; three days
> Have chased the darkness since you took some food.]

Phèdre's insomnia, which is exacerbated by malnourishment, also constitutes an expression of desire. Her attraction to the darkness of night is the converse of her aversion to the bright light of day:

> Misérable! Et je vis? Et je soutiens la vue
> De ce sacré Soleil, dont je suis descendue?
> J'ai pour Aïeul le Père et le Maître des Dieux.
> Le Ciel, tout l'Univers est plein de mes Aïeux.
> Où me cacher? Fuyons dans la Nuit infernale.
> Mais que dis-je? Mon Père y tient l'Urne fatale.
> Le Sort, dit-on, l'a mise en ses sévères mains.
> Minos juge aux Enfers tous les pâles Humains.
>
> (4.6.1273–80)

> [Wretch! And I live!
> And I endure the sight of sacred Phœbus
> From whom I am derived. My ancestor
> Is sire and master of the gods; and heaven,
> Nay all the universe, is teeming now
> With my forbears. Where then can I hide?
> Flee to eternal night. What do I say?

> For there my father holds the fatal urn,
> Put by the Fates in his stern hands, 'tis said.
> Minos in Hades judges the pale ghosts.]

In Phèdre's case there can be no escape, neither into the dark of night nor even in death, where Minos performs the austere duty of judging mortals as they descend into Hades.[15]

Caught between night and day, and between life and death, Phèdre's attitude is decidedly ambivalent. Œnone reminds us of her mistress's indecision in regard to the day at hand: "Elle veut voir le jour. Et sa douleur profonde / M'ordonne toutefois d'écarter tout le monde . . ." [She wants to see the light of day. And her profound sorrow / Commands me still to keep others away (*my translation*)] (1.2.149–50). Phèdre's approach to the tragic day is marked by contradiction and by a vision, beyond the present time frame, of her own death:

> Noble et brillant Auteur d'une triste Famille,
> Toi, dont ma Mère osait se vanter d'être Fille,
> Qui peut-être rougis du trouble où tu me vois,
> Soleil, je te viens voir pour la dernière fois.
>
> (1.3.169–72)

> [Author of my sad race, thou of whom my mother
> Boasted herself the daughter, who blush perhaps
> At these my sufferings, I see you now
> For the last time.]

Phèdre's ambivalent reaction to daylight places emphasis squarely on the detailed temporality of tragedy. We thus become painfully aware, over the time of the tragedy, that Phèdre is living out the last moments of her life. She blames Œnone for having prolonged an existence that might have been finished by now: "Au jour que je fuyais c'est toi qui m'as rendue" [and when I fled / You brought me back] (4.6.1310). Imagining the lives of the lovers Hippolyte and Aricie, Phèdre compares their experience of diurnal temporality with her own lot:

> Tous les jours se levaient clairs et sereins pour eux.
> Et moi, triste rebut de la Nature entière,
> Je me cachais au jour, je fuyais la lumière.
> La Mort est le seul Dieu que j'osais implorer.
> J'attendais le moment où j'allais expirer.
>
> (4.6.1240–44)

[And every day, for them, broke clear and calm!
While I, sad castaway of Nature, hid
From day and light. Death is the only god
I dared invoke; and I waited him.]

Her tragic situation thus leads to a focus on the ultimate moments of her existence, on the very threshold of death, a shadowy zone that she occupies from the beginning to the end of this tragedy: "Jusqu'au dernier soupir de malheurs poursuivie, / Je rends dans les tourments une pénible vie" [Dogged by miseries / To the last gasp, in torture, I render up / A life I long to lose] (4.6.1293–94).[16] The final moment takes the physical form of the last breath, which Phèdre anticipates as the tragic action unfolds. A key component of the modern esthetic construction of this tragedy, the subjective experience of the threshold of death grows out of the development of the thematics of subjective instability. The individual, leaving the safe shores of formerly defined selfhood, wanders into the night of difference, of otherness, and ultimately of death.

ON THE BANKS OF THE ACHERON

In an attempt to distract Phèdre from her morbid focus on the last instants of terrestrial life, Œnone tries to convince her that the time still available to her, though scant, can still be put to good use:

Mais ne différez point, chaque moment vous tue.
Réparez promptement votre force abattue,
Tandis que de vos jours prêts à se consumer
Le flambeau dure encore, et peut se rallumer.

(1.3.213–16)

[But don't delay: each moment threatens life.
Repair your weakened strength, while yet life's torch
Can be rekindled.]

Phèdre, however, sees the remaining moments of her life not as a potential resource to be utilized, but rather as an already excessive temporality: ".J'en ai trop prolongé la coupable durée" [I have too much prolonged / Its guilty span] (1.3.217). Time is guilty and thus excessive. Time itself is to be rejected, to be used up as quickly as possible. The infatuated stepmother insists not on staving off the final moments of her life but rather on seeking them out, placing herself willfully at the crossing to her death. She reproaches Œnone for trying to turn back the clock on her life and demands that she be able to rid herself of her already waning vitality:

> Je t'ai tout avoué, je ne m'en repens pas,
> Pourvu que de ma mort respectant les approches
> Tu ne m'affliges plus par d'injustes reproches,
> Et que tes vains secours cessent de rappeler
> Un reste de chaleur, tout prêt à s'exhaler.
>
> (1.3.312–16)

> [I have confessed
> All my dark secret; and I won't regret it
> If you respect now my approaching death,
> And do not wound me with unjust reproofs,
> Or with vain remedies keep alive within me
> The last faint spark of life.]

Once again, time takes the visceral form of a human breath, the last vestiges of the body heat that will disappear in the throes of death. Panope observes the symptoms of Phèdre arriving at death's door:

> J'ignore le projet que la Reine médite,
> Seigneur. Mais je crains tout du transport qui l'agite.
> Un mortel désespoir sur son visage est peint.
> La pâleur de la mort est déjà sur son teint.
> Déjà de sa présence avec honte chassée
> Dans la profonde mer Œnone s'est lancée.
> On ne sait point d'où part ce dessein furieux.
> Et les flots pour jamais l'ont ravie à nos yeux.
>
> (5.5.1461–68)

> [My lord, I know not what the Queen is planning,
> But yet I fear her violent distress.
> Mortal despair is painted on her face,
> Marked with Death's pallor. Œnone, from her presence
> Driven away with shame, has thrown herself
> Into the deep sea: it is not known why
> She took her desperate action; and the waves
> Have hidden her forever.]

Ironically, Œnone, whom Phèdre had blamed for prolonging an already miserable existence, has beaten her in the race to death's door. Near the end of the final act, Phèdre's demise occurs in a way that brings out the full dramatic force of the journey to the other world:

> Le fer aurait déjà tranché ma destinée.
> Mais je laissais gémir la Vertu soupçonnée.
> J'ai voulu, devant vous exposant mes remords,
> Par un chemin plus lent descendre chez les Morts.
> J'ai pris, j'ai fait couler dans mes brûlantes veines
> Un poison que Médée apporta dans Athènes.
> Déjà jusqu'à mon cœur le venin parvenu
> Dans ce cœur expirant jette un froid inconnu,
> Déjà je ne vois plus qu'à travers un nuage
> Et le Ciel, et l'Epoux que ma présence outrage.
> Et la Mort à mes yeux dérobant la clarté
> Rend au jour, qu'ils souillaient, toute sa pureté.
>
> (5.7.1633–44)

> [The sword by now
> Would have cut short my life, had I not left
> Virtue suspected. Baring my remorse
> Before you, I wished to take a slower road
> To the house of Death. I have taken — I have made
> Course through my burning veins a deadly poison
> Medea brought to Athens. Already the venom
> Has reached my dying heart, and thrown upon it
> An unimagined cold. Already I see,
> As through a mist, the sky above, the husband
> My presence outrages; and Death, that robs
> My eyes of clearness, to the day they soil
> Restores its purity.]

Death proceeds from the inside with the toxin that Phèdre has taken. In the intimate figural space of subjective experience, the poison first attacks her heart, the organ with which she has loved so passionately, before consummating the blindness that has progressively formed with Phèdre's increasing disorientation. Finally the "clarté" of the day at hand has disappeared from Phèdre's perceptions, and she descends into Hades while speaking from the threshold of death, witnessing her own demise and voicing this experience in the last of Racine's plays to stage mortals at odds with the uncertainty of their existences in a world of invisible gods.

Phèdre's death has been thematically prepared in this work by the continual development of the theme of crossing the boundaries separating the world of the living from that of the dead. The story of Thésée's descent into Hades and his eventual return places the idea of the mortal on death's doorstep at the esthetic center of this play. In his 1677 preface to the play, Racine discusses Plutarch as the key source for the story of Theseus's flirtation with death:

> C'est dans cet Historien que j'ai trouvé que ce qui avait donné occasion de croire que Thésée fût descendu dans les enfers pour enlever Proserpine, était un voyage que ce Prince avait fait en Epire vers la source de l'Achéron, chez un Roi dont Pirithoüs voulait enlever la Femme, et qui arrêta Thésée prisonnier après avoir fait mourir Pirithoüs. Ainsi j'ai tâché de conserver la vraisemblance de l'histoire, sans rien perdre des ornements de la Fable qui fournit extrêmement à la Poésie. (818)

> [It is in this historian that I have found that what gave occasion to believe that Theseus descended into the underworld to rescue Prosperpine [*sic*] was a journey that the prince had made in Epirus towards the sources of the Acheron, at the home of a king whose wife Peirithous wishes to bear off, and who took Theseus prisoner after slaying Peirithous. So I have tried to keep the verisimilitude of the story, without losing anything of the ornaments of the fable, which is an abundant storehouse of poetical imagery.]

I am arguing, then, that a significant part of the ornamentation that Racine found in his source material is what might be called an esthetics of the threshold. Along with shores and the forest's edges, the doorways to the underworld occupy a prominent place in Euripides, whose Hippolytus laments that "I am a broken man; yes, I see the gates that close upon the dead" and whose Aphrodite gleefully adds that "little he recks that Death hath opened his gates for him, and that this is his last look upon the light."[17] Seneca's character of the Nurse adds an even more sinister image: "Trust not in Dis. Though he bar his realm, and though the Stygian dog keep guard o'er the grim doors, Theseus alone finds out forbidden ways."[18] Memorable for its poetry and imagery, the idea of Thésée at the very portals of Hades functions powerfully on the level of plot.

Initially, Ismène develops the idea of the doors to death when she indulges Aricie in speculation about Thésée's disappearance:

> On dit même, et ce bruit est partout répandu,
> Qu'avec Pirithoüs aux Enfers descendu
> Il a vu le Cocyte et les Rivages sombres,
> Et s'est montré vivant aux infernales Ombres,

Mais qu'il n'a pu sortir de ce triste séjour,
Et repasser les bords, qu'on passe sans retour.

(2.1.383–88)

[It is even said—
A widespread rumor this—that he descended
To Hades with Peirithoüs, and saw
Cocytus and the gloomy banks, and living
Appeared to the infernal shades, but then
Could not emerge from those sad regions,
And cross the bourn from which there's no return.]

The "bords" evoked here are of a more elusively metaphorical nature than the seashores described in terms of conceptual geography and subjective changes of experience. Here Thésée reaches the very limits of human possibility, in the shadowy nether regions of virtual death. Characteristically, Phèdre puts his predicament in terms of sight:

On ne voit point deux fois le Rivage des morts,
Seigneur. Puisque Thésée a vu les sombres bords,
En vain vous espérez qu'un Dieu vous le renvoie,
Et l'avare Achéron ne lâche point sa proie.

(2.5.623–26)

[None has beheld the marches of the dead
A second time, my lord. Since he has seen
Those dismal shores, you hope in vain some god
Will send him back. The greedy Acheron
Never lets go its prey.]

For Phèdre, one cannot see the underworld and then come back to gaze upon the realm of the living. Similarly, she wishes to reject her vision of the day at hand in order to plunge into the eternal night that Thésée now faces.[19]

The culminating moment of the tragedy takes place along those fatal seashores where Hippolyte has for so long exercised his horses. This space, formerly the domain of Hippolyte's training and developing valor, has become destabilized by the power of the sea monster Neptune has summoned at Thésée's behest: "Ses longs mugissements font trembler le rivage" [The seashore trembled with his bellowing] (5.6.1521). His powerlessness over his horses in the unstable space of the shore leads to the disintegration of his body: "Il veut les rappeler, et sa voix les effraye. / Ils courent. Tout son corps n'est bientôt qu'une plaie" [He tried to check them; but, frightened by his voice, / They ran; and soon his body was a single wound] (5.6.1549–50). Théramène describes how parts of Hippolyte's body lead him to the scene of the disaster while marking the shores of Trézène as a site concretizing the passage to death:

> J'y cours en soupirant, et sa garde me suit.
> De son généreux sang la trace nous conduit.
> Les rochers en sont teints. Les ronces dégouttantes
> Portent de ses cheveux les dépouilles sanglantes.
> J'arrive, je l'appelle, et me tendant la main
> Il ouvre un œil mourant, qu'il referme soudain.
> *Le Ciel, dit-il, m'arrache une innocente vie.*
> *Prends soin après ma mort de la triste Aricie.*
> *Cher Ami, si mon Père un jour désabusé*
> *Plaint le malheur d'un Fils faussement accusé,*
> *Pour apaiser mon sang, et mon Ombre plaintive,*
> *Dis-lui, qu'avec douceur il traite sa Captive,*
> *Qu'il lui rende ...* A ce mot ce Héros expiré
> N'a laissé dans mes bras qu'un corps défiguré,
> Triste objet, où des Dieux triomphe la colère,
> Et que méconnaîtrait l'œil même de son Père.
>
> (5.6.1555–70)

> [There I ran, in tears,
> And his guard followed me. A trail of blood
> Showed us the way. The rocks were stained with it.
> The loathsome brambles carried bloodstained scraps
> Of hair torn from his head. I reached him, called
> To him; he stretched his hand to me, and opened
> His dying eyes, then closed them suddenly.
> "The heavens," said he, "now snatch my guiltless life.
> Look after Aricia when I am dead.
> Dear friend, if my father one day learns the truth,
> And weeps the tragic ending of a son
> Falsely accused, in order to appease
> My blood and plaintive ghost, tell him to treat
> His captive kindly, to give her . . ." At this word
> The hero died and left within my arms
> Only a corpse, disfigured, where the wrath
> Of the gods had triumphed, one which his father's eyes
> Would fail to recognize.]

The young hero's generosity speaks with particular intensity from the crossing to death, a conceptual space that becomes visible on the shores

of Trœzen. The fragmentation of Hippolyte's body, spread on the rocks
and flora of the beach, gives imagistic form to this ineffable notion. His
body has become unrecognizable and thus other. In the last scene of his
terrestrial life, Hippolyte has once again stretched the boundaries of his
identity.[20] This otherness throws into relief the sameness of the emotions that he has cultivated from the very beginning of the tragic action.
His love for Aricie remains intact and in fact becomes energized in his
final words.

Théramène describes Aricie's reaction to the awful sight of her dying
lover:

> Elle approche. Elle voit l'herbe rouge et fumante.
> Elle voit (quel objet pour les yeux d'une Amante!)
> Hippolyte étendu, sans forme et sans couleur.
> Elle veut quelque temps douter de son malheur,
> Et ne connaissant plus ce Héros qu'elle adore,
> Elle voit Hippolyte, et le demande encore.
> Mais trop sûre à la fin qu'il est devant ses yeux,
> Par un triste regard elle accuse les Dieux,
> Et froide, gémissante, et presque inanimée,
> Aux pieds de son Amant elle tombe pâmée.
>
> (5.6.1577–86)

> [She approached.
> She saw the red and reeking grass; she saw
> (What an object for a lover's eyes!)
> Hippolytus lying there a shapeless mass.
> A while she wished to doubt of her disaster
> And failed to recognize the man she loved.
> She saw Hippolytus—and asked for him still.
> At last too sure that he was lying there,
> She with a mournful look reproached the gods;
> Cold, moaning, almost lifeless, she fell down
> At her lover's feet.]

In a manner congruent to the fate of her beloved, Aricie temporarily
loses consciousness, thus arriving at a similar borderline between wake-
ful life and oblivion. Théramène, who is slightly more removed from the
situation than Aricie but still mortified by it, echoes Phèdre by cursing
the day that has allowed these events to take place:

> Et moi, je suis venu détestant la lumière
> Vous dire d'un Héros la volonté dernière,

Et m'acquitter, Seigneur, du malheureux emploi,
Dont son cœur expirant s'est reposé sur moi.

(5.6.1589–92)

[And I have come,
Hating the light, to tell you the last wish
Of a dead hero; and discharge, my lord,
The unhappy task his dying heart reposed
Upon me.]

In his report to Thésée, Théramène emphasizes once again the significance of the fact that Hippolyte spoke from death's door. Thésée has no choice but to give us the relatively happy ending of his clemency for Aricie and of the promise of a brighter future after the resolution of the tragic conflict.

Throughout *Phèdre*, Racine develops the esthetics of the threshold in a manner leading to the pair of key tragic deaths, those of Hippolyte and of Phèdre herself. In these death scenes, problems of utterance, of the organization of the tragic topography, of the changing and stretching of identities, and of the subjective experience of the passage to death all intertwine. These culminating moments contribute to what Georges Poulet considers the apotheosis of the Racinian individual's apprehension of the transcendent. In what Poulet sees as a break from the pessimistic vision of human life characteristic of Racine's earlier tragedies, in *Phèdre*,

> what shows through the most intense feeling of human indignity is the feeling, no less intense, of the prodigious dignity which in every instant the eternal act of creation confers upon and restores to this unworthy being. Thus the fatality of past cause and past evil is exorcised by the recognition of a cause which transcends all duration, and which is found immediately and almost miraculously, even in the moment of death—of the death of Phèdre, since this moment, like all moments, is the gift of God.
>
> After that, no more remains than to set forth the divine acts of this Providence in human durations. That is what Racine will do in *Esther* and *Athalie*.[21]

With *Phèdre*, Racine's last work of profane theater, we arrive at the threshold to the divine. While Poulet elegantly states that this intermediary space has been traversed and that a transcendent will can be clearly perceived in a way that redeems the tragic action, I wish to argue, in conclusion, that this ultimate passage to divinity still remains unaccomplished as the curtain falls on *Phèdre*. By the time of *Esther* (1689) and *Athalie* (1691), the crossing will have been made, as the tragedy of the threshold becomes the drama of Providence. Racine's sacred theater, premiering more than a decade after *Phèdre*, stands in stark contrast to the secular staging of tragic impasses and points of passage. Whereas with *Esther* and *Athalie* Racine invites us to take a leap of monotheistic faith, when we reread the earlier tragedies, like *Britannicus*, we always find ourselves utterly, irrevocably caught in a universe of irreducible, unredeemable tragic ambiguity.

Conclusion

FROM *LA THÉBAÏDE TO PHÈDRE,* THE TRAGIC SUBJECT SEES THE WORLD from a profoundly ambivalent perspective. Jocaste and Phèdre both apostrophize the sun, placing it at the source of what torments them. Jocaste wishes that night would last indefinitely to envelop and smother the tragic action of the day at hand. Even more pointedly, Phèdre states her desire to flee from the light of day that shows her in all her shame. To make matters worse, she is the direct descendant of Helios, and thus she rejects not only the creator of the fateful day but also her own lineage. World, sun, gods, and time itself are all sharply thrown into question in the first and last works of Racine's profane theater.

With the sacred plays, Racinian cosmology takes a different form. In verses sung from the libretto of *Athalie,* the sun is no longer a harsh light to be interrogated but becomes rather a benevolent force emanating from the unquestioned, omnipotent God who animates the world as a whole: "Il commande au Soleil d'animer la nature, / Et la lumière est un don de ses mains" [The sun all nature doth reanimate / At His command; He gives the blessed light] (1.4.328–29). No longer at the point of transition between the terrestrial and the transcendent, Racine's characters need not speculate on the nature of divine will. In *Athalie,* they are either believers or unbelievers, and the chorus informs the audience in no uncertain terms of the structure of the tragic cosmos. The limits to the divine have thus been traversed, and the truth of the Judeo-Christian God's power and benevolence becomes the privileged object of lyric reflection. As a member of the chorus in *Esther* triumphantly declares, "Dieu descend, et revient habiter parmi nous" [The Lord descends to dwell among His own] (3.9.1261).

In other words, we know things will end properly within the plays, even if the tragic action includes dangers, unforeseen circumstances, and menacing characters. Athalie herself is a frightening force in a social world dominated by the persecution of the Hebrew nation. The daughter of Jezabel and Ahab, King of Israel, Athalie had been wed to Joram, the heir to the throne. Their son was Ochosias, brother of Josabet and father of the young Joas, the first child Racine was to put onstage. The play is the story of Joas's accession to the throne, a bid for power that is threatened by the presence of Athalie, archpersecutor of the Jews. Joas, whom Josabet rescued from Athalie and Ahab's killing spree of the children of Ochosias, is being raised in the temple of the Levites by the high priest Joad. But the child's life is threatened by Athalie and her dastardly advisor Mathan. As the action of the play unfolds, Joas remains in safety, under Joad's protection in the temple, and Athalie does not yet know who he is.

Athalie, however, comes ever closer to discovering Joas's identity. In a transgressive act that astonishes and frightens those present to see it, Athalie, prepares to enter the temple:

> Dans un des parvis aux hommes réservé
> Cette Femme superbe entre le front levé,
> Et se préparait même à passer les limites
> De l'enceinte sacrée ouverte aux seuls Lévites.
> Le peuple s'épouvante et fuit de toutes parts.

(2.2.397–401)

> [Into a sanctuary reserved for men
> Entered this haughty woman, head held high,
> And made to pass into the holy precincts
> Open to Levites only. Struck with terror
> The people fled away.]

With the focus on the "limites" of the privileged space in the interior of the temple, the text draws our attention to significant points of access to the sacred space in which Joas remains in safety. As the reaction of the populace shows, Athalie holds the dangerous potential for a transgressive crossing of these boundaries, which are exclusive both in terms of religion and gender.

The dramatic tension of *Athalie* develops according to the threat of Athalie's approach. She will come closer to Joas in a sequence following her premonitory dream, in which, after Jezabel has been ripped apart by dogs, the boy appears before her, dressed as a Hebrew priest, and kills her with a dagger. She thus approaches the temple in an effort to appease the Hebrew God, for she fears this young boy.

Whereas Josabet, in a suggestion reminiscent of *Andromaque*, wishes to take Joas off to the desert to rescue him from Athalie's wrath, Joad insists that the protection provided in the temple by the Levites and by God is all that the boy will need. His utter faith in God's custody of the priests and children who are there to carry out divine will finds expression in his remark on the nature of life and death:

> Voilà donc quels vengeurs s'arment pour ta querelle,
> Des Prêtres, des Enfants, ô Sagesse éternelle!
> Mais si tu les soutiens, qui peut les ébranler?
> Du tombeau quand tu veux tu sais nous rappeler.
>
> (3.7.1119–22)

> [See what avengers arm them for thy quarrel,
> O everlasting Wisdom—priests and children!
> But if Thou dost uphold them, who can shake them?
> Thou canst, at pleasure, call us from the tomb.]

God guarantees Joas's safety inside the temple by reason of a complete control over the borderline between life and death. Crossing over this threshold means nothing if it is not God's will, for he can bring us back into the world of the living at any moment. The shadowy space between life and death, which as we have seen constitutes one of the most ambiguous and complex interstitial spaces in Racine's profane theater, has become subordinated to the univalence and coherence of divine will.

Still, in support of dramatic action and suspense, the threat of Athalie's crossing into the temple remains a key object of focus (5.1.1537–40, 5.2.1643–46). Joad instructs one of the Levites on how to deal with Athalie's imminent entry into the temple:

> Vous dès que cette Reine ivre d'un fol orgueil
> De la porte du Temple aura passé le seuil,
> Qu'elle ne pourra plus retourner en arrière;
> Prenez soin qu'à l'instant la trompette guerrière
> Dans le camp ennemi jette un subit effroi.
>
> (5.3.1681–85)

> [You, when the Queen,
> Drunk with mad pride, has crossed the Temple threshold,
> That she may not retreat the way she came
> See that the warlike trumpet at that instant
> Startles the hostile camp with sudden fear.]

In the fifth act, the doors to the temple, which have been set up earlier in the play as a key site, function as the central dramatic locus for the question of whether Athalie will kill young Joas or not. On the verge of what may befall Joas and the Hebrews, in this very liminal space the sudden reversal of the play's dénouement will occur — Athalie will acquiesce to the will of the Judeo-Christian God and let Joas live. It is this deity who has frustrated her, in her dreams, through her conflicting feelings for Joas, and this god will triumph in the end. The drama is played in the doorway to the temple, the final significant place of passage in Racine's theater.

Unlike the figurative and literal sites of transition in the secular tragedies, the key threshold in *Athalie* is a space that unambiguously signifies the omnipotence of the Judeo-Christian God. Thus with the sacred theater the space of crossing appears after a key traversal has been made, the one to absolute faith. It is fitting, then, that the esthetic experimentation with the threshold should end here, at a point from which, for Racine, there will be no return. The final traversal has been made, and in a linear movement of apotheosis the book is closed on moments of tragic passage.

And yet the profane tragedies, from *La Thébaïde* to *Phèdre*, continue to pose the irreducible question of the threshold, as an open-ended dynamics of difference, to present-day readers and spectators of Racine. I have tried in the preceding analyses to elucidate the figurative richness of these in-between spaces and times that some of Racine's most memorable characters have to confront. Jocaste opens this exploration with an interrogation of divine will, and her tragedy ends with her sons' experiences of the borderline to the nether world. Alexandre drives this inquiry to the ends of the earth in his military conquests. In *Andromaque*, the limits between past and present and present and future lead to the dawning of a new reign and the new possibilities represented by the absent character Astyanax. The concept of the threshold to a political future takes a more pessimistic turn with the emergence of the monstrous Néron. In *Bérénice*, the question of political succession becomes above all an issue of subjective experience as the eponymous heroine's fate takes shape with an excruciating slowness of dramatic suspension. *Bajazet* stages an entirely different tragic experience, a sadistic drawing-out of the moment of death, in Roxane's plans for Bajazet and in her own demise. With *Mithridate*, the subject's own willfullness shapes the point of transition to the world of the dead, as the practitioner of poisons makes a final escape from the world of the living. *Iphigénie* highlights the anticipation both of death and of a politico-military future. This extreme drama of waiting overfills characters with the weight of their destinies and prompts dispersions of identity in space. Finally,

Phèdre places the broken and battered subjectivity of Hippolyte on the shores of his destiny, in an irrevocable departure from selfhood.

These tragedies all depict key crossings in progress, between one realm of experience and another. In reading them or seeing them performed, we also make a traversal, through the paratextual mediation of prefaces and rising curtains, into a stylized world of poetry and tragic action that offers glimpses of ambiguous regions of self and world. These are times and spaces of in-betweenness that figure the universal human predicament of being caught in a universe that offers points of entry into its understanding but that also prompts further, indeed endless questioning.

The open-endedness of Racine's works testifies to their signifying power across the centuries. Literature that is most worth rereading speaks to us differently over time, requiring us to evaluate its historically anchored meanings as well as its potential to elucidate issues of our own times. From the faith in technology that characterized the high modern area of industrial progress, we have arrived at the era of biospheric limitations. As humanity in the twenty-first century becomes increasingly aware of the global scale of its impact on its natural environment, the interrogation of world limits becomes a more urgent task. The question of the sustainability of our collective relationship to the earth demands our attention in unprecedented ways, as misuses of natural resources and unchecked practices of pollution strain the capacity of the world as we know it. The pressing problem of world limits is to a significant extent a scientific one, as we look to climatologists, biologists, and population researchers to redefine humanity's interactions with its natural environs in ways that may offer hope for the future. But it is also a human problem. As we consult the precise instruments that describe the changing parameters of our biological existence, we must also simply consult ourselves by examining carefully how we understand our world, dwell in it, and perceive its limits.

Although their author could never have foreseen the ecological predicament in which twenty-first-century humanity is now caught, Racine's secular tragedies, in their unending inquiry into the boundaries of the human condition, continue to shed light on some of the present time's most crucial questions. As we reread these works, resituating them in new contexts to engage contemporary problems, we, along with characters like Phèdre, interrogate our individual and collective destinies by simultaneously looking into ourselves and scanning (what is left of) our horizon.

Notes

INTRODUCTION

1. All references to Racine's tragedies and their prefaces are to Racine, *Œuvres complètes*, vol. 1, ed. Georges Forestier. Specific passages of the plays will be followed, as will other works of theater, by parenthetical citations including act, scene, and lines of verse, as in this quotation from *Phèdre:* (1.3.153). Quotations from Racine's prefaces will be accompanied by parenthetical page references to the Forestier edition.

2. See Barthes, *On Racine;* Campbell, *Questioning Racinian Tragedy;* Delcroix, *Le sacré dans les tragédies profanes de Racine;* Emelina, "L'espace dans les tragédies romaines de Racine"; Freudmann, "*Iphigénie:* A Study in Solitude"; Goodkin, *The Tragic Middle;* Mourgues, *Racine or the Triumph of Relevance;* Sussman, "*Bérénice* and the Tragic Moment"; Szuszkin, *L'Espace tragique dans le théâtre de Racine;* Venesoen, "*La Thébaïde* et les dieux de Racine."

3. Maulnier, *Racine,* 70.

4. Muratore, "Racinian Stasis," 113.

5. Racine is a slippery artist. As Marcel Gutwirth points out, his greatest trick may have been to "have managed to pass off to his society the celebration of the rebel as the catechism of order" (*Jean Racine,* 45). This is a useful warning against taking Racine too literally or unproblematically. Negativity and apparent lacunae especially merit a careful look, beyond their surface, negative value. Maulnier argues forcefully against associating Racine's characters with national ideologies or myths of progress: "They do not die in the service of scientific progress or of an oppressed class. They are filled with hatred and love; they are like no one else. It is impossible to dress up these characters in a national costume, to give them the hair, the figure, or the profile of a people or a race, to put flags or emblems in their hands. Their lips are made for lies and love, for insults and complaints, not for sermons or speeches" (*Racine,* 12).

6. Goodkin, *The Tragic Middle,* 22.

7. Ibid., 164.

8. For Maulnier, the antithesis is even sharper: "Corneille is a playwright of conservation: he shows how man holds firm, triumphs heroically, affirms himself even in death; Racine is tragic, which is to say a playwright of destruction" (*Racine,* 160).

9. Aristotle, *On Poetics,* 32–33, 1452b-1453a. I have left out the remarks that appear in parentheses in this translation, in order more concisely to present Aristotle's concept of a character who is neither entirely good nor entirely bad. As Goodkin puts it, "The tragic hero is a middle case: neither purely good nor purely bad, he seems to be defined as an average taken between extremes, an example of the ethical middle, a being who is in no essential way distinguishable—'mete arete diapheron,' 'not different'—from the collectivity" (*The Tragic Middle,* 40).

10. Goodkin, *The Tragic Middle,* 30.

11. Hopkins, *Shakespeare on the Edge*, 53.

12. Ibid., 45.

13. Ibid., 115.

14. Ibid., 120.

15. Shakespeare, *King Lear* (conflated text 4.6.57, 4.6.25–27), in *The Norton Shakespeare*. All further references to Shakespeare are to this edition and will be indicated parenthetically within the text.

16. Goodkin, *The Tragic Middle*, 10.

17. Braider, *Indiscernible Counterparts*, 330.

18. Ellen McClure's recent discussion of the diplomat as an interstitial figure in seventeenth-century Europe points the way toward a politically contextualized reading of existential in-betweenness in Racine. According to McClure, the ambassador is neither fully endowed with the powers of his sovereign nor fully in possession of an independent identity; "he is betweenness itself" (123). For a seminal reading of Racine in the context of politics under Louis XIV, see Apostolidès, *Le prince sacrifié*. For interpretations of Corneille and Racine from the perspective of postcolonial theory, see Longino, *Orientalism in French Classical Drama*. For a recent methodological discussion of the question of history for Racine studies, see Schröder, "Situation des études raciniennes," in Declercq and Rosellini, eds., *Jean Racine*, 11–24.

19. For a recent discussion of Racinian cartography, see Horowitz, "East/West: Mapping Racine."

20. Soare, *"Bajazet,"* 33.

21. Ibid., 33. For a study of the multiple uses of the liminary terms descriptive of seashores in Racine ("bord(s)," "rivage(s)," and "rive(s)"), see Soare, *"Phèdre* et les métaphores du labyrinthe."

22. Hopkins, *Shakespeare on the Edge*, 8.

23. See Murray, "Digital Baroque," for a discussion of representations of thresholds in Bill Viola's multimedia installations. These works serve as a visual counterpart to the conceptual focus of this book.

24. My reading of the threshold as a site expressive of the tragic predicaments of Racine's characters necessarily excludes his only comedy, *Les Plaideurs*, from consideration here. This by no means indicates, however, that *Les Plaideurs* bears no relevance to the corpus of Racine's tragedies. In his analysis of the staging of the plays, for example, David Maskell has shown how "[t]he whole range of his theatrical techniques appear in humorous form in *Les Plaideurs*. The décor, with the doors of Dandin and Chicanneau, is seen again in the doors of *Britannicus* and *Bérénice*" (*Racine: A Theatrical Reading*, 241).

25. Heidegger, *On the Way to Language*, 70.

26. Ibid., 120.

27. Ibid., 161.

28. Ibid., 119.

29. Mardas, "On Language as the Translation of Being."

30. Jacques Derrida examines the multiple meanings of the term "aporia" in a philosophical reflection on borders, crossings, and death: "The 'I enter,' crossing the threshold, this 'I pass' puts us on the path, if I may say, of the *aporos* or of the *aporia:* the difficult or the impracticable, here the impossible, passage, the refused, denied, or prohibited passage, indeed the nonpassage, which can in fact be something else, the event of a coming or of a future advent which no longer has the form of the movement that consists in passing, traversing, or transiting" (*Aporias,* 8).

31. Bachelard, *The Poetics of Space*, 217.

32. Ibid., xii. Further, for Heidegger, "[t]he poet experiences his poetic calling as a call to the word as the source, the bourn of Being" (*On the Way to Language*, 66).

33. Heidegger, *Poetry, Language, Thought*, 204.

34. Derrida, *Dissemination*, 214.

35. Ibid., 215.

36. In a discussion of ambiguity in Racine, Christian Biet examines the effects of lack and absence on our understanding of Racine:

> What is striking in the Racinian universe is . . . that it gives no clear lessons. The theater, by definition, is not an essay and thus allows for different points of view simultaneously. The combination of these positions may, but does not have to, lead to a demonstration or a lesson. Racine knows all of this and plays on it. The characters he shows evolving onstage never have the legitimacy, the strength, or the brilliance that would lead one to hope for a triumph of positive values, whatever those may be. The crisis which the tragedies explore never limits itself to being a point of access to an immaculate legitimacy, even were it to be found offstage. There is always a lack, a suspicion, a failure in Racine, a flaw in the hero that prevents him/her from achieving victory and from changing the world. It is impossible for the will to arrive at its ultimate objective.
>
> Racine in no way seeks to provide a homogeneous doxa, neither by defining a fixed esthetics, nor by establishing a homogeneous ideological lesson, for he clearly does not want his theater to carry a single, unified message. On the contrary, Racine plays on a fundamental lack, on the absence of absolute models, thus leaving his audience prone to reflection, to doubt, and to mourning at the end of his plays without ever providing, on the horizon of his tragedies, any glimmer of theoretical or practical hope. ("*Mithridate*, ou l'exercice de l'ambiguïté," 95)

In the end, however, Biet is unwilling to leave the ambiguities where they are, and he responds to them with an essentializing notion of tragic "larmes" [tears] which, as he argues, connect Racine, his characters, and his spectators in shared mourning for the uncertainties of the human condition. See Biet, *Racine ou la passion des larmes*.

Christopher Braider has also recently developed a complex and insightful approach to classical dramatic texts' resistance to reductive latter-day readings. For Braider, the best classical dramas shirk our ideological, theoretical, historicizing, psychoanalyzing, in a word distorting readings of them by anticipating these approaches. A complex ironic double to performance emerges after the fact and resists any unequivocal interpretation: "To read the plays of classical France is to stand in the presence of deliberate monuments intended to serve as incontrovertible paradigms of the greatness they embody. But the very texts by which these paradigms commit themselves to posterity teach us to detect, as it were behind the imposing monuments that meet us at first glance, the critical double formed by the historical coercions that attend their creation" (*Indiscernible Counterparts*, 322). This counterpart to performance or to initial readings of the text works silently and subtly over time "to preempt its own documentary ruin" (ibid., 79).

37. *On the Way to Language*, 192. Alfred Bonzon has drawn on Heidegger to find in Racine not a textual space of difference and ambiguity, but rather a single "global impression" or truth, that of the "tristesse majestueuse" [majestic sadness] that Racine mentioned as a central component of tragedy in the preface to *Bérénice* (*Racine et Heidegger*, 79). Bonzon does not discuss the dynamics of difference that Heidegger locates in poetic language, nor does he make a sustained connection between Heidegger and Ra-

cine, limiting his study to a suggestive but cursory reading of *Andromaque* in the context of the idea of *dasein* and to a few remarks on *Britannicus* and *Phèdre*.

38. *On the Way to Language*, 192.

39. Campbell, *Questioning Racinian Tragedy*, 33–34.

40. Ibid., 54.

41. Goldmann, *The Hidden God*, 328. See also Niderst, *Les tragédies de Racine, Diversité et unité*, 7–8, 184–85.

42. Campbell, *Questioning Racinian Tragedy*, 30.

43. Ibid., 83.

44. Goldmann, *The Hidden God*, 36.

45. Goodkin, *The Tragic Middle*, 20. This philosophical inquiry into humanity's interstitial positioning refers to Pascal's famous description in the fragment on the "Disproportion of Man": "That is our true state. It is what makes us incapable of certain knowledge and of absolute ignorance. We drift along on a vast middle, always uncertain and floating, pushed from one end toward the other; whatever is the end to which we think we can attach ourselves and anchor ourselves, it shakes free and gets away from us" (quoted in Goodkin, *The Tragic Middle*, 19).

46. Goldmann, *The Hidden God*, 67–68.

47. Ibid., 68.

48. Ibid., 71.

49. Orphaned at a young age, Racine fell under the care of a strict Jansenist grandmother, who enrolled him in the Jansenist school at Port-Royal. While the extent of Racine's indoctrination remains unclear, it is well known that the young Racine received rigorous classical training there, particularly in ancient Greek. At the age of eighteen Racine left his theological studies at Port Royal for Paris, where he would eventually enter the world of the theater. For Alain Viala, Racine's conformist adherence to Jansenist doctrine during adolescence constituted a *habitus*, a way to adapt to circumstances and acquire the knowledge and training that would serve him later in his career (*Racine*, 43–44).

50. Campbell, *Questioning Racinian Tragedy*, 152.

51. Delcroix, *Le sacré dans les tragédies profanes de Racine*, 353–57. Marc Fumaroli's erudite discussion of the poetic "plasticity" of pagan deities in Racine informs the present study's assessment of the potential theological dimensions of the secular tragedies ("Entre Athènes et Cnossos," 61). I do not, however, follow Fumaroli's argument to its reductive conclusion that Racine's secular tragedies are the work of a Christian moralist dressing up his lessons in Greco-Roman costume (ibid., 186). As I will show, Racinian invocations of divinity lead to stark yet thought-provoking ambiguities.

52. Goldmann, *The Hidden God*, 33.

53. Hopkins, *Shakespeare on the Edge*, 2.

54. Clearly, Racine's plays, although they can be understood as texts, were initially works to be performed onstage, and the question of the staging of the tragedies remains central to our understanding of Racine. For thought-provoking recent discussions of questions of staging, see Declercq and Rosselini, eds., *Jean Racine*, 3–8, 25–39, 53–74.

55. Pavis, *Dictionnaire du théâtre*, 151.

56. Ibid., 152.

57. Ibid., 153.

58. Maskell, *Racine: A Theatrical Reading*, 210.

59. Barrault, *Mise en scène de* Phèdre, 83 n. 11.

60. Ibid., 31.

61. Emelina, "L'espace dans les tragédies romaines de Racine," 125.

62. An indication of the numerous potential areas of inquiry into interstitial space in tragedy can be found in Patricia Dorval's discussion of threshold esthetics in a film version of Shakespeare's *Othello:* "[Oliver] Parker's 1995 film adaptation of Shakespeare's *Othello* is rife with images of doorways or thresholds of all sorts invested mostly by the sneaking ensign, Iago, who becomes the living embodiment of the Roman double-faced god of doors and passageways, Janus, also god of beginnings, initiating the visual and verbal perception, seeing and saying things (doing things) backwards as much as forwards" ("Shakespeare on Screen," ¶ 14). The open and variegated nature of Shakespearean stage space entails an entirely different treatment of interstitiality than we find in Racine, where threshold space is above all a site of minimalist tragic concentration.

63. Maskell, *Racine: A Theatrical Reading,* 167. A similar image is evoked in Jean-Louis Barrault's staging of the beginning of the second act of *Phèdre,* where "Aricie stops in the middle of the stage but without inhabiting it, still standing on one foot. She is extremely agitated" [Elle est "dans tous ses états"] (*Mise en scène de* Phèdre, 101 n. 3).

64. Ubersfeld, *Reading Theatre,* 150.

65. Maskell, *Racine: A Theatrical Reading,* 77.

66. Ibid., 154.

67. Barthes, *On Racine,* 5.

68. Pascale-Anne Brault, in her study of threshold space in Sophocles and Racine, comments on the

> importance of the arrangement of scenes according to definite limits, as the gate or door, that which hides, separates and relates inside and outside, partakes in the evolution of the hero and of the tragic event. Each time that a door or boundary is crossed, the protagonists are set into not only physical but existential motion. The tension created by the interrelation of inside/outside, private/public, free will/necessity, ignorance/knowledge, and so on, opens up what might be called 'thresholds of the tragic'—that is to say, places of communication (or miscommunication) and translation, places which define the boundary situation, revealing it to the protagonist at the precise moment when this place of translation is completely unveiled.
>
> This understanding of the inevitability of one's fate makes of the tragic character, there, at the threshold, a tragic hero. ("Thresholds of the Tragic," 239)

My understanding of these places of passage differs from this reading in that, rather than seeing an esthetics of accomplishment and subjective evolution, I focus on the painful, unproductive occupation of threshold space that so often plagues Racinian characters.

69. Emelina, "L'espace dans les tragédies romaines de Racine," 127.

70. Ibid., 129.

71. Barthes, *On Racine,* 4.

72. Poulet, "Notes on Racinian Time," in *Studies in Human Time,* 117–30.

CHAPTER 1. *LA THÉBAÏDE*

1. Adam, *Histoire de la littérature française,* 306.

2. Brody, "Racine's *La Thébaïde: An Analysis,*" 200.

3. For Gutwirth, politics in *La Thébaïde* "is not the science of governance, but rather the art of getting to the throne" (*Jean Racine*, 21).

4. Barthes, *On Racine*, 65–66.

5. Unlike Racine's later plays, the first version (1664) of *La Thébaïde* differs considerably from the 1697 version. As Forestier points out,

> *La Thébaïde* is the work which Racine revised the most extensively: as is indicated in the preface that he added to the play in 1675, at the moment when he made the most changes, he intended to erase the elements that most clearly revealed—according to him—the first hesitant steps he had taken in his career as a tragedian.
>
> In this first collective edition, there were 231 modifications in comparison with the original edition: 160 had to do solely with punctuation; 52 affected a word or a verse; and 19 are deletions of groups of verses. But these deletions had a considerable effect since there were thus 128 verses that were cut.
>
> The 1687 revision brought no major changes: the text only underwent 63 changes, out of which 50 concerned punctuation alone. No group of verses was cut.
>
> The final revision (1697) was more thoroughgoing: 133 changes can be identified; 62 concern punctuation alone (a considerable number of commas replaced by periods at the ends of verses); 67 are modifications of a word or a verse; three are deletions (16 verses cut); and one constitutes the only addition that Racine brought to his revisions (4 verses in scene 1 of act 4). (Racine, *Œuvres complètes*, 1250–51)

If we consider, for example, that Racine added fewer than ten lines of verse in the revision of his dramatic corpus, and that four of these verses appear in *La Thébaïde* (the rest belong to *Bérénice*), which is also the play from which the author deleted the greatest number of verses, we can take full account of the fact that *La Thébaïde* constitutes an exceptional case. Racine clearly saw his début as the least certain of the initial steps in his literary and theatrical career.

6. In a study of *Mithridate*, Michael O'Regan explains how tensions, irresolution, and striving function within the esthetics of Mannerism, a significant element that emerges in tension with classical symmetries in *La Thébaïde:*

> The forms, however, conventional in themselves, become elongated (whence the oval ground-plan in architecture), distorted into strange, difficult shapes and postures, curved or twisted. Because these forms are juxtaposed without apparent connection, their relationship is obscure; the combinations are other than what is expected. There seems to be a "refusal to satisfy expectation." One infers some abstract, intellectual intention, symbolic or allegorical, which is not clear, "in forma d'enigma," avoiding "that superfluous facility of being at once understood." The effect is thus of disproportion or dislocation, of balance either disturbed or precarious, of undecidedness, irresolution or vacillation. This may lead further to an impression of "unresolved tensions and contradictions," of "paradoxical combination of opposites," of a combination of "apparently incompatible themes into a whole," a "union of apparently irreconcilable opposites," a "union of . . . tension-filled principles and incompatible contrasts," a "union of extremes." It sometimes seems to some critics that Mannerism paid no attention "to the whole fitting together into a harmonious unity," that it was "deprived of . . . unity," that it lacked the "unifying principle" which always prevails in a baroque work, that it pursues variety, not the "structural," "energetic" and "organic unity" of the Baroque. None of this is arrived at by accident, for Mannerism is always a conscious art, artificial, cultured, the art of the virtuoso. (*The Mannerist Aesthetic*, 68)

This Mannerist esthetics contributes to the representation of failed becoming as a constantly renewed, yet ultimately unproductive effort. For Goodkin, the image of Créon's striving evokes Zeno's paradox: "Créon, like a sort of Zenonian arrow or 'trait' is, as Jocaste observes, pure tension: 'attente,' 'tendez,' 'attendez,' 'tend,' all indicate this latent contained energy of Créon's, as if he were simply waiting for the creation of a unifying process by which his individual moments of plotting might realize their momentum and allow him to spring forward toward his final goal, the throne" (*The Tragic Middle*, 74). In the end, Créon's effort at individuation through the acquisition of sovereign power will fail.

7. As Barthes puts it, "Eteocles and Polynices are so much alike that between them hatred constitutes a kind of internal current running through the same substance. Hatred does not divide the two brothers. Racine keeps telling us that it brings them closer together; they need each other in order to live and in order to die, their hatred is the expression of a complementarity and derives its force from this very unity: they hate each other for being unable to tell each other apart" (*On Racine*, 61).

8. Corneille, *Œuvres complètes*, ed. André Stegmann (1.5.307–8). All further references to Corneille are to this edition and will be indicated parenthetically within the text.

9. In Corneille's *Héraclius* (1647), the throne is hotly contested by Héraclius and Martian, who strive to determine which of them is the sovereign Phocas's son; as in *Rodogune*, the seat of power in *Héraclius* is unequivocally occupied by Phocas, who threatens everyone around him from his stable site of authority.

10. The word "couronne" appears 12 times out of a total of 22 times in all the tragedies; the verb "couronner" appears twice, its conjugated form "couronnez" once, and the past participle "couronné" 4 times. A similar term, "diadème," occurs 13 times out of a total of 34. Strikingly, the noun "trône" appears 47 times out of a total of 104 occurrences. See Freeman and Batson, *Concordance*, for this and all subsequent analyses of the frequency with which specific terms occur in Racine's dramatic works.

11. Barthes, *On Racine*, 62.

12. My reading contests Greenberg's assertion that the body is absent from Racinian tragedy (*Baroque Bodies*, 209). It is the visceral character of the enemy brothers' hatred that renders this animosity so inexorable, as is shown in the famous image of the intra-uterine war. See Montbertrand, "La mort dans les gènes."

13. Goodkin, *Birth Marks*, 162.

14. Cave, "Corneille, Oedipus, Racine," 94.

15. Venesoen, "*La Thébaïde* et les dieux de Racine," 762. For a close reading of Jocaste's call to the gods, see Delcroix, *Le sacré dans les tragédies profanes de Racine*, 254–55. Eléonore Zimmermann considers Jocaste to be the strongest, most coherent persona of *La Thébaïde*: "In the midst of a set of contradictory characters, Racine managed to create a coherent character whose stature imposes itself on us, a great figure of lamentations" ("La Tragédie de Jocaste," 570). Zimmermann describes the ambiguity of transcendent authority, and Jocaste's suspiciousness of this authority, as a dominant esthetic element of this tragedy.

16. Dubu, "De Corneille à Racine," 26.

17. Ibid., 26. Dubu argues that other changes in the text over the years were motivated by the experience of court life, which Racine was also on the verge of entering in the early stages of his career.

18. For Heidegger, the liminary moment of dawn, which he associates with the pain of the threshold, initiates an inquiry into the potential unconcealment of being in the human experience of becoming: "Pain conceals itself in the stone, the petrifying pain

that delivers itself into the keeping of the impenetrable rock in whose appearance there shines forth its ancient origin out of the silent glow of the first dawn—the earliest dawn which, as the prior of beginning, is coming toward everything that is becoming, and brings to it the advent, never to be overtaken, of its essential being" (*On the Way to Language*, 182). The significance of the moment of dawn for this experience of the possibility of grasping one's being manifests itself in the painful apprehension of this point of temporal transition: "The primal early brightness of all dawning being trembles out of the stillness of concealed pain" (ibid., 183). The pain and frustration of Racine's characters may be understood as this kind of trembling of "dawning being."

19. Poulet, *Studies in Human Time*, 127–29.

20. As Goodkin explains, Racine's tragic time in general is a time of in-betweenness, caught between past and future: "If tragedy is the genre which, more than any other, begins in the middle of things, during a crisis which has been building since some undefined cause or 'beginning' and which will subsequently demand some sort of resolution or 'ending,' it is nonetheless a genre which takes place in a middle time of irresolution, caught between a backward-looking exploration of the causes of its crisis and a forward-directed search for a solution" (*The Tragic Middle*, 3).

21. Racine, *Œuvres complètes*, 1262 n. 4.

22. The political and historical setting of the action of *Britannicus* during the initial years of Néron's notoriously criminal reign takes up once again the tragic notion of the first steps in an itinerary of criminality. The idea of incremental steps toward crime also assumes a prominent position in Hippolyte's self-defense in *Phèdre:*

> Examinez ma vie, et songez qui je suis.
> Quelques crimes toujours précèdent les grands crimes.
> Quiconque a pu franchir les bornes légitimes
> Peut violer enfin les droits les plus sacrés.
> Ainsi que la Vertu le Crime a ses degrés.
>
> (4.2.1092–96)

> [I urge you to examine
> My life. Remember who I am. Small crimes
> Always precede the great. Whoever crosses
> The bounds of law may violate at last
> The holiest rights. There are degrees of crime
> Just as of virtue.]

For an assessment of this passage as a possible adaptation from Saint-Réal's *Dom Carlos* (1672), see Racine, *Œuvres complètes*, 1654 n. 2.

23. Ibid., 117.

24. Goodkin connects Créon's ambiguous ontological status at the fall of the curtain to the issue of failed individuation in Racine, or what he calls "The (Still) Birth of the Racinian Individual": "Créon can watch death's departure here and watch it again and again, but the play, by ultimately emphasizing the mediocrity of the living, blocks his access to the domain of tragic individuation. . . . *La Thébaïde* obstinately refuses to destroy or to create Créon as an individual. Créon keeps talking because the Racinian individual is still being born" (*The Tragic Middle*, 79). This analysis of Créon's failed process of becoming strongly challenges Barthes's assertion that Créon is an emancipated, fully formed individual.

25. Biet, "Sophocle, Euripide, Séneque/Corneille, Racine, Dryden," 221–22.

26. In his study of history and sexual difference in Corneille, Mitchell Greenberg has discussed Derrida's notion of the hymen and of the threshold as a way to understand the major political and historical transitions that Corneille's dramas represent:

> [T]he historical moment Corneille chooses for his tragedies is always a "dramatic," fraught, moment, a moment of "history" becoming, a moment of passage, a threshold where what has been vanishes into what must be. Corneille's historical tragedies, from *Le Cid* to *Polyeucte,* are always situated at the point where ideologies collide. Corneille's history always appears threatened with a return to chaos, to social and cultural disintegration. Curiously, all of these plays reflect this moment of passage in the twists of their plots and in the inscription of this "threshold" at the very center of their "dramatic" dilemmas. In a large sense the moment of representation, the moment we are called upon to witness, is the threshold (the "hymen") of History. (*Subjectivity and Subjugation,* 54)

Greenberg examines the tremulous, uncertain moments, for example, of the beginnings of Castilian monarchy in *Le Cid,* but his main focus is on the accomplishment of these major transitions, as for example in the move from republican Rome to empire in *Cinna,* or the passage from paganism to Christian monotheism in *Polyeucte,* such that "all of Corneille's major dramas are sacred moments of metamorphosis" ("L'hymen de Corneille," 134–35). This analysis of historical transition is complemented by a study of how the political world is mirrored in Cornelian familial relations, and specifically sexual relations, in which male appropriation of the hymen is an attempted act of patriarchal domination of an irreducible space of difference that frustrates that attempt. While Greenberg focuses on history and sexual politics in Corneille, my interest in threshold space in Racine relates to existential and ontological questions concerning individual characters' experience of the tragic world. In *La Thébaïde,* the focus on these questions of human experience is facilitated by the lack of meaningful political change represented by Créon's ultimate failure.

27. The play implicitly refers to the story of the struggle between Jacob et Esau (Genesis, 25:22–25).

28. Montbertrand, "La mort dans les gènes," 239.

29. In *Macbeth,* a concise but detailed spatiotemporal description of the effects of hatred already explores some of this dramatic territory, albeit in a different, nonfamilial context. Macbeth, whom the Scottish thane Banquo sees as his archenemy, expresses his own deep-seated animosity: "So is he mine, and in such bloody distance / That every minute of his being thrusts / Against my near'st of life" (3.1.117–19). To the biological image of hatred penetrating to the heart, "my near'st of life," Shakespeare adds the notion of the temporality, "every minute," of the enemy's heartbeat.

30. Biet, "Sophocle, Euripide, Sénèque/Corneille, Racine, Dryden," 224.

31. Greenberg, *Baroque Bodies,* 229–30.

32. For Michael Edwards, the main thrust of the play is discord, or a kind of "non-relation or even anti-relation among those tied by blood" (*La Thébaïde de Racine,* 17).

Chapter 2. *Alexandre le Grand*

1. Racine's fictional exploration of the limits of the known world implicitly raises the historical question of the construal of countries', continents', and indeed of earth's

boundaries in early modern maps. On the history of cartography and the question of boundaries, see Peters, *Mapping Discord*, 28, 147–76.

Maskell discusses geographical boundaries, and especially rivers, from the perspective of the staging of *Alexandre le Grand:*

> The scenery for *Alexandre* is a long way from the banal antechamber so often associated with Racinian tragedy. It is precise to the extent that it shows tents and is not a *palais à volonté*. It is also precise to the extent that it represents a specific military camp, that of Taxile. Racine exploits this precision to give a spatial and geographical dimension to the action of *Alexandre*. Not only does the camp serve as a prison for Axiane, but the rivers mentioned in the text—the Euphrates, the Hydaspes, the Indus, the Ganges—mark the steps of Alexander's all-conquering progress. It is on the banks of the Hydaspes that Taxile's camp is pitched. The conqueror has passed the Euphrates; the Indus and the Ganges lie ahead. The spatial elements are thus indispensable for the unfolding of the action and for an understanding of the precise historical moment represented in *Alexandre*. (*Racine: A Theatrical Reading*, 20)

2. Adam, *Histoire de la littérature française*, 4:307.

3. Ibid., 310. Saint-Evremond complained that, rather than appearing as an Indian king, Porus was nothing more than an exotically disguised Frenchman (Racine, *Œuvres complètes*, 182).

4. Adam, *Histoire de la littérature française*, 4:311. Picard sees this play as the potential Racine: "The *Alexandre* is a marvelous instrument for understanding Racine; clearly, Racine had not yet found himself, but he was on the verge of his own revelation. Between this tragedy and those that will follow, there is only a nuance, difficult to define clearly, but that sums up Racine" (Racine, *Œuvres complètes*, ed. Raymond Picard, 192).

5. See Bruneau, "Racine historiographe"; Hawcroft and Worth, eds., *Alexandre le Grand*, xix–xxii; Reiss, "Banditry, Madness, and Sovereign Authority," 116, 134–35; Ferrier-Caverivière, *L'image de Louis XIV*, 94.

6. Reiss, "Banditry, Madness, and Sovereign Authority," in *Homage to Paul Bénichou*, 135.

7. Quoted in Reiss, "Banditry, Madness, and Sovereign Authority," in *Homage to Paul Bénichou*, 133.

8. Boileau, *Œuvres complètes*, 43.

9. Racine, *Œuvres complètes*, 124.

10. In the preface of the 1675–76 edition of his works, Racine insists that "il n'y a pas un vers dans la Tragédie qui ne soit à la louange d'Alexandre, que les invectives même de Porus et d'Axiane sont autant d'Eloges de la valeur de ce Conquérant" [there is not a single verse in this tragedy that does not contribute to glorifying Alexander, and that even Porus and Axiane's insults bear testimony to this conqueror's valor (*my translation*)] (192).

11. Occurrences of key terms provide evidence of the widespread nature of the theme of world and world limits in *Alexandre le Grand*. The word "terre" occurs 9 times out of a total of 75 in the Racinian corpus (thus more than in any other secular tragedy; the play with the most occurrences is *Esther*, with 16). "Univers" appears 14 times out of 82 total (*Alexandre* is second only to *Bérénice*'s 16 occurrences). "Monde" occurs 6 times out of a total of 56 (the most of any secular tragedy other than *La Thébaïde*, which also has 6 occurrences). "Partout" appears 15 times out of 71 total (*Mithridate* has the second-most occurrences, with 14).

12. Quoted in Racine, *Œuvres complètes*, 1310 n. 2.

CHAPTER 3. *ANDROMAQUE*

1. The transitional moment staged in *Andromaque* bears a similarity to what takes place, according to Greenberg, in Corneille's major tragedies, which also represent historical transitions (see chapter 1, n. 26 above). What remains specific to Racine's treatment of historical transition, as I argue, is its focus on individual failures against the backdrop of historical becoming.

2. For a study of related mythological themes in Ronsard, Corneille, and Desmarets de Saint-Sorlin, see Niderst, "Ronsard, *Andromaque* et *Attila*."

3. Gutwirth describes the transitional temporality of *Andromaque* as follows: "Caught between an inexpiable past and an inexorable present, [Andromaque] discovers tragic time, this time-out-of-time which is a promontory swept by all of the winds of temporality" (quoted in Goodkin, *The Tragic Middle*, 108). On tragic time as a temporality of in-betweenness, see chapter 1, n. 20.

4. Tobin, *Racine Revisited*, 46.

5. In response to the criticism that Pyrrhus inadequately exercises his functions as a (would-be) lover, the first preface states that "Pyrrhus n'avait pas lu nos Romans" [Pyrrhus had not read our romances] (197).

6. Barthes, *On Racine*, 78; Bersani, *A Future for Astyanax*, 49.

7. Barthes, *On Racine*, 73–74.

8. In her agitated stasis, Hermione experiences the tension of opposing forces that trap her in a moment of unrealized striving: "Toujours prête à partir, et demeurant toujours" [She is always ready / To leave Epirus, but she always stays] (1.1.131).

9. Man, according to Nietzsche, wears the chain of the past and thus can only envy the ability that animals have to forget the past and live in the present moment. Like Racine's Oreste (1.1.44), Nietzsche's man is weighed down by the chain of history: "[H]owever far and fast he runs, the chain runs with him" (*On the Advantage and Disadvantage of History for Life*, 8).

10. Here I refer to the famous "Songe, songe" passage (3.8.996–1015) and to the repeated invocation of Hector that so frustrates Pyrrhus: "Cent fois le nom d'Hector est sorti de sa bouche" [a hundred times she uttered / The name of Hector] (2.5.654).

11. On Andromaque's ability to visualize a different kind of future for Astyanax, see Bach, "Fatal Identity."

12. Barthes, *On Racine*, 77.

13. Ibid., 75 n. 12.

14. Bersani, *A Future for Astyanax*, 49.

15. Horowitz, "The Second Time Around," 24. The notion of a dominating past is part of the intellectual inheritance of Georges Poulet. See *Studies in Human Time*, 117–18, 121.

16. On the question of Racine's esthetics and the dramaturgical construction of the future, I follow on Muratore's concluding statement: "The future of art lies somewhere between the ideological constraints of Pyrrhus's mimetic recycling and the chaotic freedom of Oreste's unanchored referents. And it is to the discovery of this future that Racine dedicates his artistic endeavor" (Muratore, "The Pleasures of Re-Enactment in *Andromaque*," 68–69).

CHAPTER 4. *BRITANNICUS*

1. This epigraph suggests, beyond my reading of conceptual dramatic space in *Britannicus*, a sociological analysis of doors and antechambers in the context of

seventeenth-century court life. Ubersfeld refers to the well-established connection between onstage intersubjectivity and social structures based on rank: "It is commonplace
to demonstrate how spatial relations among characters (for example the background
position of the confidants in classical theatre) correspond to a material hierarchiciza-
tion, how the classical 'vestibule'—that simultaneously closed and open space, socially
protected and undifferentiated—corresponds to the sociopolitical workings of the
court, and how the bourgeois salon, shut off, isolated from nature, with a strict code
governing access, is the mime of the social relationships among the upper bourgeoisie"
(*Reading Theatre*, 104). Maskell refers additionally to the significance of transitional
spaces in early modern civility manuals like Antoine de Courtin's *Traité de la civilité*
[*Treatise on Civility*]: "Courtin's *Civilité* shows how, in the seventeenth century, behav-
iour at the door, entering a room, waiting in an antechamber are activities fraught with
significance" (*Racine: A Theatrical Reading*, 235).

   2. As Tacitus recounts in *The Annals*, Nero's tutor Seneca, defending himself against
accusations that he was undermining his emperor's reputation, praised Nero for his
actual and potential power: "You have yet before you a vigorous prime, and that on
which for so many years your eyes were fixed, supreme power" (Book XIV, section 54,
page 154 [Citations from *The Annals* will henceforth appear in the following format:
XIV.54.154]). Nero ironically responds to this with the claim that "as for myself, I am
but treading the threshold of empire" (XIV.56.154).

   3. What Néron aims to suppress is what Michel de Certeau calls *accidental time*.
In contrast to the programmed time of practices of control, Certeau identifies a more
inconsistent, unpredictable temporality: "Accidental time appears only as the night that
creates accident and lacuna within the area of production. It is a lapse in the system, its
diabolical adversary;" simultaneously with the "modern mutation of time into controlla-
ble space," then, the historian can examine the "daily practices, based on a relation to
opportunity, that is to say to accidental time, practices that are scattered all along the
line of duration" (*L'Invention du quotidien*, 295, 134, 295).

   4. Gearhart, "Racine's Politics," 41.

   5. Barthes, *On Racine*, 87.

   6. See Foucault, *Discipline and Punish*, 200–203.

   7. Tacitus, *The Annals*, XIII.5.126.

   8. The rushed conversations that Néron's subjects seek to engage resemble the re-
quests and complaints that courtiers registered with Louis XIV as he descended the
steps of the palace of Versailles on his way to a walk in the gardens. See Levron, *La vie
quotidienne à la cour de Versailles*, 49.

   9. Maskell, *Racine: A Theatrical Reading*, 23.

   10. Quoted in ibid., 24.

   11. On the use of doors, curtains, and other spatial dividers and obstacles in the
staging of *Britannicus* by Michel Laurent and other decorators at the Hôtel de Bourgogne, Roger W. Herzel observes that

> after stating, "Theatre este un palais a volonte," [The theater is any given palace] Laurent adds
> "Il faut 2 portes, 2 fauteille pour le 4e acte; des rideaux" [There must be two doors, two chairs
> for the fourth act, and curtains]. Even in comedy practical doors were not especially common.
> Laurent notes the need for them for a few plays, sometimes finding it necessary to remind him-
> self that they should open and close. . . . [t]hough the script of *Britannicus* refers to doors twice,
> it is somewhat surprising to find Laurent punctiliously providing physical examples of them.
> Perhaps Racine insisted that it was necessary to show the visual image of the mother waiting in

frustration at her son's door (1.1.4) and to give full dramatic value to Junie's first entrance (2.2.525). In the same way, the curtains are not strictly necessary as the place of concealment from which Néron eavesdrops on Britannicus and Junie (2.6): Néron could have simply hidden behind a wing, though that movement might have been hard to distinguish from an ordinary exit. But the curtains allowed Néron to remain onstage, though concealed—to be visibly invisible, so that his sadistic presence would weigh as heavily on the audience as on the hapless Junie. ("Racine, Laurent, and the *Palais à Volonté,*" 1067)

12. Lyons, "Au seuil du panoptisme général," 280.

13. Gearhart, "Racine's Politics," 41.

14. By contrast, Lyons explains how the protagonist of *La Princesse de Clèves,* under the constant surveillance of her social milieu, not only has to control her every action and appearance, but must also internalize the workings of the power that constrains her. Thus, for Lyons, *La Princesse de Clèves* marks a significant development in the subjective dimension of an early modern protopanopticism ("Au seuil du panoptisme général," 284).

15. Conroy, in *Racine: The Power and the Pleasure,* 56.

16. Foucault, *Discipline and Punish,* 202.

17. Ibid., 26.

CHAPTER 5. *BÉRÉNICE*

1. Tobin views *Bérénice* as a turning point in Racine's theater . . . because of his imaginative deployment of time in all the plays from this point forward. Though ideal time in all Racinian tragedies is characterized by being modified in relation to the intensification of tragic emotion, in *Bérénice* it assumes such proportions that it competes with Rome for the primary role as an 'invisible presence'" (*Racine Revisited,* 88).

2. Campbell refers to "that sense of suspended time that is the great tragic illusion explored in *Bérénice*" (*Questioning Racinian Tragedy,* 57). In order to describe the slow but inexorably rhythm of the play, Campbell connects suspense and suspension:

> It is this suspension that generates suspense, defined by the *OED* as "a state of mental uncertainty, with expectation or desire for decision, and usually some apprehension or anxiety." Racine exploits the uncertainty created by this suspension to raise the emotional pressure: "Je ne respire pas dans cette incertitude" (644). For the clearer it becomes that Titus must leave Bérénice, and cannot do so, the steeper becomes the curve of emotional tension, and the greater the impact of an inevitable but ironically unpredictable outcome. Put simply, the audience cannot know to what extreme measures either of the main protagonists might resort.
>
> Racine's use of suspension and suspense is evident in his exploitation of the different reactions of characters, oscillating unpredictably between fear, hope, and desire in situations that are volatile and unbearable. (ibid., 50–51)

3. No one knows exactly how the story of *Bérénice* and *Tite et Bérénice* was selected as the terrain for Racine and Corneille's theatrical competition of 1670. Forestier questions the legendary account whereby Henriette d'Angleterre would have proposed the tale of Titus's tragically frustrated love as a challenge to the two playwrights (Racine, *Œuvres complètes,* 1446–56). Forestier argues that the choice of *Bérénice* was more likely

the result of a competition between the Hôtel de Bourgogne and the Palais-Royal the-
aters than of a direct order from the Duchess of Orléans.

4. Racine uses a similar temporal comparison in the preface to *Britannicus*, to argue
for the importance of the simplicity of action. He imagines the kind of fragmented action that his critics may endorse, in a sharp *reductio ad absurdum*:

> Que faudrait-il faire pour contenter des Juges si difficiles? . . . Au lieu d'une action simple,
> chargée de peu de matière, telle que doit être une action qui se passe en un seul jour, et qui
> s'avançant par degrés vers sa fin, n'est soutenue que par les intérêts, les sentiments, et les pas-
> sions des Personnages, il faudrait remplir cette même action de quantité d'incidents qui ne se
> pourraient passer qu'en un mois. (374)

> [What would one have to do to please such difficult judges? . . . Instead of a simple plot bur-
> dened with little matter, such as a plot that takes place in only one day must be, a plot which
> progresses step by step to its end, which is only sustained by the interests, the sentiments, and
> the passions of the characters, it would be necessary to fill this very plot with a heap of inci-
> dents, which could take place only in a month.]

5. For a discussion of the functions of prefaces as paratexts, see Genette, *Seuils*,
164–98. For Genette, the paratext is the intermediary space in which the author presents her/his work as a fictional universe which the reader is free to enter or leave. Genette uses the spatial metaphors of vestibules, forest's edges, and fringes to describe these
transitional textual zones (ibid., 7–12).

6. The same tension is taken up in 3.4 and 5.5 of *Bérénice*.

7. As Ellen McClure puts it, "Antiochus . . . is condemned to perpetual betweenness" as he uncomfortably occupies "his intermediary position between the two main
characters" ("Sovereign Love," 313).

8. *Bajazet* is a distant second, with 23 occurrences, followed by *Mithridate*, with 22,
out of a total of 169 occurrences of "moment" and "moments" in Racine's dramatic
corpus.

9. Sussman, "*Bérénice* and the Tragic Moment," 241.

10. For Brault, the cabinet marks the point of conjunction of public and private life:
"The cabinet is no longer a sentimental territory but an enlargement of the city's boundaries, an irremediable engulfment of the internal by the external" ("Thresholds of the
Tragic," 239). Thus for Brault public duty invades private space once Titus makes his
decision. The cabinet is the point of tension between these two spheres of existence.
Forestier describes how this space, which initially framed encounters between lovers,
comes to represent lonely separation: "Titus no longer dares to cross the threshold of
his mistress's apartment. Formerly the place of happy encounters, this 'superb and solitary cabinet' is transformed into a place of suffering solitude, and its positioning at a
halfway point symbolizes the definitive rift between the lovers" (Racine, *Œuvres complètes*, 1471 n. 3).

11. Mourgues, *Racine or the Triumph of Relevance*, 12. Titus has earlier remarked on
Bérénice's painful temporal experience of waiting for him:

> Etrangère dans Rome, inconnue à la Cour,
> Elle passe ses jours, Paulin, sans rien prétendre
> Que quelque heure à me voir, et le reste à m'attendre.
> Encor si quelquefois un peu moins assidu
> Je passe le moment, où je suis attendu,

Je la revois bientôt de pleurs toute trempée.
Ma main à les sécher est longtemps occupée.

(2.2.534–40)

[In Rome a stranger, knowing not a soul,
She passes all her days with scarce a smile,
Happy only if I see her awhile:
And sometimes if, detained by cares of State,
I go to visit her a little late,
I'm sure to find with tears her fair face stained:
My hand in drying them is long detained.]

12. Campbell argues that Bérénice attempts to cultivate her love outside of time altogether, in an immobile, atemporal dimension created by desire to escape the destructive forces of dramatic time ("Playing for Time in *Bérénice*," 26). I propose, by contrast, that Bérénice undergoes her experience not outside of time but rather all the more deeply within a subjectively constructed temporality of hope and anticipation. This approach in a different way reinforces Campbell's fundamental point that *"Bérénice* is in every sense a tragedy of time" (ibid., 28).

13. Titus's internal conflicts, which I examine here in terms of how Racine represents them poetically, over against the experience of Bérénice, constitute the subjective effects of a political transition. Biet discusses the tragic moment represented in *Bérénice* in terms of the historical and political progression from Vespasian's past rule to the reign to come of Titus:

> The five acts of *Bérénice* take place in the space of the comma in the juridical and political adage: "The King is dead, long live the King!" Titus's mourning is essential here, for it signals the passage from the role of son and dauphin to that of sovereign, the passage from humanity to royalty. Between two political roles, one already past and the other, alas, already present, Titus deliberates, hearing his father Vespasian's voice, the people's voice, in the distance, a voice that judges him and wants to believe in him, and hearing the voice of the law, the voice of Paulin who for his dogmatic discourse could just as well be called Paul. (*Droit et littérature,* 148)

On the question of historical and political transitions represented in tragic action, see chapter 1, n. 26.

14. McClure describes the disparity between the continuous lovers' time Bérénice wishes to cultivate and the disconnected moments that constitute her lived reality: "What Bérénice demands (but not necessarily what she wants) is precisely what Titus, due to his status as emperor, cannot give her—a love predicated not on discrete moments, however full, but rather on continuous *temps*" ("Sovereign Love," 311).

15. Campbell highlights the significance of inaction as a device that contributes to the representation of stasis in this tragedy: "The appearance of immobility in *Bérénice* is reinforced by what might be seen as non-activities: waiting, delaying, and frustrated seeking, what Bérénice calls 'cette longueur'" (*Questioning Racinian Tragedy,* 60).

16. As Maskell has shown, the temporalities of in-betweenness in *Bérénice* mirror the spatial struggles that can take clear shape on the stage: "There is a struggle at the threshold. At the end of Act IV the spectator sees Titus torn between the two doors. Antiochus entreats him to come to the queen, to prevent her from committing suicide. Paulin exhorts him to return to his apartment where the senators await him. It is a theatrical tableau. Titus's dilemma is represented visually, as Paulin and Antiochus im-

plore him to leave the stage in their respective directions through one or other of the two doors" (*Racine: A Theatrical Reading,* 26). Once again, the door as object and transitional space provides the opportunity for the director of a performance to frame visually the struggles and indecision of characters.

17. For Maskell, "[t]he exit of Racine's Bérénice in tragic isolation carries connotations of death, since final exits are repeatedly glossed by Racine to signify death" (ibid., 213).

CHAPTER 6. *BAJAZET*

1. See Campbell, "*Bajazet* and Racinian Tragedy: Expectations and Difference."
2. Racine, *Œuvres complètes,* 1493.
3. The concept of Damocles' sword figures also in *Andromaque,* where the eponymous character laments the fact that her captor Pyrrhus holds the power of life and death over her son Astyanax: "Mais cependant, mon Fils, tu meurs, si je n'arrête / Le fer, que ce Cruel tient levé sur ta tête" [But yet, my son, you die, if I arrest not / The sword that is uplifted o'er your head] (3.8.1037–38).
4. For Kathryn Hoffmann, "The crisis of controlling this labyrinthine space quickly becomes a crisis of doors; doors that form the limits of the world of the seraglio and the beginning of the outer world" (*Society of Pleasures,* 47).
5. Barthes, *On Racine,* 100.
6. Brody describes Roxane in terms of her inability, throughout most of the play, to make the transition from tragic blindness to the acceptance of truth: "Her immobility contrasts sharply with the bustling resiliency of a particularly energetic and enterprising cast of characters" ("*Bajazet,* or the Tragedy of Roxane," 274). Whereas "the stalemate between Roxane and Bajazet seems always at the brink of resolution," her refusal to come into a full awareness of the impossibility of her love for him prevents the further development for action, for "the impulse needed to carry a wavering consciousness over the threshold of lucidity has still to be supplied" (ibid., 274, 276). The result, at least prior to the bloody dénouement, is the entropic transformation of action into stasis.
7. A salient characteristic of *Bajazet* is the characters' (especially Roxane's) detailed awareness of time. As discussed in the previous chapter, *Bajazet* includes the second-most frequent occurrences of the term "moment(s)"—the word appears 23 times—in the Racinian dramatic corpus (see chapter 5, n. 8). Forestier shows that *Bajazet* is the most fragmented of Racine's plays, with the greatest number of scenes in comparison to others, thus contributing to a pronounced effect of acceleration of events, especially as the play approaches its dénouement (Racine, *Œuvres complètes,* 1506).
8. Racine took the image of secret passages and imminent departure from Corneille's *Nicomède* (1650–51), where the Roman ambassador Flaminius intends to light out quickly to pursue the eponymous Prince of Bythinia, a rebel against the will of the empire: "Ma galère est au port toute prête à partir, / Le palais y répond par la porte secrète" [My galley is at port, ready to depart, / The palace leads to it by this secret door] (5.5.1606–7). The plan is to capture him and to let the Roman senate decide on who will succeed the King Prusias to the throne of Bythinia, the choice having come down to Nicomède and his half-brother Attale. The generous Attale will rescue Nicomède in extremis, and everyone will be won over by Nicomède's uncompromising

virtue. As we have seen, no such happy ending can transpire in *Andromaque*, and things turn out even worse in *Bajazet*.

9. The dark, labyrinthine corridors of the seraglio in *Bajazet* point the way toward the subterranean passageways that Sade's Justine must navigate on her way to undergoing sexual torture by strangulation (*Justine*, 247). While in Sade extreme cruelty will achieve explicit clarity, in Racine it is poetically suggested as a menacing potential.

10. Barthes, *On Racine*, 101, 102–3. Tobin finds evidence for the significance of the strangulation theme in the fact that the term "nœud(s)" appears in *Bajazet* more often than in any other of Racine's tragedies—seven out of thirty-three total occurrences. Tobin discusses the figurative and literal significance of breathing and strangulation in the play:

> The . . . metaphor about "breathing" (510) appears to be simply a trite substitute for "living." Given, however, the method by which one was often slain in the harem—garroting—, the metaphor becomes demetaphorized to disclose a brutal reality. This recharging of traditional and often euphemistic images with a passionate content is one of Racine's signal contributions to French literature. He is also a master at turning ambiguity to his best, ironic advantage. When, to cite an instance, characters speak of a "knot," it can mean either the bond of marriage or the means of strangulation. Roxane offers both to Bajazet at one time or another and indulges in frightening sadism when, near the end, she tells Atalide that she will unite her to Bajazet "by eternal knots" (1625). (*Racine Revisited*, 96)

11. Barthes, *On Racine*, 100.

CHAPTER 7. *MITHRIDATE*

1. Campbell, "Tragedy and Time in Racine's *Mithridate*," 591. See also *Questioning Racinian Tragedy*, 67.

2. Campbell calls the play an "imitation of inaction" where "it is as though all were shadowboxing, and nothing in reality could be done. In that reality, where acts have consequences, he who would set out to march into Rome now finds himself tracked down by the Romans to the extreme limits of what in the real present is the Roman world. The great king and general is unable even to control the parcel of land to which the remnant of his army has withdrawn" (ibid., 74). In *L'Illusion comique* (1.2), Corneille concretely stages the threshold between dramatic action and inaction: the magician Alcandre presents the spectator Pridamant with an inert stage containing the costumes of actors on the verge of performing a play within the play.

3. These spaces are further evoked later in the play when Pharnace holds his troops to the shore, and some of them even embrace it: "Les uns avec transport embrassent le rivage. / Les autres qui partaient s'élancent dans les flots, / Ou présentent leurs dards aux yeux des matelots" [Some in excitement hug the very shore; / Others, on board, are jumping in the waves / Or jab their javelins in the sailors' eyes] (4.6.1432–34). Jean Emelina discusses how, in comparison to the other, claustrophobic Roman tragedies of *Bérénice* and *Britannicus*, dramatic space in *Mithridate* opens onto extensive vistas of shore and sea ("L'espace dans les tragédies romaines de Racine," 129–30, 138). Although I do not agree with his conclusion that *Mithridate* stages heroism, Emelina's discussion of the specifically expansive nature of dramatic space in *Mithridate* is indispensable for the study particularly of imaginary space as it relates to character development.

4. According to Kuizenga, "[S]he is more a potential than an actual heroine" (*"Mithridate:* A Reconsideration," 282); for Campbell, "Monime for her part is still waiting to live and breathe" (*Questioning Racinian Tragedy,* 70).

5. Racine, *Mithridate,* 54 n. 1.

6. Plutarch, *Lives,* 514.

7. Plutarch tells of how in Mithridates' memoirs "[t]here were several judgments upon the interpretation of dreams, which either he himself or some of his mistresses had had" (ibid., 517).

8. Hubert, *Essai d'exégèse racinienne,* 165.

9. Plutarch, *Lives,* 515.

10. Quoted in O'Regan, *The Mannerist Aesthetic,* 50.

11. Plutarch, *Lives,* 515.

12. Kuizenga comments on the awkward tardiness of Mithridate's death: "Ironically, he does not die, so to speak, on time. To have been killed in combat, believing in the illusory allegiance of Monime, would have been Mithridate's personal *belle mort*" (*"Mithridate:* A Reconsideration," 284).

13. O'Regan, *The Mannerist Aesthetic,* 84.

14. Goldmann, *Le Dieu caché,* 395; *The Hidden God,* 355. See Goodkin, "The Death(s) of Mithridate(s)," 215–16 n. 3 for a critique of Goldmann's interpretation.

15. Campbell, *Questioning Racinian Tragedy,* 77.

16. Hubert, *Essai d'exégèse racinienne,* 175.

17. Ekstein, *"Mithridate,* Displacement, and the Sea," 110.

18. Phillips, *Racine:* Mithridate, 66.

Chapter 8. *Iphigénie*

1. The liminal moment of dawn at the opening of the tragedy symbolizes both the confusion and pain of Agamemnon and Arcas and the emergence of potential insight into the question of being and of the being of language. On the poetic and philosophical significance of dawn for the experience of being, see chapter 1, n. 18.

2. We may recall here the scene in which Euripides' Agamemnon anticipates the meaningful sobs of Iphigenia's younger brother: "Orestes, from his station near us, will cry in childish accents, inarticulate, yet fraught with meaning" (*The Plays of Euripides,* 429).

3. According to Richard Goodkin, Eriphile's failure at communication contributes to Racine's implicit questioning of heroic mythography: "Half outside and half inside, Eriphile and her half-silent tears thus teach a lesson at the play's midpoint: that heroic representation allows external expression of only half of oneself, and silences the rest" (*The Tragic Middle,* 133).

4. Barthes, *On Racine,* 114. For Barthes, "Agamemnon is not a monster, but a mediocre man, an average soul" (ibid.). In his analysis of Agamemnon as a model of the Aristotelian tragic hero, Forestier examines the complexities of the king's situation and thus tempers Barthes's view (Racine, *Œuvres complètes,* 1574). For a study of Agamemnon's difficulties with language and utterance, see Ahmed, "Racine's Agamemnon: The Problem of Voice in *Iphigénie.*"

5. In a study of processes of representation and knowledge formation, Sylvie Romanowski has analyzed the central role of uncertainty in *Iphigénie:* "While referring to

the necessity for clarity and unequivocal reference, the play is one long representation of confusion and ambiguity" ("Sacrifice and Truth in Racine's *Iphigénie*," 145). Agamemnon's perplexity in the role of sovereign recalls King Lear's lament: "You see me here, you gods, a poor old man, / As full of grief as age; wretched in both!" (2.4.267–68).

6. Felix R. Freudmann, "*Iphigénie:* A Study in Solitude," 140.

7. *La Chanson de Roland*, 111–13, 257–61.

8. Ekstein, "The Destabilization of the Future in Racine's *Iphigénie*," 919. See chapter 3 above for an examination of the significance of the future in *Andromaque*.

9. In a close reading of *Othello*, Hopkins examines the figurative significance of water and bodily fluids: "As well as focusing on literal waters and their edges, . . . *Othello* is also a play greatly concerned with the tides and fluids flowing within the body as well as those outside" (*Shakespeare on the Edge*, 96). The potential mixing of external liquids and internal humors leads, as it does in *Iphigénie*, to a destabilization of identities: "The play's characters, in short, are like islands, uneasily afloat, dangerously permeable, and subject to attack on all sides from fluids which threaten to engulf entirely their already imperilled individuality" (ibid., 101).

10. In an attempt to rescue Astyanax from the blackmail of Pyrrhus and the jealous rage of Hermione, Andromaque proposes a willing exile that would allow the child's military potential to lie forever dormant: "Laissez-moi le cacher en quelque Ile déserte. / Sur les soins de sa Mère on peut s'en assurer, / Et mon Fils avec moi n'apprendra qu'à pleurer" [Let me conceal him / On a desert island. I'll look after him, / And he will only learn to weep with me] (3.4.882–84).

11. As Apostolidès describes it, "Time in *Iphigénie* is a stretched-out moment of suspension, a short period of hesitation that prolongs itself for five acts: everything is held in the balance, everything is still possible, and yet everything has already played out" (*Le prince sacrifié*, 117). Koch discusses a "non-time or rather a between-time" that structures the suspended action of *Iphigénie*, where entropic stasis pervades the scene set on Aulis's shores: "On the road to Troy, the Greek machine of war has been reduced to a state of entropy, that natural state in which all ordered movement comes to a halt. Like movement, time itself has been suspended; it is merely the perpetuation of the same moment" ("Tragic Disclosures of Racine's *Iphigénie*," 163, 162).

12. Heidegger, *On the Way to Language*, 59.

13. Iphigénie also evokes the image of Eriphile taking Achille's heart away from her, as she herself willingly participates in this disarticulation of her lover's and her own selfhood: "Moi-même à votre char je me suis enchaînée. / Je vous pardonne, hélas! des vœux intéressés, / Et la perte d'un cœur, que vous me ravissez" [I've chained myself instead to your proud car. / I pardon you alas! your selfish dream, / And a lost lover you have snatched from me] (2.5.694–96).

14. In a discussion of the philosophical concept of unhomeliness or uncanniness [*Unheimlichkeit*] in Heidegger, Will McNeill explains the connections between the unhomely wandering of mortality and the anguished experience of being: "Unhomeliness is disclosed in one's anxiety in the face of (*vor*) and about (*um*) being-in-the-world as such. The uncanny unhomeliness of anxiety thus stands at the threshold, at the threshold of the home" ("*Heimat*," 322). I would propose, following on this philosophical reading of anxiety and displacement, that Racinian characters' inability to find themselves in space leads them, as does their frequent aphasia, to brushes with language *qua* language: "The experience of unhomeliness marks, as it did already in *Being and Time*, the

very threshold of language" (ibid., 324; see also Heidegger, *Being and Time*, 203–10). McNeill raises the question of the inherence of unhomeliness in human experience in general: "What if the task of dwelling were precisely to become 'at home' in unhomeliness? What if *Unheimlichkeit* were the proper *Heimat* [home] of mortals? What if, more precisely, our seeking of *Heimat* were our being *unheimlich* [unhomely]?" ("*Heimat*," 327).

15. For Apostolidès, the eventual departure for Troy signals not only the reconstitution of the army and the Greek nation, but also the passage from tribal social organization to the modern world of nation-states at war with one another (*Le prince sacrifié*, 116).

16. The "Autel" [altar] is a key site of potential passage, from the world of the living to the world of the dead, from the inertia of peacetime to the war on Troy. Of the ninety-six total occurrences of the term, in its singular and plural forms, in Racine's dramatic corpus, *Iphigénie* has the greatest number, with thirty-six. *Athalie* is next with twenty-four.

17. Barthes, *On Racine*, 108–9; Mauron, *L'Inconscient dans l'œuvre et la vie de Racine*, 139.

18. One of the meanings given in the 1690 *Dictionnaire de l'Académie française* for the verb "se répandre," which Eriphile uses in line 520, is the following: "On dit aussi fig. de la peste, d'un mal contagieux, *qu'Il s'est respandu dans tout le pays*" [One also says figuratively of the plague, of a contagious disease, that *it has spread throughout the whole country*].

19. Montaigne, *Essais*, 1:11.

20. Montaigne, *The Essays*, 6.

CHAPTER 9. *PHEDRE*

1. *The Plays of Euripides*, 232. Goodkin identifies a reference to Homer in the difficult conversation Phèdre has with Œnone in Thésée's absence:

> Indeed, the rumor of Thésée caught in the underworld and unable to cross the Acheron in the other direction becomes a metaphor for the nature of language in the play: "Malheureuse, quel nom est sorti de ta bouche?" [Wretch! What name has issued from your mouth?] (206), Phèdre's initial reaction to Œnone's mention of Hippolyte's name, echoes the Homeric image of scandalous or shocking words crossing the barrier of the teeth and unable to be taken back. The mouth itself, the link between inside and outside, then becomes the "bords qu'on passe sans retour" [bourn from which there's no return.] (*The Tragic Middle*, 166)

2. *Seneca's Tragedies*, 365.

3. For Marc Fumaroli, the well-known interplay between light and darkness in verses like "Soleil, je te viens voir pour la dernière fois" [O shining sun . . . I see you now / For the last time] (1.3.172) represents the emergence of the tragic character on-stage and points to that character's difficult acts of utterance: "So many classical images, referring to the theater as a bringing to light, identifying it with the solemn passage of the character from night and absence to her dazzling apparition on the illuminated stage. As Phèdre slowly takes the stage, the theater itself reflects and consummates itself in this same movement. A second set of metaphors, of confession in tension with retraction and silence, completes the metaphorical definition of theater: it is the

genesis not only of the visible but of the word" (*Héros et orateurs*, 508). In an elegant metadramatic exploration that is nonetheless tinged with anachronism, Fumaroli argues that *Phèdre* somehow self-consciously sounds the deathknell of French classical tragedy at a time when Racine would leave profane theater and when opera would increase in popularity. With the benefit of centuries of hindsight—we know now (but who knew then?) that *Phèdre* was Racine's last secular tragedy and that it has proven to be the pinnacle of the genre—Fumaroli describes *Phèdre* as an act of dramaturgical suicide in which the metatheatrical dimension determines the meaning of the entire play. I stop short of this kind of monolithic interpretation and aim to situate the metatheatrical dimension among a variety of levels of meaning.

4. Parish, *Racine*, 104, 106.

5. Ubersfeld, "The Space of *Phèdre*," 206. The image of the trapped animal squares with Barrault's visualization of Thésée, who has just learned of Œnone's suicide (5.5.1480) and agitatedly darts between the limits of the stage like an insect flying into a lampshade (*Mise en scène de* Phèdre, 181 n. 12).

6. Barrault, *Mise en scène de* Phèdre, 31, 83 n. 11. See introduction no. 59, n. 60.

7. Ubersfeld, "The Space of *Phèdre*," 204.

8. Racine, *Œuvres complètes*, 1643 n. 1.

9. Although Theseus is known for his ability to move between the world of the living and the world of the dead, as Gutwirth points out, Thésée's crossings in Racine remain in a sense incomplete. As a result, this character only brings our attention more pointedly to the ambiguity of transitional space: "Thanks to [Thésée] the tragedy straddles three shores: those of Crete, of Trœzen, and of the Acheron. He himself has not ventured far enough into any of these haunted territories to understand their nature. . . . He who once landed at Crete to kill the Minotaur, he who made the shores of both seas safe by slaying their monsters and thieves, has unwittingly completed the circuit of mortality. . . . A hero who until now has been running from one end of the universe to the other, now makes the mistake of standing still. The shore has revealed itself, to this superficial being, in all its incomprehensible depth" (*Racine*, 138). Thésée thus remains as inexorably caught in transitional space as the rest of the main characters of *Phèdre*. Thésée's ignorance and nonchalance to what surrounds him have kept this potential hero from making any definitive crossings.

10. The terms designating shores—"bords," "rives," and "rivages"—figure prominently in this play, most often as metonymic indicators for spatial entities. For example, Hippolyte locates the beginnings of tragic action on the shores of Trézène: "Cet heureux temps n'est plus. Tout a changé de face / Depuis que sur ces bords les Dieux ont envoyé / La Fille de Minos et de Pasiphaé" [Alas, that happy time / Is now no more. For everything has changed / Since to these shores the gods despatched the Queen, / The daughter of Minos and of Pasiphaë] (1.1.34–36). His death is foreshadowed by the evocation of his habitual activity of driving his chariot on the seashore: "On vous voit moins souvent, orgueilleux, et sauvage, / Tantôt faire voler un char sur le rivage" [You're seen less often, proud and solitary, / Racing the chariot on the shore] (1.1.129–30). In recounting her family history, Phèdre points to the importance of seashores in the tragic story of her sister's abandonment: "Ariane ma Sœur! De quel amour blessée, / Vous mourûtes aux bords où vous fûtes laissée!" [My sister Ariadne, / Stricken with love, upon a desolate coast / Despairing died] (1.3.253–54). When Phèdre names Hippolyte, Œnone reacts to the confession as follows: "Voyage infortuné! Rivage malheureux, / Fallait-il approcher de tes bords dangereux?" [Disastrous voy-

age! O unlucky coast! / Why did we travel to your perilous shores?] (1.3.267–68) Œnone describes the city metonymically as "ces bords heureux" [these happy shores] (1.5.358) and "Les superbes Remparts que Minerve a bâtis" [the lofty ramparts / Minerva built (*my translation*)] (1.5.360). For a systematic analysis of the use of these key terms in all of Racine's tragedies, see Soare, "*Phèdre* et les métaphores du labyrinthe," 148 n. 9.

J. D. Hubert comments on the prominence of the term "bord" in *Phèdre*, but only in reference to the idea of the "gouffre" [abyss] that is situated on the other side of the borderline, and the monsters that threaten to devour those who cross over (*Essai d'exégèse racinienne*, 206–7). What I aim to explore further in this chapter is the situation of the tragic character at this very point of crossing.

In a discussion of "the edge-shore paradigm" that organizes dramatic space in *Phèdre*, Ubersfeld assesses the potential of seashores for the staging of the tragedy: "[W]hat can we say about the 'borders of Trézène' where the action unfolds? One can show these borders or not. The whole possible interplay of on-stage and off-stage objects offers much scope both to the work of the director and to the imagination of the reader-spectator" (*Reading Theatre*, 107, 121).

11. Thésée will make a similar statement about his own past actions when invoking the aid of Neptune:

> Et toi, Neptune, et toi, si jadis mon courage
> D'infâmes Assassins nettoya ton rivage,
> Souviens-toi que pour prix de mes efforts heureux
> Tu promis d'exaucer le premier de mes vœux.

> (4.2.1065–68)

> [And thou, O Neptune!
> If formerly my courage cleansed your shores
> Of infamous assassins, remember now,
> That for reward of all my happy efforts,
> Thou promisedst to grant one prayer of mine.]

12. Ubersfeld, "The Space of *Phèdre*," 203.

13. Goodkin, *The Tragic Middle*, 156. For Goodkin, it is a matter in *Phèdre* of "trying not to recognize what is at the center of one's being" (ibid., 153). Ultimately, the process of subjective unraveling that we witness in this tragedy functions to call into question the idea of the tragic hero:

> But if one ever understands how artificial this centrifugal movement is, if it ever comes to seem inauthentic, that is when the heroic illusion which forms the basis for any conception of unity of personality is destroyed. That is when one loses the only trump card proper to the human condition, and more particularly to the tragic effort to transcend it, the possibility of struggle itself; when one becomes, like Phèdre, or like Néron in *Britannicus*, a monster, a creature which no longer fights against itself, which has accepted its contradictory and irresolvable nature. In becoming a simple agent of the goddess, Phèdre loses the heroic potential of being like the gods by fighting against them, of defining herself by fleeing herself. If heroism is itself, like the idea of the unity of the individual, artificial, fully understanding its artifice means no longer being able to use it. (ibid., 165)

14. When Œnone tells him her account of events, Thésée himself will experience a similar degree of uncertainty of identity, which takes the form, for the world traveler

and conqueror, of disorientation in space: "Je ne sais où je vais, je ne sais où je suis" [I know not where I'm going, nor what I am!] (4.1.1004).

15. Phèdre's anguished sense of having nowhere to run or hide, even in death, receives further elucidation in the context of McNeill's exegesis of Heideggerean *unhomeliness*, or *uncanniness* (see Heidegger, *Introduction to Metaphysics*, 158–76):

> In their active violence human beings cut their way through beings as a whole; they are *pantoporos*, "everywhere underway" in their breaking out into the midst of the prevailing of sea, earth, and animal life (in short, of *phusis*). At the same time they become *aporos*, "without way out" in the face of the "Nothing" of death, in the face of their essential thrownness. The site of their essential being is named as the *polis*, in which they dwell as *hupsipolis apolis*: towering high in the place of history, yet at the same time without site, unhomely and solitary, essentially "lone-some ones" (*Ein-same*) insofar as they are confronted with the overwhelming violence of being through their constant exposure to death. . . . The human being is without any way out in the face of death not at the point where he or she comes to die, but "constantly and essentially," "insofar as the human being *is*." ("*Heimat*," 333)

Thus, on this reading, Phèdre's dying is not only the culmination of her tragic situation; it touches off a reflection on the human condition as the repeatedly renewed experience of the aporia of death.

16. In Barrault's stage directions, Phèdre's living-dead status takes clear shape in the performer's moribund attitudes: "C'est une loque humaine" [She is a human rag]; she is "comme un pantin brisé" [like a broken puppet]; "Phèdre n'est plus qu'un chiffon . . . . [L]'état de Phèdre est semblable à celui d'un malade que l'on vient de piquer à la morphine" [Phèdre is no more than a tatter. . . . Phèdre's state is similar to that of an invalid who has just been given a dose of morphine] (*Mise en scène de* Phèdre, 137 n. 16, 137 n. 18, 139 n. 23).

17. *The Plays of Euripides*, 236, 225.

18. *Seneca's Tragedies*, 335.

19. Thésée recounts his own imprisonment in the following terms: "Moi-même il [le tyran d'Epire] m'enferma dans des Cavernes sombres, / Lieux profonds, et voisins de l'Empire des Ombres" [He shut me up / In dismal caverns underground that neighbored / The empire of the shades] (3.5.965–66).

20. In his close reading of the disintegration of Hippolyte's body, Leo Spitzer examines the indeterminacy of processes of representation in the "Récit de Théramène":

> Ce héros expiré stands for *l'expiration, la mort de ce héros*—or rather, we should say that *ce héros expiré / N'a laissé dans mes bras qu'un corps défiguré* is ambiguous by intent: is it the person of the hero (who happened to be dead), or his death, which left the sad vestiges? This type of expression, which ascribes to the agent what really belongs to the resulting action, and which remains on the borderline between the abstract and the concrete, gives an intellectual, sophisticated flavor ("can a dead hero act?") to a passage which otherwise speaks so directly to the heart. Finally, the personality of Hippolyte, of that "object," is further reduced by the use of the relative adverb où, which seems to refer not to a person but to a locality: the object has become a "place where" the Gods have sated their anger. This où, of which modern symbolistic poets might have been proud, immediately renders visualization impossible: we are in a No Man's Land somewhere between an object and a place, between the visible and the abstract, the emotional and the intellectual, between a picture and a definition. ("The 'Récit de Théramène,'" 112)

Spitzer's reading situates the esthetics of *Phèdre* at a point of tension between the classical and the baroque.

21. Poulet, *Studies in Human Time*, 129–30.

Bibliography

Adam, Antoine. *Histoire de la littérature française.* Vol. 4. Paris: Del Duca, 1954.

Ahmed, Ehsan. "Racine's Agamemnon: The Problem of Voice in *Iphigénie.*" *Romanic Review* 79.4 (November 1988): 574–84.

Apostolidès, Jean-Marie. "La Belle aux eaux dormantes." *Poétique* 58 (April 1984): 139–53.

———. *Le prince sacrifié. Théâtre et politique au temps de Louis XIV.* Paris: Minuit, 1985.

Aristotle, *On Poetics.* Translated by Seth Benardete and Michael Davis. South Bend, IN: St. Augustine's Press, 2002.

Bach, Ray. "Fatal Identity: Parents and Children in Racine's *Andromaque.*" *Stanford French Review* 16.1 (1992): 9–18.

Bachelard, Gason. *The Poetics of Space.* Translated by Maria Jolas. New York: Orion, 1964.

Barrault, Jean-Louis. *Mise en scène de* Phèdre *de Racine.* Paris: Seuil, 1946.

Barthes, Roland. *On Racine.* Translated by Richard Howard. New York: Hill and Wang, 1964.

———. *Sur Racine.* Paris: Seuil (Coll. "Points"), 1963.

Bersani, Leo. *A Future for Astyanax: Character and Desire in Literature.* Boston: Little, Brown and Co., 1976.

Biet, Christian. *Droit et littérature sous l'Ancien Régime. Le jeu de la valeur et de la loi.* Paris: Champion, 2002.

———. "*Mithridate,* ou l'exercice de l'ambiguïté: «Que pouvait la valeur dans ce trouble funeste?»" In *La Rochefoucauld, Mithridate, Frères et sœurs, Les Muses sœurs. Actes du 29e congrès annuel de la NASSCFL,* edited by Claire Carlin, 83–98. Tübingen: Narr, 1998.

———. *Racine ou la passion des larmes.* Paris: Hachette, 1996.

———. "Sophocle, Euripide, Séneque/Corneille, Racine, Dryden: les interprétations du mythe de la Thébaïde au XVIIe siècle." In *France et Grande Bretagne de la chute de Charles Ier à celle de Jacques II (1649–1688), edited by C. Smith et al.,* 207–29. Norwich: University of East Anglia, 1990.

Bonzon, Alfred. *Racine et Heidegger.* Paris: Nizet, 1995.

Braider, Christopher. *Indiscernible Counterparts: The Invention of the Text in French Classical Drama.* Chapel Hill: University of North Carolina Press, 2002.

Brault, Pascale-Anne. "Thresholds of the Tragic: A Study of Space in Sophocles and Racine." *Theatre Research International* 14.3 (Autumn 1989): 229–41.

Brody, Jules. "*Bajazet,* or the Tragedy of Roxane." *Romanic Review* 60 (1969): 273–90.

———. "Racine's *La Thébaïde:* An Analysis." *French Studies* 13.3 (July 1959): 199–213.

Bruneau, Marie-Florine. "Racine Historiographe: *L'Epître au Roi* et *Alexandre le Grand.*" *Papers on French Seventeenth Century Literature* 14.27 (1985–86): 537–49.

Campbell, John. "*Bajazet* and Racinian Tragedy: Expectations and Difference." *Dalhousie French Studies* 49 (Winter 1999): 103–18.

———. "Playing for Time in *Bérénice.*" *Nottingham French Studies* 32.2 (1993): 23–28.

———. *Questioning Racinian Tragedy.* Chapel Hill: University of North Carolina Press, 2005.

———. "Tragedy and Time in Racine's *Mithridate.*" *Modern Language Review* 92.3 (July 1997): 590–98.

Cave, Terence. "Corneille, Oedipus, Racine." In *Convergences: Rhetoric and Poetic in Seventeenth-Century France,* edited by David Lee Rubin and Mary B. McKinley, 82–100. Columbus: Ohio State University Press, 1989.

Certeau, Michel de. *L'Invention du quotidien. 1. Arts de faire.* Paris: Gallimard, 1990.

La Chanson de Roland. Edited and translated by Pierre Jonin. Paris: Gallimard, 1979.

Corneille, Pierre. *Œuvres complètes.* Edited by André Stegmann. Paris: Seuil ("L'Intégrale"), 1963.

Delcroix, Maurice. *Le sacré dans les tragédies profanes de Racine.* Paris: Nizet, 1970.

Derrida, Jacques. *Aporias.* Translated by Thomas Dutoit. Stanford: Stanford University Press, 1993.

———. *Dissemination.* Translated by Barbara Johnson. Chicago: University of Chicago Press, 1981.

Dorval, Patricia. "Shakespeare on Screen: Threshold Aesthetics in Oliver Parker's *Othello.*" *Early Modern Literary Studies* 6.1 (May 2000): 15 paragraphs.

Dubu, Jean. "De Corneille à Racine: *La Thébaïde* de 1664 à 1697." *Papers on French Seventeenth Century Literature* 27.52 (2000): 15–27.

Edwards, Michael. *La Thébaïde de Racine, clé d'une nouvelle interprétation de son théâtre.* Paris: Nizet, 1965.

Ekstein, Nina. "The Destabilization of the Future in Racine's *Iphigénie.*" *French Review* 66.6 (May 1993): 919–31.

———. "*Mithridate,* Displacement, and the Sea." In *La Rochefoucauld,* Mithridate, *Frères et sœurs, Les Muses sœurs. Actes du 29e congrès annuel de la NASSCFL,* edited by Claire Carlin, 85–98. Tübingen: Narr, 1998.

Emelina, Jean. "L'espace dans les tragédies romaines de Racine." *Littératures Classiques* 26 (1996): 125–38.

Euripides. *The Plays of Euripides.* Translated by Edward P. Coleridge. Chicago: Britannica, 1952.

Ferrier-Caverivière, Nicole. *L'Image de Louis XIV dans la littérature française de 1660 à 1715.* Paris: PUF, 1981.

Foucault, Michel. *Discipline and Punish: The Birth of the Prison.* Trans. A. Sheridan. New York: Pantheon, 1977.

———. *Histoire de la folie à l'âge classique.* Paris: Gallimard, 1972.

———. *Madness and Civilization.* Translated by R. Howard. New York: Random House, 1965.

Freeman, B. C., and A. Batson. *Concordance du théâtre et des poésies de Jean Racine.* 2 vols. Ithaca, NY: Cornell University Press, 1968.

Freudmann, Felix R. *"Iphigénie:* A Study in Solitude." *L'Esprit Créateur* 8.2 (Summer 1968): 138–48.

Fumaroli, Marc. "Entre Athènes et Cnossos: les dieux païens dans *Phèdre.*" *Revue d'histoire littéraire de la France* 93.1 (1993): 30–61; 93.2 (1993): 172–90.

———. *Héros et orateurs: rhétorique et dramaturgie cornéliennes.* Geneva: Droz, 1990.

Gearhart, Suzanne. "Racine's Politics: The Subject/Subversion of Power in *Britannicus.*" *L'Esprit créateur* 38.2 (Summer 1998): 34–48.

Genette, Gérard. *Seuils.* Paris: Seuil, 1987.

Goldmann, Lucien. *Le Dieu caché. Étude sur la vision tragique dans les* Pensées *de Pascal et dans le théâtre de Racine.* Paris: Gallimard, 1959.

———. *The Hidden God: A Study of Tragic Vision in the* Pensées *of Pascal and the Tragedies of Racine.* Translated by Philip Thody. London: Routledge & Kegan Paul, 1964.

Goodkin, Richard. *Birth Marks: The Tragedy of Primogeniture in Pierre Corneille, Thomas Corneille, and Jean Racine.* Philadelphia: University of Pennsylvania Press, 2000.

———. "The Death(s) of Mithridate(s): Racine and the Double Play of History." *PMLA* 101.2 (March 1986): 203–17.

———. *The Tragic Middle: Racine, Aristotle, Euripides.* Madison: University of Wisconsin Press, 1991.

Greenberg, Mitchell. *Baroque Bodies: Psychoanalysis and the Culture of French Absolutism.* Ithaca, NY Cornell University Press, 2001.

———. "L'hymen de Corneille: Classicism and the Ruses of Symmetry." In *Pascal, Corneille, Désert, Retraite, Engagement. Actes de Tuscon,* edited by Jean-Jaques Demorest and Lise Leibacher-Ouvrard, 127–51. Paris; Biblio 17, 1984.

———. *Subjectivity and Subjugation in Seventeenth-Century Drama and Prose: The Family Romance of French Classicism.* Cambridge: Cambridge University Press, 1992.

Gutwirth, Marcel. *Jean Racine. Un itinéraire poétique.* Montreal: Les Presses de l'Université de Montréal, 1970.

Heidegger, Martin. *Being and Time.* Translated by John Macquarrie and Edward Robinson. New York: Harper & Row, 1962.

———. *Introduction to Metaphysics.* Translated by Gregory Fried and Richard Polt. New Haven, CT: Yale University Press, 2000.

———. *On the Way to Language.* Translated by Peter D. Hertz. New York: Harper & Row, 1971.

———. *Poetry, Language, Thought.* Translated by Albert Hofstadter. New York: Harper & Row, 1971.

Herzel, Roger W. "Racine, Laurent, and the *Palais à Volonté.*" *PMLA* 108.5 (October 1993): 1064–82.

Hoffmann, Kathryn A. *Society of Pleasures: Interdisciplinary Readings in Pleasure and Power during the Reign of Louis XIV.* New York: St. Martin's, 1997.

Homage to Paul Bénichou. Edited by Sylvie Romanowski and Monique Bilezikian. Birmingham, AL: Summa, 1994.

Hopkins, Lisa. *Shakespeare on the Edge: Border-crossing in the Tragedies and the* Henriad. Burlington, VT: Ashgate, 2005.

Horowitz, Louise K. "East/West: Mapping Racine." In *Intersections. Actes du 35e congrès annuel de la NASSCFL,* edited by Faith Beasley and Kathleen Wine, 247–54. Tübingen: Narr, 2005.

———. "The Second Time Around." *L'Esprit Créateur* 38.2 (1998): 23–33.

Hubert, J. D. *Essai d'exégèse racinienne.* Paris: Nizet, 1956.

Jean Racine. 1699–1999. Actes du colloque Ile-de-France—La Ferté-Milon. Edited by Gilles Declercq and Michèle Rosellini. Paris: Presses Universitaires de France, 2003.

Juvenal. *The Satires of Juvenal.* Translated by Hubert Creekmore. New York: Mentor, 1963.

Koch, Erec R. "Tragic Disclosures of Racine's *Iphigénie.*" *Romanic Review* 81.2 (March 1990): 161–72.

Kuizenga, Donna. "*Mithridate:* A Reconsideration." *French Review* 52.2 (Dec. 1978): 280–85.

La Bruyère, Jean de. *Les Caractères.* Edited by Pierre Ronzeaud. Paris: Librairie Générale Française, 1985.

Levron, Jacques. *La vie quotidienne à la cour de Versailles aux XVIIe et XVIIIe siècles.* Paris: Hachette, 1965.

Longino, Michèle. *Orientalism in French Classical Drama.* Cambridge: Cambridge University Press, 2002.

Lyons, John D. "Au seuil du panoptisme général." *XVIIe siècle* 56.2 (2004): 277–87.

———. *Kingdom of Disorder: The Theory of Tragedy in Classical France.* West Lafayette, IN: Purdue University Press, 1999.

Mardas, Nancy. "On Language as the Translation of Being, or Translation as the Language of Being." *Diotima* 2.1 (Spring 2001): <http://college.holycross.edu/diotima/n1v2/nancy.htm>

Maskell, David. *Racine: A Theatrical Reading.* Oxford: Clarendon Press, 1991.

Maulnier, Thierry. *Racine.* Paris: Gallimard, 1936.

Mauron, Charles. *L'Inconscient dans l'œuvre et la vie de Racine.* Gap: Ophrys, 1957.

McClure, Ellen. "Sovereign Love and Atomism in Racine's *Bérénice.*" *Philosophy and Literature* 27.2 (October 2003): 304–17.

———. *Sunspots and the Sun King: Sovereignty and Mediation in Seventeenth-Century France.* Urbana: University of Illinois Press, 2006.

McNeill, Will. "*Heimat:* Heidegger on the Threshold." In *Heidegger toward the Turn: Essays on the Work of the 1930s,* edited by James Risser, 319–49. Albany: SUNY Press, 1999.

Molière. *Œuvres complètes.* Edited by Georges Couton. 2 vols. Paris: Gallimard, 1971.

Montaigne, Michel Eyquem de. *Essais.* Vol. 1. Edited by Maurice Rat. Paris: Garnier, 1962.

———. *The Essays.* Great Books of the Western World. Vol. 25. Edited by W. Carew Hazlitt. Translated by Charles Cotton. Chicago: Britannica, 1952.

Montbertrand, Gérard. "La mort dans les gènes, une biocritique du théâtre de Racine: *La Thébaïde* et *Phèdre.*" In *Actes de Lexington,* Edited by Jean Charron and Mary Lynne Flowers, 233–49. Paris: Biblio 17, 1995.

Mourgues, Odette de. *Racine or the Triumph of Relevance.* Cambridge: Cambridge University Press, 1967.

Muratore, M. J. "The Pleasures of Re-Enactment in *Andromaque*." *Dalhousie French Studies* 24 (1993): 57–70.

———. "Racinian Stasis." In *Re-Lectures Raciniennes: Nouvelles approches du discours tragique*, edited by Richard L. Barnett, 113–25. Paris: Biblio 17, 1986.

Murray, Timothy. "Digital Baroque: Via Viola or the Passage of Theatricality." *SubStance* 31.2/3 (2002): 265–79.

A New History of French Literature. Edited by Denis Hollier. Cambridge, MA: Harvard University Press, 1989.

Niderst, Alain. "Ronsard, *Andromaque* et *Attila*." *Travaux de littérature* 4 (1991): 117–26.

———. *Les Tragédies de Racine, diversité et unité*. Paris: Nizet, 1975.

Nietzsche, Friedrich Wilhelm. *On the Advantage and Disadvantage of History for Life*. Translated by Peter Preuss. Indianapolis: Hackett, 1980.

O'Regan, Michael. *The Mannerist Aesthetic: A Study of Racine's* Mithridate. Bristol: Bristol University Press 1980.

Parish, Richard. *Racine: The Limits of Tragedy*. Paris: Papers on French Seventeenth Century Literature, 1993.

Pavel, Thomas. *L'Art de l'éloignement: Essai sur l'imagination classique*. Paris: Gallimard (Folio essais), 1996.

Pavis, Patrice. *Dictionnaire du théâtre*. Paris: Editions sociales, 1980.

Peters, Jeffrey N. *Mapping Discord: Allegorical Cartography in Early Modern French Writing*. Newark: University of Delaware Press, 2004.

Phillips, Henry. *Racine:* Mithridate. London: Grant and Cutler, 1990.

Picard, Raymond. *Nouvelle critique ou nouvelle imposture*. Paris: Pauvert, 1965.

Plutarch. *The Lives of the Noble Grecians and Romans*. Translated by John Dryden. Chicago: Britannica, 1952.

Poulet, Georges. *Studies in Human Time*. Translated by Elliott Coleman. New York: Harper Torchbooks, 1959.

Racine, Jean. *Alexandre le Grand*. Edited by Michael Hawcroft and Valerie Worth. Exeter: University of Exeter Press, 1990.

———. *Complete Plays*. Translated by Samuel Solomon. 2 vols. New York: Random House, 1967.

———. *Five Plays*. Translated by Kenneth Muir. New York: Hill and Wang, 1960.

———. *Mithridate*. Edited by Georges Forestier. Paris: Gallimard (Folio), 1999.

———. *Œuvres complètes*. Edited by Raymond Picard. Paris: Gallimard, 1950.

———. *Théâtre complet*. Edited by Maurice Rat. Paris: Garnier, 1960.

———. *Œuvres complètes*. Vol. 1. Edited by Georges Forestier. Paris: Gallimard, 1999.

Racine: The Power and the Pleasure. Edited by Edric Caldicott and Derval Conroy. Dublin: University College Dublin Press, 2001.

Ronsard, Pierre de. *Œuvres complètes*. Vol. 1. Edited by Jean Céard, Daniel Ménager, and Michel Simonin. Paris: Gallimard, 1993.

Rotrou, Jean. *Antigone*. In *Œuvres de Jean Rotrou*, 4: 1–87. Paris: Th. Desoer, 1820.

Sade, Donatien-Alphonse-François, marquis de. *Justine ou les malheurs de la vertu*. Paris: Union générale des éditions (10/18), 1969.

Seneca. *Seneca's Tragedies*. Translated by Frank Justus Miller. Vol. 1. Cambridge, MA: Harvard University Press, 1917.

Shakespeare, William. *The Norton Shakespeare. Tragedies*. Edited by Stephen Greenblatt, Walter Cohen, Jean E. Howard, and Katharine Eisaman Maus. New York: Norton, 1997.

Soare, Antoine. "*Bajazet* dans l'imaginaire racinien." In *Racine et l'Orient. Actes d'un colloque international tenu à l'Université de Haïfa, 14–16 avril 1999*, edited by Isabelle Martin and Robert Elbaz, 33–51. Tübingen: Narr (Biblio 17), 2003.

———. "*Phèdre* et les métaphores du labyrinthe: les tracés et les formes." In *Les épreuves du labyrinthe. Essais de poétique et d'herméneutique raciniennes. Hommage tricentenaire*, edited by Richard-Laurent Barnett. *Dalhousie French Studies* 49 (Winter 1999): 145–57.

Spitzer, Leo. "The 'Récit de Théramène.'" In *Linguistics and Literary History: Essays in Stylistics*, 87–134. Princeton, NJ: Princeton University Press, 1948.

Stone, Harriet. "Inheriting the Father's Image with His Blood: Mithridate's Legacy to Xipharès and Thésée." *Papers on French Seventeenth Century Literature* 25.48 (1998): 267–78.

Sussman, Ruth. "*Bérénice* and the Tragic Moment." *L'Esprit Créateur* 15.1–2 (1975): 241–51.

Szuszkin, Marc. *L'Espace tragique dans le théâtre de Racine*. Paris: L'Harmattan, 2005.

Tacitus. *The Annals and the Histories*. Translated by Alfred John Church and William Jackson Brodribb. Chicago: Britannica, 1952.

Tobin, Ronald W. *Jean Racine Revisited*. Boston: Twayne, 1999.

Ubersfeld, Anne. *Reading Theatre*. Edited by Patrick Debbèche and Paul Perron. Translated by Frank Collins. Toronto: University of Toronto Press, 1999.

———. "The Space of *Phèdre*." *Poetics Today* 2.3 (Spring 1981): 201–10.

Venesoen, Constant. "*La Thébaïde* et les dieux de Racine." *Revue d'histoire littéraire de la France* 79 (1979): 755–71.

Viala, Alain. *Racine. La stratégie du caméléon*. Paris: Seghers, 1990.

Vinaver, Eugène. *Racine and Poetic Tragedy*. Translated by P. Mansell Jones. New York: Hill and Wang, 1957.

Zimmermann, Eléonore. "La Tragédie de Jocaste: le problème du destin dans *La Thébaïde* de Racine." *French Review* 45.3 (February 1972): 560–70.

Index

action, questioning of, 15, 23–24. See also *Alexandre Le Grand; Andromaque; Athalie; Bajazet; Bérénice; Britannicus; Esther; Iphigénie; Mithridate; Phèdre; Thébaïde, La*

Adam, Antoine, 38, 62–63

æsthetics. *See* esthetics

agnosticism, 49

Ahmed, Ehsan, 204 n. 4

Alexandre le Grand (Racine), art of, 70; criticisms of, 62–63; death in, 66; esthetics of, 62–63; limits in, 66, 70; power in, 62–72; prefaces to, 196 n. 10; space in, 65–66, 71; staging of, 195 n. 1; subjectivity in, 64; thresholds in, 71; vocabulary of, 196 n. 11; world in, 35, 60–72, 185, 195 n. 1, 196 n. 11

ambiguity, 25, 29, 181, 189 n. 36, 190 n. 51. See also *Andromaque; Britannicus; Iphigénie; Mithridate; Thébaïde, La*

Andromaque (Racine), action in, 27, 74; ambiguity in, 90; becoming in, 76, 197 n. 8; death in, 84–85; esthetics of, 88, 90, 197 n. 16; exile in, 205 n. 10; generational transition in, 35, 74–90; identity in, 73–74, 76, 87; power in, 74, 82, 85; prefaces to, 74–75, 89, 197 n. 5; rhetoric in, 76–77, 82–83; sovereignty in, 18, 40, 86; subjectivity in, 87; suspension in, 202 n. 3; thresholds in, 74, 88; time in, 35–36, 72, 74–90, 113, 185

Antigone (Rotrou), 60

Apostolidès, Jean-Marie, 188 n. 18, 205 n. 11

Aristotle, 17–18, 74

art, that of Racine, 15–16, 18, 28, 38–39, 63, 70

Athalie (Racine), action in, 182–84; death in, 184; limits in, 182–83; power in, 183; sovereignty in, 27; space in, 183–85;

suspense in, 184; thresholds in, 184–85; vocabulary of, 206 n. 16; world in, 37, 180–82, 184

Bach, Ray, 197 n. 11

Bachelard, Gaston, 22

Bajazet (Racine), action in, 123; death in, 31, 115–27, 185, 203 n. 10; esthetics of, 115, 117, 120; inaction in, 202 n. 6; limits in, 117; passions in, 116; power in, 115–27; rhetoric in, 118, 122–23; sovereignty in, 118; space in, 116–27, 202 n. 4; subjectivity in, 119; suspense in, 115, 118; suspension in, 115, 202 n. 3; thresholds in, 115–27, 119; time in, 120–21, 125, 127, 202 n. 7; torture in, 124–27, 203 n. 9, 203 n. 10; vocabulary of, 200 n. 8, 202 n. 7, 203 n. 10

baroque. *See* esthetics

Barrault, Jean-Louis, 32, 164, 191 n. 63, 207 n. 5, 209 n. 16

Barthes, Roland, 26; on *Andromaque*, 80, 83, 88; on *Bajazet*, 118, 125; on *Britannicus*, 96, 103, 125; on *Iphigénie*, 145, 149, 156, 204 n. 3; on *Thébaïde, La*, 34, 40, 46, 193 n. 7

becoming, failures of, 21; Greenberg on, 195 n. 26; Heidegger on, 22, 193 n. 18; Racine's characters caught in, 15, 17, 60. See also *Andromaque; Bérénice; Britannicus; Mithridate; Thébaïde, La*

being, in Corneille, 17; in Derrida, 24; in Heidegger, 22, 193 n. 18; and nothingness, 22; tension with becoming, 15. See also *Hamlet; Iphigénie; Phèdre*

Bentham, Jeremy, 96–97, 99

Bérénice (Racine), action in, 104–8, 113–14; becoming in, 108; death in, 110, 114, 202 n. 17; desire in, 109; des-

tiny in, 109, 111; esthetics of, 108, 114; inaction in, 27, 108, 114, 200 n. 6, 201 n. 15; passions in, 112; preface to, 104–8, 114; revisions of, 192 n. 5; space in, 109, 114, 188 n. 24, 200 n. 10, 201 n. 16; subjectivity in, 36, 103–14, 185, 201 n. 13; suspense in, 104, 199 n. 2; suspension in, 104, 106, 185, 199 n. 2; thresholds in, 103–4, 107–8, 113–14, 201 n. 16; time in, 36, 103–14, 199 nn. 1 and 2, 200 n. 11, 201 nn. 12 and 14; torture in, 108; vocabulary of, 196 n. 11, 200 n. 8
Bersani, Leo, 80, 88
Beugnot, Bernard, 29
bienséances, 32
Biet, Christian, 55, 59, 189 n. 36, 201 n. 13
body, 102. See also *Phèdre*
Boileau, Nicolas, 67–68
Bonzon, Alfred, 189 n. 37
boundaries. *See* limits
Braider, Christopher, 19, 189 n. 36
Brault, Pascale-Anne, 191 n. 68, 200 n. 10
Britannicus (Racine), action in, 92; ambiguity in, 181; becoming in, 20, 94, 103; death in, 96; esthetics of, 95, 103; gaze in, 95, 100; inaction in, 95, 96; Néron as potential villain in, 18, 194 n. 22; power in, 36, 42, 47, 91–103, 111; rhetoric in, 101; sovereignty in, 27, 41, 103; space in, 91–93, 96–103, 109, 188 n. 24, 197–98 n. 1, 198 n. 11; subjectivity in, 95, 99–100, 103; thresholds in, 92, 97–98, 103, 198 n. 2; time in, 90, 92–96, 101–3, 111, 185, 198 n. 3; torture in, 124; utterance in, 95
Brody, Jules, 38–39, 202 n. 6
Bruneau, Marie-Florine, 196 n. 5

Campbell, John, 25–27, 128, 141, 199 n. 2, 201 nn. 12 and 15, 203 nn. 1 and 2, 204 n. 4
Cassius Dio Cocceianus, 137
Cave, Terence, 48, 55
Certeau, Michel de, 198 n. 3
Cid, Le (Corneille), 99, 195 n. 26
Cinna (Corneille), 195 n. 26
classical. *See* esthetics
Conroy, Derval, 101
Corneille, Pierre, 197 n. 2; exaltation of

being in, 17; political inquiries in, 18; as predecessor to Racine, 74, 199 n. 3. See also *Cid, Le; Cinna; Héraclius; Horace; Illusion comique, L'; Rodogune; Œdipe; Nicomède; Polyeucte; Tite et Bérénice*
Courtin, Antoine de, 197–98 n. 1

death, deferral of, 18; of Orpheus, 22; in Shakespeare, 18; staging of, 31–32; thresholds to, 53, 55; and worlds, 18, 22, 31. See also *Alexandre Le Grand; Andromaque; Athalie; Bajazet; Bérénice; Britannicus; Iphigénie; Mithridate; Phèdre; Thébaïde, La*
Declerq, Gilles, 188 n. 18, 190 n. 54
Delcroix, Maurice, 29, 193 n. 15
Derrida, Jacques, 23–25; 188 n. 30, 195 n. 26
desire, for action, 33; in tension with duty, 15. See also *Bérénice; Iphigénie; Phèdre*
Desmarets de Saint-Sorlin, Jean, 197 n. 2
destiny, 22. See also *Bérénice; Iphigénie; Mithridate; Thébaïde, La*
Dorval, Patricia, 191 n. 62
dramaturgy, 18, 32, 38–39, 75, 104–7. See also Racine
Dubech, Lucien, 97
Dubu, Jean, 49, 193 n. 17

Edwards, Michael, 195 n. 32
Ekstein, Nina, 142, 148–49
Emelina, Jean, 32, 34, 203 n. 3
Esther (Racine), action in, 182; vocabulary of, 196 n. 11; world in, 37, 180–82
esthetics, baroque, 192 n. 6; classical, 41, 206 n. 3; fluidity of, 189 n. 36; liminary, 15; mannerist, 41, 97, 192 n. 6; of minimalism, 20, 30, 32, 34, 36–37, 104; of the threshold, 36, 108, 185; of the unspoken, 19. See also *Alexandre le Grand; Andromaque; Bérénice; Britannicus; Iphigénie; Mithridate; Phèdre; Thébaïde, La*
Euripides, 74. See also *Hippolytus; Iphigenia at Aulis; Phœnician Maidens, The*

fate. *See* destiny
Ferrier-Caverivière, Nicole, 196 n. 5
Forestier, Georges, 39, 52–53, 115, 130,

165–66, 187 n. 1, 192 n. 5, 199 n. 3,
   200 n. 10, 202 n. 7, 204 n. 4
Foucault, Michel, 36, 92, 96, 99, 102–3
Freudmann, Felix, 145–46
Fumaroli, Marc, 190 n. 51, 206 n. 3

gaze, 44–45, 102. See also *Britannicus*
Gearhart, Suzanne, 95, 100
Genette, Gérard, 200 n. 5
Goldmann, Lucien, 26–29
Goodkin, Richard, 17–20, 28, 46, 169,
   187 n. 9, 192 n. 6, 194 nn. 20 and 24,
   204 n. 3, 206 n. 1, 208 n. 13
Greenberg, Mitchell, 59–60, 193 n. 12,
   195 n. 26, 197 n. 1
Gutwirth, Marcel, 187 n. 5, 192 n. 3,
   197 n. 3

Hamlet (Shakespeare), 18
Hawcroft, Michael, 196 n. 5
Heidegger, Martin, 21–25, 153, 193 n. 18,
   205 n. 14, 209 n. 15
Héraclius (Corneille), 193 n. 9
Herodotus, 74
heroism, in Aristotle, 187 n. 9; questioning
   of, 17–18. See also *Iphigénie; Mithridate;*
   Phèdre
Herzel, Roger, 198 n. 11
Hippolytus (Euripides), 160, 176
Hoffmann, Kathryn, 202 n. 4
Homer, 206 n. 1
Hopkins, Lisa, 18–20, 29–30, 205 n. 9
Horace, 74
Horace (Corneille), 146
Horowitz, Louise, 88–89, 188 n. 19, 197 n.
   15
Hubert, Judd, 136, 142, 207–8 n. 10
hymen, 23–25, 195 n. 26

identity, disintegration of, 15, 37; Racine's
   vision of, 15. See also *Andromaque; Iphi-*
   génie; Mithridate; Phèdre, Thébaïde, La
Illusion comique, L' (Corneille), 203 n. 2
inaction, 15–16, 33. See also *Bajazet; Bri-*
   tannicus; Bérénice; Iphigénie; Mithridate;
   Phèdre
Iphigenia at Aulis (Euripides), 204 n. 2
Iphigénie (Racine), action in, 148; ambigu-

ity in, 144, 204 n. 5; anticipation in, 27,
   143, 147; being in, 152–53, 155, 204 n.
   1; death in, 143, 149, 185; desire in,
   146–47, 149, 155, 158; destiny in, 37,
   49, 144–45, 148, 150–51; esthetics of,
   153–54; heroism in, 204 n. 3; identity in,
   37, 143, 150, 154–58, 205 n. 9; inaction
   in, 142, 152; opening scene of, 49;
   power in, 157; rhetoric in, 149–50, 152;
   space in, 20, 142, 147–49, 151, 154,
   158, 185; subjectivity in, 52, 142, 146,
   154–58, 205 n. 13; suspense in, 148–49,
   157; thresholds in, 142–44, 149–50,
   153, 158; time in, 52, 143–46, 148–52,
   156–58, 204 n. 1, 205 n. 11; utterance
   in, 143–45, 152–53, 158, 204 n. 4; vocabulary of, 206 nn. 16 and 18; world
   in, 143–44, 146, 149, 152, 154–55, 158

Jansenism, 26–30
Janus, 191 n. 62

King Lear (Shakespeare), 19, 204–5 n. 5
Koch, Erec, 205 n. 11
Kuizenga, Donna, 204 nn. 4 and 12

La Mothe Le Vayer, François de, 67–68
language, in Heidegger, 21–24; of Racine,
   17, 30; of Racine's characters, 16. *See*
   also utterance
Laurent, Michel, 198 n. 11
Le Brun, Charles, 62–63
Levron, Jacques, 198 n. 8
limits, of human condition, 22; in Racine,
   30; in Shakespeare, 18–19; of utter-
   ance, 17. See also *Alexandre le Grand;*
   Athalie; Bajazet; Mithridate; Phèdre; Théb-
   aïde, La.
Longino, Michèle, 188 n. 18
Louis XIV, 63, 68, 198 n. 8
Lukàcs, Georg, 28
Lyons, John D., 99, 199 n. 14

Macbeth (Shakespeare), 18, 195 n. 29
Mallarmé, Stéphane, 23–25
Mannerism. *See* esthetics
Mardas, Nancy, 22
Maskell, David, 31–33, 97, 188 n. 24,

195 n. 1, 197–98 n. 1, 201 n. 16, 202 n. 17
Maulnier, Thierry, 15–16, 187 n. 5
Mauron, Charles, 26, 156
McClure, Ellen, 188 n. 18, 200 n. 7, 201 n. 14
McNeill, Will, 205 n. 14, 209 n. 15
mimesis, 23–24
minimalism. *See* esthetics
Mithridate (Racine), action in, 127, 129, 140, 142; ambiguity in, 129, 142; becoming in, 133; death in, 31, 36, 127–29, 131, 135–42, 185, 204 n. 12; destiny in, 130–31, 134, 140; esthetics of, 128, 130; and heroism, 136–37, 141, 203 n. 3; identity in, 130; illustrations of, 32–33; inaction in, 129, 132, 141–42, 203 n. 2; limits in, 129–30, 142; and positivism, 141; power in, 130–31, 134–35, 141; rhetoric in, 135; silence in, 131; space in, 127, 130, 135, 203 n. 3, 142; subjectivity in, 128, 132, 140; suspension in, 128, 131–33, 137, 141; thresholds in, 129, 130, 134–35, 138–39, 141; time in, 27, 141; utterance in, 129, 131–32, 141; vocabulary of, 196 n. 11, 200 n. 8; world in, 129, 135
Montaigne, Michel Eyquem de, 157
Montbertrand, Gérard, 58, 193 n. 12
Mourgues, Odette de, 110
Muratore, M. J., 16–17, 197 n. 16

negativity, 16, 25, 187 n. 5
Nicomède (Corneille), 202 n. 8
Niderst, Alain, 197 n. 2
Nietzsche, Friedrich, 197 n. 9

Œdipe (Corneille), 49–50
Oedipus, 17
O'Regan, Michael, 141, 192 n. 6
Orpheus, 22, 60
Othello (Shakespeare), 191 n. 62, 205 n. 9

paradox, 15, 16, 19, 24
Parish, Richard, 163
Pascal, Blaise, 27–28, 190 n. 45
passions, of Racine's characters, 16; staging of, 32. See also *Bajazet; Bérénice; Phèdre; Thébaïde, La*

Pavis, Patrice, 31
Peters, Jeffrey, 195 n. 1
Peyron, Pierre, 32–33
Phædra (Seneca), 160, 176
Phèdre (Racine), action in, 15, 160, 163–64, 179; being in, 208 n. 13; body in, 174, 177–79, 209 n. 20; death in, 15, 31, 49, 104, 159–65, 168, 170, 172–81, 209 n. 15, 209 n. 16; desire in, 160, 171; esthetics of, 163–64, 168, 173, 176, 180, 209 n. 20; heroism in, 167, 208 n. 11; identity in, 17, 37, 168–73, 179, 180, 208–9 n. 14; inaction in, 160, 164; innocence in, 194 n. 22; limits in, 71, 164–70, 175–77; 207–8 n. 10; passions in, 159; power in, 159, 167; prefaces to, 176; silence in, 162, 164; space in, 28, 163–68, 177, 180, 207–8 n. 10; staging of, 32, 164, 191 n. 63, 207 n. 5, 209 n. 16; subjectivity in, 162, 164, 166–73, 175, 180, 185; suspension in, 15, 162, 164; thresholds in, 160–63, 168–70, 173, 175–76, 180–81; time in, 171–74, 182; utterance in, 158, 160–64, 180; world in, 71, 165–67, 175–76, 180, 182
Phillips, Henry, 142
Phœnician Maidens, The (Euripides), 60
Picard, Raymond, 196 n. 4
Plaideurs, Les (Racine), 188 n. 24
Plato, 23
Plutarch, 136–37, 176, 204 n. 7
Poetics (Aristotle), 17
poetry, Heidegger on, 21–25, of Racine, 22, 186
Polyeucte (Corneille), 195 n. 26
positivism, 16. See also *Mithridate*
Poulet, Georges, 36, 49, 180, 197 n. 15
power, and the antechamber, 34; thresholds to, 45–46, 53. See also *Alexandre Le Grand; Andromaque; Athalie; Bajazet; Britannicus; Iphigénie; Mithridate; Phèdre; Thébaïde, La*
Princesse de Clèves, La (Lafayette), 199 n. 14
progress, 16, 187 n. 5

Quintus Curtius Rufus, 62, 71

Racine, Jean, career of, 38, 75, 199 n. 3; dramaturgy of, 15, 18, 32, 38–39, 75,

104–7, 113, 206 n. 3; format of quotations from, 187 n. 1; language of, 19; and Port-Royal, 29, 190 n. 49; present-day readership of, 185–86. See also *Alexandre le Grand; Andromaque; Athalie; Bajazet; Bérénice; Britannicus; Esther; Iphigénie; Mithridate; Phèdre; Plaideurs, Les; Thébaïde, La*

Reiss, Timothy, 66–67, 196 n. 5

representation, 23–25

rhetoric, in the service of Louis XIV, 68–69; of perfection, 16; in Racine's prefaces, 74–75, 105–7, 200 n. 4. See also *Andromaque; Bajazet; Britannicus; Iphigénie; Mithridate; Thébaïde, La*

Rodogune (Corneille), 45–48, 54

Romanowski, Sylvie, 204–5 n. 5

Romeo and Juliet (Shakespeare), 132

Ronsard, Pierre de, 89, 197 n. 2

Rotrou, Jean. See *Antigone*

Sade, Donatien-Alphonse-François, marquis de, 125, 203 n. 9

Saint-Evremond, Charles de Marguetel de Saint-Denis, seigneur de, 62, 196 n. 3

Schröder, Volker, 188 n. 18

Seneca, 74. See also *Phædra*

Shakespeare, eschatology in, 29–30; language of, 19; polyphony in, 18. See also *Hamlet; King Lear; Macbeth; Othello; Romeo and Juliet*

silence, in Heidegger, 21; interplay with utterance, 15, 17, 33. See also *Mithridate; Phèdre*

Soare, Antoine, 20, 207–8 n. 10

Sophocles, 74, 191 n. 68

sovereignty. See *Andromaque; Athalie; Bajazet; Britannicus*

space, dramatic, 20, 31; in Shakespeare, 18, 30; and power, 40–48; scenic, 31; staging of, 30–35, 197–98 n. 1, 198 n. 11; transitional, 15, 29–30, 34; of thresholds, 20, 24–25. See also *Alexandre le Grand; Andromaque; Athalie; Bajazet; Bérénice; Britannicus; Iphigénie; Mithridate; Phèdre; Thébaïde, La*

speech. See utterance

Spitzer, Leo, 209 n. 20

staging, space of, 30–34. See also *Alexandre le Grand*

subjectivity. See *Alexandre le Grand; Andromaque; Bajazet; Bérénice; Britannicus; Iphigénie; Mithridate; Phèdre; Thébaïde, La*

suspense, 33. See also *Bérénice; Bajazet; Iphigénie; Thébaïde, La*

suspension, 16. See also *Bérénice; Bajazet; Iphigénie; Mithridate; Phèdre*

Sussman, Ruth, 109

sylleptic projection, 20

Tacitus, 36, 97, 198 n. 2

Thébaïde, La (Racine), 38–60; action of, 40, 53; ambiguity in, 49, 193 n. 15; becoming in, 38–39, 43, 47, 195 n. 26; conflict in, 35, 37; death in, 18, 39, 45, 49, 53–60, 140; destiny in, 39, 47–50, 55; esthetics of, 38, 50, 52, 60, 97; identity in, 56, 59–60; limits in, 58–60; modernity of, 59; passions in, 59; power in, 38–50, 58, 60, 192 n. 6; premiere of, 38; published versions of, 192 n. 5; rhetoric in, 41, 52; space in, 41, 40–48, 52, 55, 57–60; subjectivity in, 52–53, 59; suspense in, 46; thresholds in, 38–60; time in, 48–52, 54, 89, 182; vocabulary of, 193 n. 10, 196 n. 11; world in, 38–39, 47, 182, 185

threshold, conceptualization of, 20, 60; in Derrida, 23–25, 195 n. 26; in Heidegger, 21–24, 205 n. 14; Racine's dramaturgy of, 15, 38; to self-actualization, 17; staging of, 30–34; of textuality, 107; of the tragic, 161, 191 n. 68. See also *Alexandre Le Grand; Andromaque; Athalie; Bajazet; Bérénice; Britannicus; Esther; Iphigénie; Mithridate; Phèdre; Plaideurs Les;* space; *Thébaïde, La*

time, and death, 54; dramatic, 20; future, 48; of tragedy, 49, 194 n. 20, 197 n. 3; transitional, 15. See also *Andromaque; Bajazet; Bérénice; Britannicus; Iphigénie; Mithridate; Phèdre; Thébaïde, La*

Tite et Bérénice (Corneille), 199 n. 3

Tobin, Ronald, 76, 199 n. 1, 203 n. 10

torture. See *Bérénice; Bajazet*

tragedy, 15; and destiny, 22; hybridity in, 17; Racinian, 25, 27–28, 59–60, 90, 104–7; and time, 49, 194 n. 20; and world limits, 71
Trakl, Georg, 21–24

Ubersfeld, Anne, 33, 164–65, 168, 197–98 n. 1, 207–8 n. 10
utterance, interplay with silence, 15, 19, 29, 33; limits of, 17. See also *Britannicus; Iphigénie; Mithridate; Phèdre*

Venesoen, Constant, 48
Vergil, 74, 105–6
verisimilitude, 105–6

Viala, Alain, 190 n. 49
Vinaver, Eugène, 17

Weber, Max, 101

world, 186; of the dead, 18, 22, 31, 34; dimensions of, 60; humanity and, 32; passages between, 18, 57; views of in Goldmann, 26–27. See also *Athalie; Alexandre le Grand; Esther; Iphigénie; Mithridate; Phèdre; La Thébaïde*

Zeno, 18
Zimmermann, Eléonore, 193 n. 15